A BASIC
CHRISTIAN
THEOLOGY

A BASIC CHRISTIAN THEOLOGY

A. J. CONYERS

ACADEMIC
Nashville, Tennessee

Published by B&H Publishing Group,
Nashville, Tennessee

978-0-8054-1092-1

Dewey Decimal Classification: 230
Subject Heading: Doctrinal Theology
Library of Congress Card Catalog Number: 94-25096

Page design by Trina D. Hollister

Library of Congress Cataloging-in-Publication Data
Conyers, A. J., 1944-
    A basic Christian theology / A. J. Conyers.
        p.   cm.
    ISBN 0-8054-1092-9 $18.99
    1.Theology, Doctrinal. I. Title.
BT75.2.C66   1995
230—dc20   94-25096
                                                                CIP

            19 20 21 22 23   14 13 12 11

To

Emily & John

CONTENTS

PREFACE

Many charitable efforts and encouraging words from friends stand behind the production of this work. My co-workers saw, as I did, the need for a clear, introductory guide to Christian theology for those just entering their theological studies. Trent Butler first envisioned the project; and John Landers expertly performed the work of an editor, advising, coaxing, and encouraging, all at the right time and in the right degree. My colleagues at Charleston Southern University provided many helpful suggestions, especially with regard to bibliography, and David Roof, my graduate intern during 1993–94, was of great help in suggesting material for the sidebars in the early chapters. The librarians at CSU and Bill Hair, the theological librarian at Baylor University, my most recent home, have all been of immense assistance.

INTRODUCTION

Translating only somewhat freely, the word *theology* means "conversation about God." In much of the Bible, the very idea that we can say something about God, other than what he has said about himself, is a very questionable notion. From Job, who concludes that he himself had "uttered what I did not understand, things too wonderful for me, which I did not know," to the psalmist, who writes that God's own knowledge is "too wonderful for me . . . I cannot attain it," we find a deep respect for the distance between the God who has created everything and the questioning human being.

Before we look at some of the most settled results of two thousand years of Christian theology, therefore, we need to face squarely two important questions. The first question is, "Can we really say anything about God?" Isn't it a bit presumptuous, we chide ourselves, to think that we can comprehend anything very significant about God, whose immensity and eternity overwhelm our imaginations? One of the church's earliest theologians, Origen, compared this enterprise to an ant's understanding of a colossal statue as it crawled around the base.

An old German proverb captures the problem: "A comprehended God is no God!" The moment we think we have understood God, we have only imagined him from our own level of thought and experience, thus proving that we are not thinking about the true God at all. We have grasped instead a faint shadow of reality that accommodates our small minds but has little to do with the living God. Thus we are faced with the difficulty—and some would say the impossibility—of thinking about God. It is a matter we must face forthrightly in the very first chapter.

The other question has to do with the *necessity* of theology. If Scripture reveals that which is essential to the knowledge of God, why should we seek to add to it with our theology? Are we, in any way, denying the sufficiency of Scripture when we raise questions and give answers that are outside the language and doctrine that are specifically found in the Bible itself? If the Bible says nothing of a Trinity, for instance, can we justify the many attempts to teach such an idea, even making it often a test of orthodoxy?

In spite of appearances, these questions are no threat to theology at all. In fact, they describe the real beginnings of any genuine Christian theology. From the earliest days of the church, the great exemplars of Christian thought have recognized that theology begins with humility and gratitude. It begins with the humility of recognizing that God is much too great for our small minds and our practical experience. It also begins with gratitude for what God has revealed about himself.

The questions that we have posed, far from denying the work of a theologian, actually reflect the undergirding virtues necessary to any Christian understanding of God. It is a settled conviction of all the major streams of Christian theology that to speak of God is possible only because of God's desire to communicate himself to us. It is an enterprise so vital to our well-being that we must place ourselves and our questions humbly before that which God has disclosed, hoping in this way to better understand so that we might better obey. In the following discussion of a definition of theology, we can at least see that, though the human enterprise is limited and altogether dependent upon God's revelation, the questions presented by theology cannot be avoided.

Taking note in this way of the limits and the possibilities of Christian theology, we can now think about how to define Christian theology. Even if the student is not well acquainted with the works of theologians, he or she could hardly have missed the fact that a broad range of quite different ideas has been presented as Christian doctrine. The theology of John Calvin can be distinguished at several points from the theology of Martin Luther, although both of these are closer to each other than to the theology of Thomas Aquinas or Duns Scotus. We also can find significant changes in the approach taken by theologians of antiquity, such as Origen and Augustine, when compared to medieval thinkers, such as Anselm of Canterbury, or modern theologians, such as Karl Barth or Jürgen Moltmann.

What can be said about the work of all these thinkers— ancient or modern, from one tradition or another—that helps us define what they are attempting to do and how they do it as "theology"?

A Basic Definition

In his 1642 book, called *The Marrow of Sacred Theology,* William Ames met the critics of his attempt at summarizing Christian theology by first acknowledging that "When the speech is carried on like a swift stream, although it catch many things, of all sorts, yet you can hold fast but a little."[1] That, in a word, is the difficulty of all theology. For the instrument that purports to capture the main lines of thought in something as vast and comprehensive as the Christian view of God, humanity, the world, and that seeks to draw some kind of system out of those lively, varied, and powerful writings of the prophets and apostles that form the foundation of Christian thought, must necessarily be a loosely-woven net.

Christian theology, therefore, cannot hope to answer all questions. The moment it pretends to do so, it ceases to be

---

1. Cited in William Adams Brown, *Christian Theology in Outline* (New York: Scribners, 1906), xv.

Christian theology and becomes instead an ideology. Christian theology is satisfied to ask the proper questions and,
through its attempts to answer them, illuminate reality for
the Christian believer. An ideology, by contrast, wants to
capture reality, explain it, and make reality fit its system.
Christian theology admits that God and his creation are too
immense to be explained. An ideology, on the other hand,
requires a small world and a manageable god. That distinction tells us that theology begins not as a project to explain
all things, but as one to help the Christian believer approach the Christian faith—and the reality of God—with
wonder and gratitude, and the beginnings of understanding.

But if theology does not even hope to answer all questions, what is its value? The work of theology, as Gustaf
Aulén stated, is first of all based on a conviction that "Christian faith is by its nature completely theocentric, and thus
determined by an act of God in Christ." For that reason,
Aulen continued, "The presentation of its content must appear as one organic whole."[2] The oneness of God, and his
complete sovereignty over creation, must mean that all of
reality reflects the nature of God in some measure. Furthermore, all truth leads ultimately to God.

These premises are commonplace in a Christian understanding of God; and they presuppose the value of doctrine
as general statements, comprehensive truths derived from
revelation and faithfully reflecting the nature of human experience, and providing wisdom as a basis for action. Thus
theology attempts to draw general truths from the variety
of revelation to help believers understand human experience and act with wisdom. This is the work of theology, and
points toward its basic definition.

Let's look at two common instances of how theology can
be true to Scripture and yet go beyond the words that are
given. If the New Testament witnesses that Jesus is human, as it does, and if it also presents Jesus as the very incarnation of God, then we naturally are faced with the task
of articulating the reality of God who became man without

2. Gustaf Aulen, *The Faith of the Christian Church*, trans. Eric Wahl-
strom (Philadelphia: Fortress, 1960), 2.

diminishing his deity, or of a man who is God incarnate yet remains one with us in humanity. Once that step beyond Scripture is made, in the form of a question, even while striving to be wholly faithful to Scripture, one has come into the realm of theology.

Often it has been noted that the Trinity (God as Father, Son, and Holy Spirit) is nowhere mentioned in Scripture. Yet when Scripture presents the strongest possible testimony to the reality of God as Father, the incarnation of God as Son, and the presence of God as Spirit, then we are faced with the inevitable question about the unity of God, who manifests himself in distinct "persons." *Theology, then, is the articulation of comprehensive and general truths about God, his creation, and his redemptive actions, based upon (1) the variety in revelation, and (2) the presupposition of the unity of all truth.* It is a work that is grounded in the most fundamental of all statements about God, one that was uttered as the fundamental tenet of the Hebrew faith, and without which there would be no Christian faith: "Hear, O Israel: The Lord our God is One" (Deut. 6:4). With the oneness of God, thought follows a certain progression: one reality, one world, one humanity, one ethic, one essential truth. Theology—the idea that one can speak a word (*logos*) about the one God (*theos*) and thus come to an understanding of other realities (the world, humanity, sin, redemption, and so on)—can only be accomplished on the basis of this fundamental belief in God's oneness.

Systematic Theology

From this fundamental unity of all things in the one God is derived the idea of an approach to theology that is systematic. In other words, because all things relate to that center that is God, then an understanding of God (theology proper) illuminates the meaning of the world (cosmology), humanity (anthropology), and the end or goal of all things (eschatology). Revelation, coming to us in Scripture, can therefore be expressed in view of its various themes: the doctrine of the person and work of Christ (Christology), the doctrine of the Spirit of God (pneumatology), salvation (soteriology), sin and forgiveness, the church, and Christian hope.

That which distinguishes theology as *systematic* is its exposition of these themes. That is why it is sometimes called thetic theology. Biblical theology differs from systematic theology by its attempt to isolate the theology of the biblical writings. It speaks of the "theology of the prophets," for instance, or of "deuteronomic theology," or of the "theology of Paul." I hasten to say that biblical theology is no more based upon the Bible than is a systematic approach: both depend upon the Bible as their fundamental source, though one deals with theology in systematic themes on the assumption that there is a fundamental unity of all revelation; and the other draws its categories from the biblical texts themselves on the assumption that there are important distinctions in biblical texts. Both, however, at their best, express the truth of Scripture.

Systematic Theology and Revelation

Christian theology, even in its systematic mode of expression, is not simply another variety of philosophy. In harmony with philosophy, it does claim that its findings illuminate reality and that they are verified by the practical wisdom and strong virtues that they support. Theology distinguishes itself from philosophy, however, in that it is based upon God's disclosure of himself in human history; it is based upon revelation. Only by virtue of God's intention to make himself known in the world does theology claim any special capacity to speak about God.

Theologians differ on the question of the scope and nature of revelation, which is a topic we will discuss in the first chapter. But all Christian theologians agree that there is a canon, a specific body of literature, that serves as a standard and a witness to God's self-disclosure. This canon, this Scripture, is the means by which God has continued to communicate all that he has done, is doing, and will do in the midst of human lives.

The Value of Theology

Most of us are acquainted with Scripture just enough so that we do not even notice that it comes to us from distant lands and times, with customs and modes of thinking that are foreign to our everyday experience. Some time ago J. B. Priestly wrote of how, upon returning to England, he was struck by this remarkable incongruity of modern life and ancient texts:

> Now, returning to it [the worship service] after a long absence, I saw how odd it was that these mild Midland folk, spectacled ironmongers, little dressmakers, clerks, young women from stationers' shops, should come every Sunday morning through the quiet streets and assemble here to wallow in wild oriental imagery. They stood in rows, meek-eyed and pink-cheeked, to sing modestly about the Blood of the Lamb. . . . They sat with bent heads listening to accounts of ancient and terribly savage tribal warfare, of the lust and pride of hook-nosed and raven-bearded chieftains, of sacrifice and butchery on the glaring deserts of the Near East. They chanted in unison their hope of an immortality to be spent in cities built of blazing jewels, with fountains of milk and cascades of honey, where kings played harps while maidens clashed cymbals; one could not help wondering what these people would do if they really did find themselves billeted forever in this world of the Eastern religious poets. What, in short, had these sober Northern islanders to do with all this Oriental stuff?[3]

This incongruity, this gap between what is revealed and what we experience and practice, is precisely the occasion, and points to the value, of theology. Let's think about the way theology arises out of this need to bridge the gap between Scripture and contemporary experience and practice.

What happens when a person reads Scripture and then seriously reflects upon his or her experience in life? The most typical response is to ask a question, or perhaps a series of questions. Whatever form these questions take, they

---

3. J. B. Priestly, *English Journey* (1934), 109f, cited in S. M. Mayo, *The Relevance of the Old Testament for Christian Faith* (Washington, D.C.: University Press of America, 1982), 1–2.

are each asking, "How do I relate this Scripture, which comes from some point in the dim, almost forgotten past, and out of a very different culture, to my present experience?" This question can mean, "How do I *verify* these things?" But it doesn't have to mean that. It could mean, "How do I *respond* to what I read in my present experience?" In any case, the questions that arise from Scripture have to do with bridging the gap between the writer of Scripture and the contemporary reader of the Bible.

The value of theology is simply that it faces the task of bridging the gap between what God has disclosed for all time—disclosed in ways sometimes peculiar to a very ancient time—and how it can be understood in our time. It asks a variety of questions, such as: "What can I say about the reality of God?" "What is the significance of God's incarnation in Jesus Christ?" "What is sin, and how might one escape the bondage of sin?" "Who is the Holy Spirit, and how shall I understand the work of the Spirit?" All of these, and many like them, lead us finally to ask the question, "What must I do, if these things are so?" Right understanding, in Christian theology, is never isolated from a personal response. The whole fabric of theology, if it is in fact Christian, has to do not simply with circumscribing God, or some idea of God, within some system of thought, but it has to do with drawing human beings into the circle of God's redemptive purpose. We are called upon to understand so that we might trust and obey. Anything short of this intention fails the most critical test of Christian theology.

PART I

God and His Creation

WHAT CAN WE POSSIBLY KNOW ABOUT GOD?

The Christian Idea of Revelation

Something of the scope of the Christian idea of revelation is suggested in the words of Ambrose, the fourth century Bishop of Milan, who said, "As in Paradise, God walks in the Holy Scriptures, seeking man." The word "revelation," especially in its Greek form, *apocalypse*, suggests an unveiling. Something is disclosed that is otherwise hidden. That which is unavailable to the natural senses is now brought into view. In Christian theology, however, the idea of revelation suggests that this disclosure is not a neutral or impersonal event, but its character is "God seeking man." It is not gained by human powers of perception, but is a divine gift.

In one sense, of course, all knowledge is received knowledge. We see accurately only by the perception of that which is truly given in reality. Physical sciences engage in the description of what is *there*, and is given in reality. This science is enhanced by accuracy, by avoiding the distortion of prejudice or imagination in its observation (even though imagination may play an important part in its later hypotheses). In a similar way, moving now to another area of thought, the historian endeavors to receive—by many kinds of tradition, some written and some not—what is otherwise inaccessible: the past. Through one means or another, we come to a greater understanding of the world by seeing what is there to be seen, and by wishing only to see honestly and accurately.

We may use powerful instruments to aid our senses or refined methods of research to enhance the historic memory, but we operate under the assumption that what we discover in science or history is true because it is already there to be discovered. We have not invented it or imagined it, but we have received it from outside ourselves.

The idea of revelation is different in only one important way. It assumes that some very important things *cannot* be seen, no matter how clever or diligent we might be in trying to discover them. As examples we can point to two realities immediately that everyone will say are important but cannot be seen. One is what we assume we are a part of—the universe. We can only assume the universe, for we can only see it in part and hypothesize its reality. We can imagine, perhaps, getting into an intergalactic spaceship and sailing to the outer reaches of the universe, and perhaps traveling far enough out to glimpse the "whole" of the universe. But, then, where would we be if not "in" the universe still, since you and I and all the space between us and the nearest star would still be a part of the universe? In a word, we cannot see what we cannot get outside of or beyond.

Nor, to take a second example, can we see the future. We experience the future as present and then as past. Until the future unfolds in our present, however, it has no reality for our senses. Yet no one would argue that the future is insignificant because we cannot know it. As a matter of fact, we use every device possible in our society, from economic forecasts to meteorology to astrology columns, to gain some knowledge of the future.

The reason the idea of revelation has had any currency and influence at all is that some of the greatest insights ever given us have come from the disclosure of what we would otherwise not know or "see" at all. In many ways, although there is much of importance in what we can see, what we cannot see is even greater and may be much more important. We will leave that argument to the side for one moment. We might only note its frank avowal that many true and important insights have come only by being revealed. Philosophers like Immanuel Kant sometimes have argued that revelation is only a concession to weaker minds, and that reason will sooner or later discern what is given earlier (as they readily concede) by being revealed. But even such arguments as Kant's acknowledge the reality—and even the necessity—of our being informed of truths that lie outside sense experience.

Christian faith, and thus Christian theology, arises out of a strong reliance upon that kind of knowledge. I would hope that, by the end of a course of study in Christian theology, the student would have a strong sympathy with the notion of our absolute need of revealed knowledge. In the meantime, we can at least test the intellectual waters a bit by considering the basis for thinking that some things must be disclosed that are otherwise hidden from the senses.

We have already mentioned the ideas of universe and future. There are many other matters—matters that are absolutely necessary for life, thought, and moral direction—that simply cannot be the product of sense experience. Various histories may rely upon the same set of facts, yet their determination of what is important may differ. They evidently rely upon something that is greater than, and outside of, mere historical fact. For that reason the telling of history can be quite different depending upon who is doing the telling and why. For one historian, the story of David and Goliath can signify only the futility of heavy armor; for another it signifies the providence of God. It requires a view from outside of the facts of history to make the difference.

Since this kind of knowledge is not accessible to us simply out of nature, it must break into our lives from a source utterly outside of nature. Like nature, it is a "given" thing that can now be seen and has become a part of our experience. But unlike nature, it breaks upon us in such a way that we are caused to think about its Source. Nature also has that same Source, and the Bible counsels that we think of God in light of his "handiwork" (Ps. 19). Yet because we do not, will not, and now cannot learn from nature, we must be startled and prodded and tutored by that which calls attention to the Source. Somewhere Flannery O'Connor explained her use of odd and unusual characters in her stories by saying, "To the hard of hearing you shout, and for the almost-blind you draw large and startling figures." Revelation is an occasional shout, an occasional illustration in large figures, done so men and women can understand the Word of God that whispers on every side.

■ ——————————————— ■

KARL BARTH ON REVELATION

When it refers to God's revelation as the Word of God, Christianity means Jesus Christ. What is a word? A word differs from a mere sound in that it is formed with the definite intention of calling on others to make a common cause. When I utter the simple word: "Look!" I call on others to look at something I think I have seen myself. Or if I say: "Listen!" I call them to listen to something I think I have heard myself. The primary intention of words is quite simply to be heard by others. Words cannot compel, they can only make an appeal. But every word has in view, in some sense or other, the obedient response of other persons. When I utter words I want to induce others to listen and conform to my wishes. In this sense too revelation is a word: God wants our interest, He wants us to listen, He wants to call us to decision, He wants us to obey His Word.

[From Karl Barth, *Against the Stream*, ed. Ronald Gregor Smith (London: SCM, 1954),213.]

■ ——————————————— ■

Revelation and Christian Theology

Not all religions require revelation in the sense that I've described it above. Buddhism, for instance, which does not make a distinction between nature and super-nature (that which is outside of nature), would not accept the idea of revelation. An enlightenment, yes, but not revelation. Christianity, however, appeals to what is greater than nature. God creates all things, and he creates them other than himself; which is to say that he allows them to exist as a separate reality. But this creation cannot truly be understood apart from God, who created it, sustains it, and ordains its purpose and destiny. Therefore the most essential knowledge must come from the outside, from God. This is necessary to *theism*, the view that God is other than his creation.

This reliance upon revelation is no simple bias of Christian thought, a purely arbitrary preference. Rather, it is based upon three common human experiences that I would like to outline next.

1. Revelation is essential in Christian theology because nature, by itself, is an incomplete and inadequate source of knowledge. Christian faith has no fundamental argument with the validity of science as a way of describing, with increasing precision and insight, what exists in nature. It is even open to the kind of refined scientific speculation that attempts to construct answers to questions about the limits of the universe, the structure of the atom, and the physical beginnings of the cosmos. Nor does Christianity fail to recognize the spectacular technological skills that have been acquired at ever-accelerating speeds since the middle of the nineteenth century, and that were made possible because of the insights of the natural sciences.

Yet no matter how far we have gone in describing and manipulating nature, basic questions remain unanswered by this line of thought. Bertrand de Jouvenal once pointed out that every day, because of the rapid expansion of science and technology, we can do more and more. But, he asked, "What on earth shall we do?"

Science can never answer that question: "What shall we do?" Nor can we answer, by science, the question of why anything exists at all. Nor can we have any knowledge of the true origin of things, or the final destiny of things, through science. These matters, all essential to our understanding of life, must come from another source.

Psalm 19 is an example of the biblical appreciation of nature. Yet we cannot fully see the importance of this psalm without noting how different it is from the pagan hymns to nature. For the Babylonian and the Egyptian alike, nature was suffused and intermingled with the divine; it was to be worshiped and feared. For the Israelite, however, nature gave evidence, not of its own divinity, but of the "glory of God," its maker. Nature is only "his handywork." That was a profoundly different view of things, and one with far-reaching consequences. For us, with our modern exaggeration of our ability to discover the secrets of nature, it means that even if nature yielded up all its secrets, we would not know all there is to know—or even the most important part of it. It means that nature (even with all its secrets) is always partial. The universe itself remains a dark mystery to us apart from the light of revelation.

2. Revelation is essential to Christian theology because sin distorts and falsifies human reason. Since reason begins with presuppositions based upon moral selection of what is important, valuable, and true, it is naturally influenced to see the world through the lens of pride, sensuality, greed, and sloth. Sin, in a word, invalidates reason as a means for finding value, purpose, and moral direction in the world, and for understanding the creation as that which glorifies God. Sin vitiates reason precisely because it causes the world to be viewed from a false point of view, a point centered in the self. Reason itself is not thereby rendered invalid; it is only given a defective point of reference. That is why the apostle Paul contrasted the "foolishness" of the cross to the "wisdom" of the world—the one is folly and the other wise only because of an entrenched self-centered presupposition. A full-scale assault on that entrenched selfishness was launched when the Son of God took up the cross: for "God chose what is foolish in the world to shame the wise" (1 Cor. 1:27).

3. Revelation is essential to Christian theology because, in the experience of Israel and of the church—that is, in the testimony of the Old and New Testaments—God reveals, and humanity responds to that revelation. It is not human beings who initiate out of a desire for understanding or goodwill, but it is God who initiates out of his love and his intention to save. Revelation assures that the egocentrism of the sin-vitiated reason is checked by a word from God that is in no way subject to human motives. Revelation is a given in the human experience. Therefore, human beings are faced with that to which they can only respond. It, in effect, short-circuits the manipulative possibilities that self-centeredness prefers.

Commenting on Paul's words in Romans that the gospel "is the power of God" (Rom. 1:16), the Swiss theologian Karl Barth said,

> The Gospel neither requires men to engage in the conflict of religions or the conflict of philosophies, nor does it compel them to hold themselves aloof from these controversies. In announcing the limitation of the known world by another that is unknown, the Gospel does not enter into competition with the many attempts to disclose within the known world some more or less unknown and higher form of existence and to make it accessible to men. The Gospel is not a truth among other truths. Rather, it sets a question-mark against all truths.[1]

Barth chose to emphasize here that the gospel—revelation—is not a deduction from more general truths, but it is a *given*. It is where we begin. In effect, it invites us to take a new beginning, one that no longer centers in the self, with its pride and sensuality, its demands for self-justification, or its sinking into sloth and indifference. Revelation is therefore the initiative of God, not the conclusion of human experience.

■ ——————————————————— ■

A. J. HESCHEL ON REVELATION

Revelation is not an act of . . . seeking, but of his being sought after, an act in God's search of man. The prophet did not grope for God. God's search of man, not man's quest for God, was conceived to have been the main event in Israel's history. This is at the core of all Biblical thoughts: God is not a being detached from man to be sought after, but a power that seeks,

---

1. Karl Barth, *The Epistle to the Romans*, trans. by Edwyn C. Hoskyns (London: Oxford University Press, 1968), 35.

pursues and calls upon man. The way to God is a way of God. Israel's religion originated in the initiative of God rather than in efforts of man. It was not an invention of man but a creation of God; not a product of civilization, but a realm of its own.

Revelation is the moment in which God succeeded in reaching man; an event to God and an event to man. To receive a revelation is to witness how God is turning toward man.

[Abraham Joshua Heschel, *God in Search of Man: A Philosophy of Judaism* (New York: Farrar, Straus and Giroux, 1955), 198–199.]

■ ─────────────────────── ■

The Idea of Two Classes of Revelation: General and Special

The idea of revelation often has been divided into two ways in which God makes himself known. One is called "special revelation," the disclosure of God's word to specific people in specific acts of redemption or judgment, or through the words of prophets and apostles. The other is designated "general revelation," which includes those ways in which God makes himself known to all people at all times, as in nature, and in the common features of human experience.

What Is Different about General Revelation?

The conviction that God makes himself known in specific acts of redemption, judgment, and in prophetic oracles has been seen by most theologians against the background of a general disclosure in human experience. In Psalm 19 and in Romans 1 we find clear references to nature, history, and human consciousness serving as the media of God's self-disclosure. The law of God is consonant with nature and with general human experience, and is thus a matter of common sense, available to all people at all times. No one is absolved on the basis of ignorance, but each has willfully rebelled against the truth disclosed by God.

This conviction, in Christian theology, is called *general revelation*. At times in the history of the church it has been strongly emphasized as a basis of Christian theology. For instance, Thomas Aquinas argued that a natural theology serves as a rudimentary basis for understanding the truth of Christianity, a truth more fully disclosed in Scripture. In modern times, Karl Barth argued against the validity of general revelation, arguing that Jesus Christ is the exclusive revelation of God, and that to add to that disclosure is to fall back into idolatry. His contemporary, Emil Brunner, however, contended for the more traditional view that the human capacity for receiving the gospel is a necessary assumption in any biblical understanding of revelation.

"What Is Special About Special Revelation?"

However Christian theologians have incorporated general revelation into their thinking, they have typically agreed that the human condition of sin has kept this general experience of God from being effective for salvation. Therefore, God's eternal purpose for humanity in redemption is disclosed, not in what is generally experienced, but in what is specially disclosed to God's people. As distinct from general revelation, this concept is called *special revelation*.

From this comparison of general and special revelation it can be seen that, although Christian theologians (such as Thomas Aquinas or Emil Brunner, to name two quite distinct thinkers) acknowledge the truth and the value of general revelation, they always see as *indispensable* God's special disclosure of himself in the history of Israel and the church, and centrally in the person and work of Jesus Christ. The particularity and the concreteness of this revelation cause us also to see another of the features of special revelation. Namely, it is a revelation that is passed on; it is a tradition in the sense that Paul expressed his role when he said to the Corinthian church: "For I handed to you as of first importance what I in turn had received" (1 Cor. 15:3). In a word, the medium of special revelation is necessarily Scripture, the written tradition of what God has done and said in human history, revealed in the lives and the living experience of prophets and apostles, in Israel and the church.

General Revelation	Special Revelation
Available to all people	Disclosed to particular people
Available to all times	Disclosed at particular times
Available in nature, history, and human consciousness	Often contradicts the normal experience
Discoverable in the philosophies and religious traditions of all people, even if subject to distortion	Revealed through the communication of a message, a gospel, or a prophetic oracle
Centered in general truths	Related to specific events
Repeatable or constant in human experience	Unrepeatable and unique
Suggests original wholeness of creation, but cannot restore wholeness	Soteric: It is restorative, revealing not only God's goodness, but also his power to save

The Significance of Special Revelation

From this point on, we will be focusing only on special revelation. For convenience, I will refer to this aspect simply as "revelation;" but keep in mind that we are including only that revelation which has the specific features of particularity and restorative intent that was described above. The need to focus on this species of revelation (without denying general revelation) was succinctly stated by Bernard Ramm when he noted the excesses that result when theology has attempted to build a structure upon the uncertain sands of general revelation. Commenting upon nineteenth-century religious liberalism, Ramm said:

> Unfortunately religious liberalism failed to assess properly the incomprehensibility of God, particularly as it bears upon the doctrine of revelation . . . . In developing an exaggerated doctrine of the divine immanence (and therefore an unbiblical one) it virtually made the concept of revelation so wide as to make it meaningless. It reached its extreme development with those theolo-

gians who sought to write Christian theology solely out
of religious experiences. The panentheism (the belief
that God richly pervades nature and man but is yet not
identical with either) of many other religious liberals
was a further weakening of the significance of the incomprehensibility of God.[2]

The very presence of an idea of special revelation in
Christianity has a bearing on two other ideas that are inseparable from the Christian understanding of God's self-
disclosure. The first idea is that God is *transcendent;* that is,
he is essentially unknown and incomprehensible. He is *holy,* both in terms of the human intellect and the human will.
The second idea is made more significant by the strength
and emphasis of the first: that is, this great God who cannot
be known in and of himself, who is beyond human experience, has condescended to make himself known. Each of
these ideas about God gives us an important insight into the
nature of revelation.

The Transcendence of God. The Christian understanding
of revelation must be coordinated with the experience of the
transcendence of God. The theologian must begin with the
honest admission that the things of God are too high and
wonderful for humans to know, for God is essentially incomprehensible. The psalmist proclaimed, "Such knowledge is
too wonderful for me; it is so high that I cannot attain it"
(Ps. 139:6). The prophets of Israel continually brought to
the attention of their people the vast difference between
man and God. "Do you seek the Lord?" Amos asks; then remember whom you seek: "He who made the Pleiades and
Orion, and turns deep darkness into the morning, and dark-
ens the day into night, who calls for the waters of the sea,
and pours them out upon the surface of the earth, the LORD
is his name" (Amos 5:8, RSV).

The immense distance between God and humanity is the
indispensable backdrop to a Christian idea of revelation. To
reduce God to the level of human thought and human imagination, so that we can comprehend God, is to lose a sense
of the very thing that distinguishes God as God. The whole

2. Bernard Ramm, *Special Revelation and the Word of God* (Grand
Rapids: Eerdmans, 1961), 23.

idea of revelation in Scripture began with this realization of the infinite greatness of God and man's incapacity for understanding God out of his own human nature.

Martin Luther's emphasis upon this distance between God and man, a distance that could only be bridged by God himself, is well known. The seriousness with which much of Protestant theology has taken this matter is reflected, for instance, in John Calvin's remark, in his *Institutes*, that "we certainly cannot *directly tend towards* [a knowledge of God] except under the guidance of the gospel."[3]

E. Y. Mullins, the great Baptist theologian of the early twentieth century, saw that the transcendence of God is a necessary companion concept to the idea of revelation. If God is equally present everywhere and in all things, Mullins said, then everything is divine revelation, which is also to say that nothing is divine revelation. God's distance from us allows us to enter into relationship with him. It is in this sense—that is, God as distinguished from everything in general—that we can speak of the personality of God. Mullins concludes: "This distinction is a fundamental condition of all the religious life of man. Religion means man in fellowship with God in personal terms. This implies both the immanence and the transcendence of God."[4]

For Karl Barth, the Swiss theologian of one generation later than Mullins, the idea of the "hiddenness of God" is fundamental to understanding the Christian certainty of God. When we identify God with our concepts of God, then we have wrongly assessed who comprehends whom. To say we comprehend God is to assert some kind of mastery over the things of God. "We are masters of what we comprehend," Barth wrote. "Viewing and conceiving certainly mean encompassing, and we are superior to, and spiritually masters of, what we can encompass."[5]

Nevertheless, this very realization of God's transcendence and his incomprehensibility is also the ground of the

3. *Institutes III*, ii, 6.

4. E. Y. Mullins, *The Christian Religion in Its Doctrinal Expression* (Philadelphia: Judson Press, 1917), 139.

5. Karl Barth, *The Doctrine of God: Church Dogmatics* vol. 2 pt. 1, eds. G. W. Bromiley and T. F. Torrance (Edinburgh: T. and T. Clark, 1967), 188.

confidence with which we respond to God's revelation. The hiddenness of God, once we acknowledge that fact, "is the confession of God's revelation as the beginning of our cognizance of God."[6] Therefore, we stand in our confession of faith, not on the fallible and uncertain strength of human intellect and imagination, but upon the certainty that if God is made known to us at all, it is from God's side that this becomes possible. As Barth can say, this "real knowledge of God" is "not an imperfection but the perfection, not a compromising but the certainty, not a limit but the reality of the knowledge of the knowledge of God, which . . . is indicated by the assertion of the hiddenness of God."[7]

The Condescension of God. God uses means appropriate to the limitations and conditions of humanity in order to disclose what is true of himself. This means, of course, that God discloses himself in human experience (history) and in a manner that is transmitted into the experience of a people (namely, through language).

Thus, the necessity of revelation is made clear when we consider the transcendence of God. The possibility of revelation also is disclosed when we consider God's desire to condescend to the human condition and make himself known. To consider the former alone might lead to despair. To consider the latter alone might lead to a trivializing of the things of God. So this inevitable tension between the transcendence of God and the condescension of his ways in revealing himself to us leads us, quite naturally, to ask just *what it is* that is revealed. It is, therefore, the *content* of revelation that we take up next.

The Content of Revelation. Let's begin with the notion of God's condescending to the human level of experience to make himself known. Only that sort of idea can break the impasse created by a full appreciation of the immense distance between God and his creation. Of course, we can say that is simple common sense, and it is. Nothing is truly *revealed* unless it is done in such a manner that human beings can understand and appropriate it.

---

6. Barth, *Doctrtine of God,* 192.
7. Ibid., 193.

The way in which God condescends to the human capacity for revelation, however, raises a question of some importance for the interpretation of Scripture. What exactly is the content of revelation? Is it the Word itself, taken in a literal manner, so that revelation is no more and no less than Scripture? Or does it point to a reality that is so inadequately expressed in proposition that we must rely on human impressions, the evoking of numinous feelings that are not at all confined to verbal constructions and the limits of vocabulary? Let's deal with these two opposite ways of seeing the content of revelation one at a time.

First, is revelation most accurately described as the words of Scripture? There is reason for leaning strongly in this direction. It was, after all, among the Jews, and later the Christians, that Scripture became the central focus in the living out of a religion. For Jews it was first the Torah, or instruction; then the writings of the prophets; and finally other holy writings—all of which came to us as the Old Testament. For Christians later, the New Testament shed new light on these old words and passed on a new tradition of the testimony of apostles. It is significant that, before Judaism and its further development in Christianity, religion was universally a cult—an action taken by the people to evoke the gods or to respond to the divine. Only in this *revealed* religion of the Jews and Christians (and later, by imitation, among the Muslims) did the Word become central. This is the way God condescended to the human need to understand and to obey, because that is the way we do understand. It is no wonder that the First Vatican Council (1869–70) took Scripture to be written at the "dictation of the Holy Spirit." Additionally, in some areas this idea of Scripture was no less characteristic of Protestantism than of Roman Catholicism.

There is good reason, therefore, to pause and consider carefully this persistent idea that God is the author of Scripture rather than to dismiss it out of hand, a practice too common in academic circles in recent decades. In answer to the question, "Did God write the Bible?" the distinguished biblical scholar John McKenzie wrote, "With some reservations concerning how the reply should be formulated exactly, the whole of Christian tradition from the earliest centuries answers in a unanimous and uninterrupted affirmative."[8] If someone like McKenzie, who is not wholly sympathetic with this tradition, can at least admit of its existence, then students of Christian thought should be open to asking why it exists and what it means.

If we see some merit in that tradition, it does not necessarily hold us to a notion identical to the Muslim idea that Allah wrote the Koran, or that the archangel dictated the words to Mohammed who was little more than a teletype for the heavenly message. We can, however, go a long way toward recovering a way of speaking about the Bible that is very much a part of our tradition, that is faithful to the text itself, but has suffered from a quagmire of reservations in our day. We suffer from our extreme devotion—even our prejudice, in the last half century—to the analytic side of truth. As Jürgen Moltmann has pointed out, our motto in the sciences is "divide and conquer." We think we have mastered a subject when we have disassembled it, measured and weighed its parts, and described what we have found. Thus, in biblical theology, there are only theologies—the theology of Paul, or of the Fourth Gospel, or of the Priestly tradition. We think only of historical circumstances, textual traditions, redactic conventions, rather than of eternal purposes, the consistent appeal of a loving God, and comprehensive design.

The sciences are discovering that investigation has been only partly completed, and truth only half served, through this kind of analysis. The frog under the scalpel that is severed part from part and tissue from tissue is no longer a frog. The truth partly lies in the living, breathing *whole* of something, and not only in its many, separate characteristics. The atom, the molecule, the organism, the personality, the environment, even the universe, is more than the sum of its parts. The scientist with an ounce of faith would say, with Gerald Manley Hopkins, that, "The world is charged with the grandeur of God." Such conviction comes as much from the mystery of the whole world as from the calculation of the parts.

---

8. John L. McKenzie, *The Old Testament Without Illusion* (Garden City, N.Y.: Image Books, 1980), 11.

As McKenzie affirmed, Jews and Christians have traditionally held that the Bible brought into the world and articulated in verbal form the mind and heart of God. It was certainly true—and they have mostly understood it to be true—that Amos wrote it, and Jeremiah wrote it. It was not a matter of indifference to them that Moses was distinct from Isaiah in time, place, circumstance, and personality; or that many of the things that Paul wrote never entered the mind of Ezra or Qoheleth of Ecclesiastes. Nor did it always escape their attention that the widely divergent historical circumstances, cultural influences, and literary conventions influenced what and how these men wrote.

Yet throughout a major part of its history, what was seen as distinct with regard to the Bible was not the commonplace of human agency or the distinguishing of human authorship, but the pervading presence of a divine hand. John McKenzie wrote: "The belief that God wrote the Bible existed in Judaism before Christian times and was accepted with no modification by the apostolic church. New Testament references to God's authorship of the Bible show a not surprising affinity in thought and in word to Jewish expressions of this belief."[9]

McKenzie says this in order to dispute the very concept. But the fact that he sees this conviction carried from early biblical times, through the church fathers including Augustine, down through the Reformation, and even to modern times is no accidental or peculiar point of view. It is, instead, strong testimony to the sense that if God indeed condescended to the estate of humanity, with the intention of making himself known, then the result of that condescension could only be a verbal communication of his mind and will.

The Scope of Scripture—Why "Literal" Is Not the Right Word. Mark Twain said the difference between the "right word" and "almost the right word" is the difference between "lightning" and "lightning-bug." No matter how strongly the student of Scripture holds to its authoritative nature, there are reasons that the idea of a literal interpretation jars the sensibilities and seems to conflict with the very thing that

---

9. Ibid.

makes Scripture so powerful and effective in Christian life and thought.

What is often misunderstood, or at least not fully appreciated, is the fact that words are useful because they are subtle. They are not always descriptive or imperative or analytical; they are also evocative of feelings, motives, and intuitions. They express truth through careful recording, but they also express truth through wild exaggeration: "If your right eye causes you to sin, tear it out and throw it away" (Matt. 5:29). Scripture uses description, but it also uses poetic imagination: "Moab is my washbasin; on Edom I hurl my shoe; over Philistia I shout in triumph" (Ps. 108:9). It tells history, but it also tells parables.

This tells us clearly that, while the Word is important—indeed, indispensable—the Word also points to something beyond itself. Words are subtle enough to convey experience and to suggest a reality beyond the visible.

Jeremiah's prophesy is punctuated by passages known as Jeremiah's "complaints." They are expressions of doubt and protest against God for the almost unbearable torment of Jeremiah's life. On one occasion we read: "Then I said, 'Ah, Lord God, how utterly you have deceived this people and Jerusalem, saying,"It shall be well with you," even while the sword is at the throat'" (Jer. 4:10).

Do these writings, so important to the spirit of the Book of Jeremiah, express the whole truth about God? Does he deceive his people? Or are the words intended to convey more than that? We can see this matter clearly if we appreciate the fact that these words convey to us, not just simple meanings and propositions, but the life of a man, with his God-infused experience of struggle and faith, including doubts and fears. The prophecy presents to us the full range of a man's experience as he stood before the living God. Even so, it is not the experience of Jeremiah that gives this work its importance; it is that *through it,* through the eyes of Jeremiah, we come to see God.

Returning to our question, then, "Are words and propositions the content of revelation?" The answer is yes if we mean by that the full range of what words can convey, their capability of doing more than simply declaring a truth, and making human experience a lens through which reality can be known in all its subtle shades and contours.

It is, therefore, at the very heart of biblical revelation to say that God has condescended to our capacity for language when he conveys to us the things of God verbally, in language. This is certainly what Paul meant when he said:

> God has revealed to us through the Spirit; for the Spirit searches everything, even the depths of God. For what human being knows what is truly human except the human spirit that is within? So also no one comprehends what is truly God's except the Spirit of God. Now we have received . . . the Spirit that is from God, so that we may understand the gifts bestowed on us by God. And we speak of these things in words not taught by human wisdom but taught by the Spirit, interpreting spiritual things to those who are spiritual (1 Cor. 2:10–13).

The words of Scripture convey something of God in a manner that can be appreciated in human experience. That is very different from the idea that Scripture only conveys information in an impersonal sense. That is the danger lurking in unreflective fundamentalism. But it is also more than something centered on human experience, which is actually only "a record of man's response to the presence and activity of God." Either the word taken literally (radical fundamentalism) or human experience taken as fundamental (classical liberalism) can be a way of making the Word of God opaque to the reality it is intended to convey.

To believe God speaks is to believe he makes himself known; to miss that point is to miss the connection between Scripture and revelation. Kittel's *Theological Dictionary of the New Testament,* in an article by Albrecht Oepke, puts this matter in a well-balanced manner when it states:

> Revelation is *not* the communication of supernatural knowledge, and *not* the stimulation of numinous feelings. The revelation can indeed give rise to knowledge and is necessarily accompanied by numinous feelings; yet it does not itself consist in these things but in quite essentially the *action* of Yahweh, an unveiling of His essential hiddenness, His offering of Himself in fellowship.

It is the *fullness* of divine revelation that should impress us when we consider its content. The term used in 2 Timothy 3:16 to describe the nature of Scripture is *theopneustos*, "God-breathed." As such, it is "useful for teaching, for reproof, for correction, and for training in righteousness." This means that it is necessarily verbal: the *words* are essential to the very idea of God condescending to the instruction of human beings. But one must also see that God breathes *life* into these words: they present us with more than propositions and abstract truths, or even historical facts. Instead, they bring before us the prophet, or the apostle, or the patriarch who has stood before God with a response of faith or of doubt, with sin and repentance, and with a new insight into the reality of God in his dealings with Israel and the church, as well as the world itself. This is why Protestant theology has often insisted that the content of revelation is Jesus Christ himself: "For in him all the fullness of God was pleased to dwell" (Col. 1:19). From that perspective, from the perspective of the life, death, and resurrection of Christ, we see the full disclosure of God's way with his creation. And it is in this that we find the meaning and the content of revelation.

Questions for Review and Reflection

1. How is knowledge gained through the natural sciences different from revealed knowledge? How are these two sources of knowledge alike?
2. What arguments would you give for the necessity of revelation?
3. What common human experiences argue for the validity of a supernaturally revealed knowledge?
4. What are the two classes of revelation? How are they different?
5. Give an example of what might be termed "general revelation." Give an example of "special revelation."
6. Why is the concept of "special revelation" significant in Christian theology?
7. How would you define "inspiration?" What is the meaning of "inspired" Scripture?

CHAPTER TWO

WHAT CAN WE POSSIBLY SAY ABOUT GOD?

Some basics:
God Is
God Is One
God Is Three in One

God Is

Though the Bible does not argue for the existence of God (it assumes God and never turns back from that point), we might say that the existence of God is established in the Bible by God's faithfulness to his promise. The covenant name of God, YHWH, is linguistically related to the words spoken to Moses in Exodus 3:14: "I am who I am." It's significant, however, that this mysterious self-identity can also be translated, "I will be whom I will be." It is as much as saying (to Moses), "You will see who I am, when you trust yourself to me."

If there were a biblical argument for the existence of God, it might be formulated in this way: God's existence is established by the correspondence of *promise* and *fulfillment*. God is faithful to his word. That speaks of more than "existence," it speaks of the real life experience of the living God. That is why the identity of God in the Old Testament is spoken of in terms of what he has done: "I am the LORD your God, who brought you out of the land of Egypt, out of the house of slavery" (Deut. 5:6). Or, he is identified in terms of who has known him as God: "The God of your ancestors, the God of Abraham, the God of Isaac, and the God of Jacob" (Exod. 3:15).

Mere existence—that is, apart from God's historical acts or his personal relationships—seems to be of no concern to the writers of the Bible. They are not engaged with God as a theoretical possibility, but as a living, acting reality in their lives and their communities.

Arguments for the Existence of God

So why does the problem of the existence of God come up in theology? We might say it is because of the possibility of imagining that God does not exist, and that this gives occasion to error and sin. It is the work of theology not simply to explain what is given in revelation, but to answer the errors arising from false reason and faulty imagination. That is why works in theology have grown ever more complex and extensive in the course of time.

The question about the being or existence of God has been answered classically using two lines of thought. It is convenient to think of these two as *a priori* and *a posteriori* arguments. *A priori* means an argument that proceeds from the logical necessity of the idea itself, whereas *a posteriori* means that one begins with the consequence of a certain reality and argues back to its logical necessity.

The Ontological Argument

The first and most famous *a priori* argument for the existence of God was stated by Anselm (1033–1109), archbishop of Canterbury, in his work entitled *Proslogion*. This line of reasoning we commonly refer to as the **ontological** argument for the existence of God.

The argument was perhaps more easily grasped by people of Anselm's own time, people living in an age convinced of the reality of universals **(realism)** than in an age long under the spell of **nominalism,** such as our own. Nominalism denies that universal values, such as goodness and beauty, or categories of objects, such as human and insect, exist apart from the objects they name. **Realism** accepts the idea that even if nothing perfectly beautiful exists, there is still the reality of beauty; if no insect were to exist, there is still the idea of insect as a universal category.

Keeping in mind the medieval predisposition to think in terms of the reality of universals, we can begin to appreciate the genius of Anselm's argument. The argument proceeds as follows, in the form of a prayer to God:

> We certainly believe that you are something than which nothing greater can be conceived.

> But is there any such nature, since "the fool has said in his heart: God is not"?

> However, when this very same fool hears what I say, when he hears of "something than which nothing greater can be conceived," he certainly understands what he hears.

> "What he understands stands in relation to his understanding (*esse in intellectu*), even if he does not understand that it exists. For it is one thing for a thing to stand in relation to our understanding; it is another for us to understand that it really exists. . . .

> And certainly that than which a greater cannot be conceived cannot stand only in relation to the understanding. For if it stands at least in relation to the understanding, it can be conceived to be also in reality, and this is something greater. . . .

> Therefore, something than which a greater cannot be conceived undoubtedly both stands in relation to the understanding and exists in reality.[1]

Thus Anselm's unstated premise that there is a hierarchy of being—that is, graduated qualities of being—drives him inevitably to the conclusion that for those greater realities to exist is greater than the concept without the reality. God, who is "that than which a greater cannot be conceived,"

---

1. As cited in *The Many-Faced Argument: Recent Studies on the Ontological Argument for the Existence of God*, John Hick and Arthur C. McGill, eds. (New York: The MacMillan Company, 1967), 4–6.

therefore necessarily exists. He must exist, that is, if a hierarchy of being is the undoubted nature of reality. What nominalism, as well as related philosophies of romanticism and pantheism, have done to our sense of hierarchy would be interesting for us to explore at this point. In the interest of space and time, however, let us simply say that modern people have trouble seeing this order of reality in quite the self-evident way that medieval Europeans did.

The Cosmological Argument

Modern people find the *a posteriori* argument much more congenial to the way they grasp reality. That is partly because it relates to the inductive method of modern physical sciences. These are called ***cosmological*** arguments because they begin with the apparent causes, effects, and purposes of the world itself, and reason back to the necessity of God. Thomas Aquinas summarized these in five succinct arguments. One is based on motion, the second on efficient cause, the third on the relationship of possibility and necessity, the fourth on the graduation of being, and the fifth on the purposefulness of things. This last argument is often referred to as the teleological argument.

To give a sense of how these cosmological arguments reason back to God, I want to touch briefly on the first and last of Thomas's cosmological proofs.

Thomas listed the argument from motion first because it was the most obvious and the one most easily grasped. Things in our world are clearly in motion, he wrote. And: "Whatever is in motion is put in motion by another." That mover must, in turn, have been acted on by something else. We can follow this chain of cause and effect—of moved object and mover—all the way back until we "arrive at a first mover, put in motion by no other; and this everyone understands to be God."[2] The prime mover, the first mover, is the unmoved mover. And this, Aquinas argued, is, by definition the creator God—the one who has no beginning, yet stands at the beginning of all else.

---

2. See *Philosophy of Religion: A Book of Readings*, George L. Abernethy and Thomas A. Langford, eds. (New York: The MacMillan Company, 1969), 184.

The other argument given by Aquinas that I wanted to touch upon is found in many forms, and will probably be quite familiar to the reader. Although it is properly called a cosmological argument, it is also commonly referred to as a **teleological** argument. This word derives from the Greek *teleos*, meaning "goal" or "end." It is fundamentally an argument based upon the apparent design of the world, the idea that the world seems purposeful. If there is a design, there must be a Designer. If there are purposes, there must be a Mind to whom purposes would occur. In Aquinas' words: "Therefore some intelligent being exists by whom all natural things are directed to their end; and this being is God."[3]

The ontological, cosmological, and teleological arguments for the existence of God have been articulated in various ways by a number of philosophers and theologians besides these, and although these arguments have played a part in giving answer to the crudest and most basic of atheistic arguments, they have not figured prominently in the development of Christian theology. The most serious arguments against the existence of a theistic God usually begin with the apparent contradiction in the goodness of an all-powerful God, and the existence of pain and evil in the world. These arguments are answered in the Christian response to **theodicy**, or the problem of evil.

The problem presented by speculation that God does not exist is almost altogether one that occurs to modern people and not to the ancients. For the people of biblical times, it was the existence of men and women that was precarious, not God's existence. However, the problem presented by the reality of evil in a world created by a good and all-powerful God is one that has demanded the attention of both modern people and ancient people alike. Modern theologians and thinkers such as John Hick and C. S. Lewis, philosophers such as Immanuel Kant, as well as the ancient writer of the Book of Job and the prophet Habbakkuk, all have wrestled with the problem of evil as it made an impact on belief in the goodness or the existence of God. We will return to this question of theodicy in the next chapter.

3. As cited in *Philosophy of Reason*, 185. Also see Aquinas's *Summa Theologica*, Volume 1, Third Article.

God Is One

The beginning of any biblical understanding of God must involve the idea that God is one. We refer to this concept broadly as **monotheism**. The oneness of God is given its clearest expression in what is known as the "Shema Israel," from the first two Hebrew words of Deuteronomy 6:4: "Hear, O Israel: The LORD our God is one LORD," (RSV).[4]

The importance of the oneness of God to both Judaism and Christianity—and to the world that has been so profoundly affected by this Judeo-Christian premise—is almost impossible to overestimate. Four implications come to mind very forcefully:

1. The oneness of God implies the oneness of the world. The world is not a patchwork of divine powers, unrelated and arbitrary events, under the spell of petty deities, as the pagans sensed it; it is instead the unified work of a single mind and will. The world's existence and character, therefore, can be reliably expected to reflect the character of its Maker.

2. The oneness of God implies the fundamental unity of humankind. The varieties of nations were once taken as absolute divisions in mankind; not only were there different hues of skin and different languages and customs, but also there were different gods. The rise of monotheism meant the dawn of a universal concept of humanity, for all human beings were created by the same God and were, in some sense, brothers and sisters.

3. The oneness of God also implies the uniformity of nature. What occurs in nature cannot be explained by the arbitrary will of local deities, but can be thought of as the consistent operation of God. Because of monotheism, then, we see a growing expectation of a uniform natural world. We can extrapolate from this how monotheism sets the intellectual predisposition necessary for the natural sciences. Empirical sciences depend upon the presupposition of a uniform nature. The idea of a uniform nature is, in turn, an intuitive or a religious sentiment. It is a sentiment productive

---

4. This is an alternate reading in the NRSV. The text is first rendered "Hear, O Israel: The LORD is our God, the LORD alone."

of a scientific view of the world, but it is one that is made possible by the belief in one God.

4. Monotheism also implies that human moral behavior is judged by a common universal standard. One of the most remarkable features of the Decalogue, or the Ten Commandments, is its complete lack of any necessary reference to the national or cultural life of Israel. The commandments come to us out of a world wholly preoccupied by national or tribal identities, yet these words amazingly speak as if to the whole world, without any national presuppositions. Feasts, cultic regulation, place, tribal identity all are forgotten; thus they are laws that can be applied to any individual or any nation, at any time in history.

Biblical ethics, therefore, do not emerge from the diversity of humankind, but from the simplicity of God in his love for the world. Monotheism yields monoethics.

The most difficult step for the historic church, of course, was the next one: building a bridge from the implied monotheism of the Old Testament to the implied trinitarian doctrine of the New Testament. Over a period of more than seven centuries, during which seven great ecumenical councils took place on three continents, the church hammered out important areas of agreement on the Christian concept of God as Father, as Son, and as Holy Spirit.

God Is Three in One

When we consider the very difficult Christian doctrine of the Trinity, we can begin with this observation: The monotheism of Judaism cannot be adequately defined as simply belief in one God. Monotheism can be merely the worship of the idea of a fundamental oneness. In that sense the monotheism of Islam, the monism of the Pantheist, and the monotheism of Aristotle look very similar. They all believe in one god, or at least in a unified reality. Judaic monotheism, however, was more impressed with the idea that human beings live in the presence of a God who is always and everywhere the *same*. It was not theoretical oneness they were interested in; instead, they were impressed that the God of Abraham (in Haran) was the same as the God of Isaac (in Canaan) and the God of Jacob (in Egypt). God did

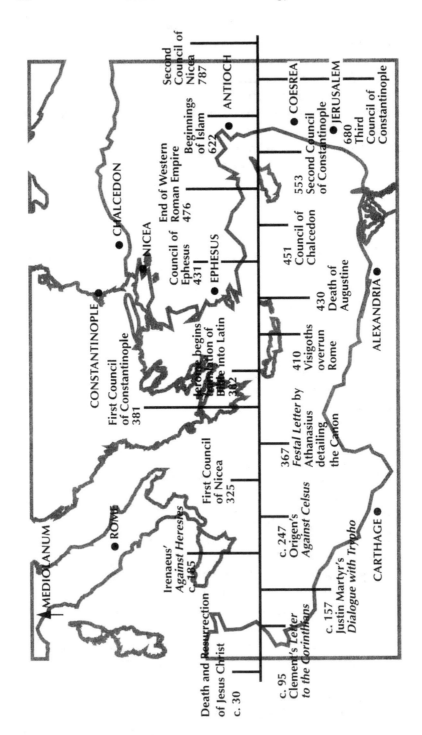

MEDIOLANUM

• ROME

CONSTANTINOPLE •

CHALCEDON •

• NICEA

EPHESUS •

ANTIOCH •

• COESREA

JERUSALEM •

ALEXANDRIA •

CARTHAGE •

Death and Resurrection
of Jesus Christ
c. 30

c. 95
Clement's Letter
to the Corinthians

c. 157
Justin Martyr's
Dialogue with Trypho

Irenaeus'
Against Heresies
c. 185

c. 247
Origen's
Against Celsus

First Council
of Nicea
325

367
Festal Letter by
Athanasius
detailing
the Canon

First Council
of Constantinople
381

Jerome begins
translation of
Bible into Latin
382

410
Visigoths
overrun
Rome

430
Death of
Augustine

451
Council of
Chalcedon

476
End of Western
Roman Empire

Council of
Ephesus
431

Beginnings
of Islam
622

553
Second Council
of Constantinople

680
Third
Council of
Constantinople

Second
Council of
Nicea
787

not change with seasons or locale or nationalities. He was constant, even when people and conditions changed.

This idea of God, as Karl Barth pointed out, is very different from the mere "glorification of the 'number one.'" "Necessarily, then, we must say that God is absolutely one, but we cannot say that the absolutely one is God." The notion of the supremacy of "the one," Barth continued, tells us little about the character of this one power. Thus the "cosmic forces in whose objectivity it is believed that the unique has been formed are varied." Moreover, it is "only by an act of violence that one of these can be given pre-eminence over the others, so that to-day it is nature, and tomorrow spirit, or to-day fate and tomorrow reason, or to-day desire and to-morrow duty. . . . For all his heavenly divinity each Zeus must constantly be very anxious in face of the existence and arrival of very powerful rivals. . . . Monotheism is all very well so long as this conflict does not break out. But it inevitably will break out again and again."[5]

Barth recognized that the monotheism of the Old Testament is not simply a matter of mathematics. It is the reliability of God's character that matters in biblical monotheism—the fact that men and women everywhere, under every circumstance, meet the same God. A theoretical oneness of some object or reality that we call "God" is not the same at all, as both Jewish and Christian thinkers have recognized.

The complexity of a God who "meets" humanity, who communicates himself to people, is therefore the first link in the connection between Jewish monotheism and Christian trinitarianism. Both speak of God's making himself known in the world, in the creation of man (Gen. 1:26), in royal representatives or messiahs (Ps. 2:7), in the Word of God (Isa. 55:11 and John 1:1), in the Spirit of God (Isa. 63:10). Both Old and New Testaments seem to require a view of God who is the same and yet varied in his manifestation. This complexity of God and this fundamental relatedness of God is expressed in the Christian doctrine of the Trinity.

---

5. Karl Barth, *The Doctrine of Reconciliation: Church Dogmatics*, vol. 2, pt. 1, ed. G.W. Bromily and T.U. Torrance (Edinburgh: T & T Clark, 1956), 448–449.

The Biblical Foundation of Trinitarian Doctrine

Even Christians will sometimes object that the idea of the Trinity is not biblical. It is true that the explicit form of a trinitarian doctrine is not found in the Bible. But clearly the basis of that formulation is there—so clearly, in fact, that we can hardly imagine the biblical references to God *not* giving rise to some kind of trinitarian conclusion about the nature of God.

The discussion of the Trinity began when the simplicity of a single God was made impossible by the witness that Jesus Christ is identified as God. The discussion over Christology gradually became discussions over the Trinity. What was obvious was the New Testament witness to the deity of Jesus Christ, including his pre-existence. John and Paul, in particular, give support to the pre-existence of Christ as divine Son or Word of God. John's prologue identifies the Word of God both with God and with Jesus (John 1:1–18). Jesus told the Jews, "Before Abraham was born, I am" (John 8:58). The divine pre-existence of Christ is also strongly stated in John 17:5 and Philippians 2:5–11.

The synoptic Gospels concentrate upon the deeds and events in Jesus' life that indicate his identity with God the Father. For instance, Jesus forgives sins and is thought by the Jews present to be blasphemous in laying claim to what only God could do (Mark 2:6–10). The Gospel of Mark makes frequent reference to Jesus as "the Son of God." Jesus' confession of his status as the Son of God leads to the Jewish condemnation, whereupon he is taken to Pilate to be put to death.

All of these matters are taken up in the chapter on the doctrine of the person of Christ (chap. 5). It is enough here simply to indicate how the picture of Jewish monotheism becomes quite complicated once this strong identity of the Messiah with God the Father is made. Added to that, we have clear references to the deity of the Spirit or the Holy Spirit. These we deal with in chapter 7. The simultaneous confession of God as the Father, along with the identity of the Son with the Father, along with the references to the Holy Spirit as God, therefore, creates the necessity of speaking about the relationship of these three, all of whom are identified as God and yet do not lose their status as separate persons.

Some biblical passages bring the three together. A notable instance would be the baptism of Jesus, in which the voice from heaven speaks as Father concerning his Son, and the Spirit of God descends upon Jesus "like a dove" (Matt. 3:16–17). If God is one, in the biblical witness, then he must also in some sense be three. It was this mystery of the biblical witness that continually pushed the church toward a full-blown trinitarian doctrine.

The Shaping of Trinitarian Doctrine

The doctrine of the Trinity did not, therefore, come self-evidently and fully stated from the Bible itself. Nor was it something that emerged overnight in the early church. Instead, it came to light in stages. First there were the Christological questions that captured the attention of thinkers in the church. Later the doctrine of the deity and personality of the Holy Spirit was taking shape. Even down into the Middle Ages, with the controversy between the Eastern and Western churches over the procession of the Spirit (see chap. 7), there were still fine points of trinitarian doctrine that were not entirely settled. As a matter of fact, there are some not settled even today.

One might well guess that they never will be. The idea of God, as the church fathers generally recognized, must be largely given over to mystery. Augustine said that we speak of the Trinity, not because we can explain this mystery, but only in order "not to be silent" and allow greater error.

Tertullian was probably the first writer to use the term "Trinity." And by the use of that term he meant what was to become the heart of Christian confessions of the Trinity: That God is essentially one and essentially manifold at one and the same time. Even before the Council of Nicea, as the church historian Phillip Schaff pointed out, the conscious necessity of the Trinity had taken hold of the mind of the church. As Schaff said, "In the article of the Trinity the Christian conception of God completely defines itself, in distinction alike from the abstract monotheism of the Jewish religion, and from the polytheism and dualism of the heathen." This idea, he said, "ruled even Ante-Nicene theology, though it did not attain its fixed definition till the Nicene age."[6]

---

6. Phillip Schaff, *History of the Christian Church*, vol. 2 (Grand Rapids: Wm. B. Eerdmans Publishing Company, 1970), 565.

By the time of the Council of Nicea (A.D. 325), it seems that the broad outlines of orthodox trinitarian theology had been articulated. The essential position of the church, as it expressed the Apostolic faith, were reduced to a few phrases in what is known as the Athanasian Creed: "We worship one God in Trinity, and Trinity in unity; neither confounding the persons, nor dividing the substance."

■ —————————————————————————— ■

This emblem of the Holy Trinity is taken from the *Handbook of Christian Symbolism,* by W. and G. Audsley (London: Day & Son, 1865), of which there is a copy in the Library of Metropolitan Museum, in New York City. The letters on the outside circles represent the three persons of the Trinity, while the center circle is designated *Deus,* or God. *P* is for *Pater,* or Father. *F* represents *Filius* or Son. *SS* is for *Spiritus Sanctus* or Holy Spirit. The whole symbol represents the central belief in the Trinity, expressed as the unity of the substance without confusion of persons. Arianism threatened the unity of substance, and Sabellianism lost the integrity of the persons. Orthodox trinitarianism embraces both the distinction of the divine persons and the fundamental unity of divine being.

■ —————————————————————————— ■

By this time it was clear, as Tertullian had earlier seen, that the Trinity was more than an apparent tripartite revelation of God; it was also essential to any idea of the nature of God. The two sides of this trinitarian concept became known as the **economic Trinity** and the **immanent Trinity** or **ontologic Trinity**. In terms of the economic Trinity, God reveals himself as Father, Son, and Holy Spirit. This has to do with the way he relates to his creation. In speaking of the immanent Trinity, however, we say that God, in himself, even apart from his self-disclosure or his operation upon the world, is three distinct persons of undivided substance.

The Idea of Person

What exactly was meant by person? Tertullian had used the term *prosopon*, which began as the word for mask and was widely used to denote a part or a character in a drama. Since it tended to imply "person" in the sense of "individual," some of the church fathers, including the great Athanasius, were reluctant to use it. By the time of the Cappadocian fathers (Basil the Great, Gregory of Nyssa, his brother, and Gregory of Nazianzus), the word *prosopon* was being replaced by *hypostasis*: God is of one *ousia* (substance) and three *hypostases* (persons).

The use of "person" to describe the three-in-oneness of God becomes confusing for the modern Christian, however, since it sounds very much like the idea of an "individual" or a private center of consciousness, the way it also sounded to Athansius. Even in English, however, the word "person" need not imply individual in the sense of private consciousness. When we think of personal characteristics, for instance, we nearly always think in relational terms. A person is "friendly," "reserved," "courageous," "observant," "thrifty," "honest"—we could make the list five pages long. Each one of the terms describes how someone *relates* to people, things, the world, God—all that is outside the self. We almost might say that we cannot adequately describe a *person* without calling upon terms that describe him or her in *relationship* to something else.

This brings us to the heart of what is meant by the persons of the Godhead. It is seen in this, in fact, that God—and, by extension, reality itself—is profoundly and even essentially relational. When Basil began to define *hypostasis*, for instance, he defined it as the relational particulars of father, son, and spirit. Gregory of Nazianzus clarified this concept and went further when he said that "The name of Father is neither a name of essence nor of action, but it indicates a relation."[7] But it was John of Damascus that gave this thought its most memorable picture, that of a *perichoretic* Trinity—a Triune God dancing in a circle. The Son exists inasmuch as he is Son of the Father; the Father exists by virture of the fact of the Son; each lives because of the love of the Spirit.

What we find developing here is not an explanation of the Trinity, which comes to us basically as a description of the biblical witness. Rather, it is the recognition of a great mystery. Both the oneness of all things and the manifold distinction of all things are realities. In pantheism, the oneness negates the significance of the many, and the deeper reality is thought to be *no distinction,* and thus *no relationship.* In materialism it is the manifold reality that overwhelms any hope of unity and thus of purposefulness or community. What is real is only what can be seen (the manifold variety of *things*). But the Trinity means that both the one and the many are real, because the deepest meaning of all things is relationship. This is certainly what is meant when John wrote, "God is love" (1 John 4:8). God is relationship; and relationship requires both distinction and unity, both individuality and community. Both are real, and both are at the heart of reality.

Principle Errors in Relation to the Trinity

The two sides of trinitarian theology, representing the two curbs on either side of orthodoxy's straight road, have to do with adhering to the faith in one God while not sacrificing the distinct reality of the three persons. The Athana-

---

7. *Or.* 29.16; cited in Edmund J. Fortman, *The Triune God* (Grand Rapids: Baker Book House, 1982), 81.

sian Creed states the matter most succinctly with the words that "We worship one God in Trinity, and Trinity in Unity, *neither confusing the Persons nor dividing the substance*" *(neque confundentes personas neque substantiam separantes).*

It always seemed clear to some of the most thoughtful of Christians, if not always to the majority, that the New Testament witness demanded adherence to both the unity of God and the three persons of God, even when efforts to reconcile them were difficult, if not impossible, to conceive, and even more difficult to the poor and simple or unlearned Christians. For the most part, trinitarian theology was pushed forward by some quite formidable attempts to deal with the problem, attempts that sought to preserve either the independence of the Son of God or the simplicity of Christian monotheism. The two errors that resulted, therefore, might well be predictable. The following is a brief description of the two major classes of trinitarian divergence.

Dynamistic Monarchianism. Paul of Samosata was the most prominent of the teachers of **dynamistic Monarchianism,** a concept of the Father and Son that is also known as **adoptionism**. He chose to emphasize the excellence of the character of Jesus, and the independence of his humanity, to such an extant that Jesus' connection with God the Father could only be seen as one of an adopted Son. Harnack expressed the argument of Paul and the other dynamistic monarchianists in this way: "Through immovable steadfastness in this relationship He united Himself intimately with God by influence of the spirit and unity of will, thus securing the power to perform miracles and fitness to become the Redeemer, and in addition attaining a permanent oneness with God."[8]

Sabellian Modalism. Early in the third century, the Roman Christian Sabellius sought to define the three persons of the Trinity as mere manifestations of God. God has three modes of revelation, he would say, as Father, as Son, and as Holy Spirit. Just as the sun has light, heat, and roundness, and yet there is only one sun, so God retains his uniqueness

---

8. A. Harnack, *History of Dogma*, 3:31ff.; cited by Otto W. Heick, *A History of Christian Thought*, vol. 1 (Philadelphia: Fortress Press, 1969), 148.

while he creates as Father, becomes incarnate as Son, and goes out to the world as Holy Spirit.

The *prosopa* are therefore not materially related, but temporally independent manifestations of God. There is no unity of community, but the simple oneness of an abstract monad; not three persons in actuality, but one Person with manifold ways of self-disclosure.

Sabellianism is a type of Monarchianism with the opposite results of dynamistic Monarchianism. While dynamistic Monarchianism preserves the independence of the persons of the Trinity but loses the unity, Sabellianism preserves the unity and loses the distinctness of the persons. The most succinct definition of modalism is to say it is the economic Trinity without the immanent Trinity.

Dynamistic Monarchianism had failed to hold to the later standard of the Athanasian Creed by dividing the substance of God; Sabellian modalism (modalistic Monarchianism) had failed in confusing the persons.

This later modalism, unlike the dynamistic Monarchianism, came as a convenient explanation of the Trinity, which had the added attraction of being decidedly monotheistic. It therefore had broad influence. In fact, the third-century church at Rome was largely under sway of a modified modalism, even though Sabellius had been expelled for his teachings.

These controversies, however, provided a bridge over which thinking Christians could move to an important new development in the thought of the church. In a way, Christians always knew that revelation called for both the reality of the Son, apart from the Father (although the status of the Spirit might not have been that clear); and they knew the dangers of dividing the reality of God into multiple deities. Yet how to be faithful in expressing both of these necessary points of revelation, and avoiding the errors, was not at all clear. This became clear only with time. In the words of Gregory of Nazianzus, the "breaking lights" of trinitarian theology, with its strong emphasis upon a *homoousian* hypostasianism (that is a same-substance personalism), began to come clear.

Questions for Review and Reflection

1. In what sense does the Bible (as distinct from theology or philosophy) speak of the reality of God?
2. How would you state the essential argument of Anselm's ontological proof for the existence of God?
3. Why do you think the ontological argument is usually less likely to persuade modern people than the cosmological arguments of Aquinas?
4. What is Aquinas's argument from motion for the existence of God?
5. What consequencies are there in our thinking once we accept the idea of one God?
6. What is it about Jewish monotheism that leads to the possibility of a trinitarian concept of God?
7. What is the difference between the "economic" Trinity and the "ontologic" or "immament" Trinity?
8. Contrast dynamistic Monarchianism and Sabellian modalism.
9. Why do you think some would say that Sabellianism was influenced by the desire of the church to express an uncompromised monotheism?
10. Do you think the concepts of the Trinity expressed in the contemporary church are sometimes more Sabellian than orthodox?
11. What practical problems of human life and thought might be solved by a trinitarian concept of God?

■ ─────────────────────── ■

CHAPTER THREE

GOD AND THE WORLD

One of the most critical questions in all theology is how God is understood to relate to the world. Five broad possibilities must come into view before we can see clearly what is distinct in the biblical vision of God and the world:

1. God is identified with the world **(Pantheism).**
2. God is identified with the world, but is more than the world **(Panentheism).**
3. God created the world, distinct from himself, and continues in dynamic relationship to the world **(Theism).**
4. God created the world and no longer operates upon that creation—he is radically distinct from the world **(Deism).**
5. God is a construction of the human mind, projecting an answer to unfulfilled material needs **(Materialism).**

In 1 and 5 the relationship of God and the world is fundamentally illusory. In 1, the illusory world is a surface manifestation of an underlying united reality. In 5, the illusion of God masks the multiplicity of real things. In neither is true relationship possible between the world and the divine, for in each the reality of either God or the world is in question.

Looking at 2 and 4, we find the recognition that God is more than the world *or* that God stands prior to the world. Both recognize the need for a transcendent God in order to explain the world. Number 2, panentheism, might see God as projected beyond (or even at the end of) the process of present creation. (Teilhard de Chardin's philosophy and *process theology* are two examples.) Number 4, deism, sees God at the very beginning of the cosmic process. In 2, God is radically dependent upon the world; in 4, the world is radically dependent upon God. In each, relationship flows one way—from God to the world, or from the world to God.

Finally, 3 represents the orthodox Christian conception of a God who creates and remains in dynamic relationship to the world. The world is both real and dependent. God is both real and transcendent. The world is a reflection of the mind of God, and the mind of God reacts to the independence of this world. Relatedness remains at the heart of this idea of reality, not a one-way cause and effect relationship, but a dialogical relationship in which the reality of both God and the world is reflected in their combination of both dependence and independence, of dialogical separateness.

This option number 3, of course, describes Christian theism. From this point we will look more closely at the distinguishing features of the Christian understanding of **cosmology,** or the doctrine of the world. Our survey of Christian cosmology includes the following: (1) *creatio ex nihilo,* the doctrine of "creation out of nothing," (2) *preservation,* (3) the independence of creation, (4) the dependence of creation, (5) the problem of evil, (6) **providence,** and (7) heaven and earth.

Creatio ex Nihilo

The basic thought in the Christian teaching on creation is that God created everything, and therefore everything is completely dependent on him. The proposition by which we attempt to say this is *creatio ex nihilo,* "creation out of nothing." In other words, God's creative act was not limited by, or conditioned by, anything at all. There was no primal matter, such as pagans mostly assumed, out of which the world and its features were fashioned. If that had been the case, we would say that the world owes its character to God *and* the primal substance or force out of which he created. With this doctrine, however, one is saying that we can credit to God alone every aspect of the created order—and the very fact that there is something rather than nothing.

Furthermore, ultimately the character of creation must be completely attributed to God and necessarily reflects the character of God. If God is good, then creation must be good. If there is evil in the world, a flaw in the constitution of humanity, then we must either attribute that to God who created, or we must find another explanation apart from the created order (we will return to the particular problem of pain or problem of evil later).

The Biblical Basis of *Creatio ex Nihilo*

The first creation passage in Genesis (1:1–2:4a) gives us the language and images for speaking of creation out of nothing. It begins by saying that when God created, "the earth was a formless void" (v. 2). Anything that we know by the senses has either form or substance, or both. When Genesis says "formless" and "void," then we must take this to mean "nothing."

As if to emphasize the point, the sequence in the six days of creation involves, first, giving form in the place of formlessness; and, second, filling the void. Notice the order of the days of creation:

Giving Form

Day one: "God separated the light from the darkness" (v. 4).

Day two: God separated the waters above from the waters below (vv. 6–7).

Day three: God separated the waters from the dry land (vv. 9–10).

Filling the Void

Day three: God called forth vegetation (vv. 11–12).
Day four: God created the moon and sun—"the greater light to rule the day and the lesser light to rule the night and the stars" (vv. 14–16).
Day five: God created animals of the sea and air (vv. 20–23).
Day six: God created the land animals, and he created humankind in his own image to have dominion over "every living thing" (vv. 24–30).

Thus, from the very beginning of the Bible, God is seen as being the one who absolutely determines all things. The idea is reflected upon in John's prologue (John 1:1–18). Only, in this case, the emphasis is placed upon the *Logos* or Word that created: "All things came into being through him, and without him not one thing came into being" (v. 3).

In Genesis the idea of the world's absolute dependence upon God is suggested in the word that God *made* (bara) the heavens and the earth, rather than "gave birth" to the cosmos. For him to fashion the world as something other than himself, rather than give birth to the world, means that God was under no necessity of nature. He freely created what he willed to create; he was not imposed upon by some process that of necessity brought the world into existence. He was utterly free to act; thus the world is utterly dependent upon his will, and it is absolutely the world he wished to design. This is why it is important that the image of God is Father rather than "mother." The Father can *only* be understood as Maker, whereas the "mother" can easily be taken as one who "gives birth."

The Goodness of Creation

Since creation is absolutely the responsibility of its Maker, it must unreservedly be a reflection of his character. For this reason, the first Genesis creation story emphasizes at every turn that what God has made is "good" (Gen. 1:4, 10, 12, 18, 21, and 24). And when all had been made, God looked upon it and said that it was "very good" (v. 31). This is the first hint that what the Bible presents about God is going to be ultimately and always "gospel"—good news. Here it becomes evident that God's intentions toward the world, and toward humankind, are always and irrevocably good. There is no ambiguity in the will of God, and there is no fundamental ambiguity in nature.

The reality of evil must at least never be understood as a necessity of the created order. Sin, furthermore, cannot be blamed on nature. Sin and evil are fundamentally *against* nature, not a result of nature. This conviction has important consequences for the moral order of a society and the moral responsibility of the individual. The fuller implications here are fascinating; we will take up the more important ones in chapter 4.

■ ——————————————————— ■

Creatio ex Nihilo

But how didst Thou make the heaven and the earth, and what was the instrument of Thy so mighty work? For it was not as a human worker fashioning body from body, according to the fancy of his mind, in somewise able to assign a form which it perceives in itself by its inner eye. And whence should he be able to do this, hadst not Thou made that mind? And he assigns to it already existing, and as it were having a being, a form, as clay, or stone, or wood, or gold, or such like. And whence should these things be, hadst not Thou appointed them? Thou didst make for the work- man his body—Thou the mind commanding the limbs—Thou the matter whereof he makes anything— Thou the capacity whereby he may apprehend his art, and see within what he may do without—Thou the sense of his body, by which, as by an interpreter, he may from mind unto matter convey that which he doeth, and report to his mind what may have been done, that it within may consult the truth, presiding over itself, whether it be well done. All these things praise Thee, the Creator of all. But how dost Thou make them? How, O God, didst Thou make heaven and earth? Truly, neither in the heaven nor in the earth didst Thou make heaven and earth; nor in the air, nor in the waters, since these also belong to the heaven and the earth, nor in the whole world didst Thou make the whole world; because there was no place wherein it could be made before it was made, that it might be; nor didst Thou hold anything in Thy hand wherewith to make heaven and earth. For whence couldest Thou have what Thou hadst not made, whereof to make anything? For what is, save because Thou art? Therefore Thou didst speak and they were made, and in Thy Word Thou madest these things.

[Augustine, "The Confessions of St. Augustine," Book XI, 7, *The Nicene and Post-Nicene Fathers of the Church*, Vol. 8, First Series, ed. Philip Schaff (Grand Rapids: Wm. B. Eerdmans Publishing Company, 1988), 165.]

■ ──────────────── ■

Preservation

Beyond creation at the beginning, God also preserves his created order despite the fact that, through humanity, it has been given an independence that is contrary to God; the disaster of the fall, in other words, has not been allowed to undo utterly the good of creation.

This view is different from the doctrine of *creatio continua*, which asserts that God's creation takes place not simply "at the beginning," but along with each moment of existence. Creation, in the formulation of this doctrine, becomes not just a "once and for all" event at the beginning, but a continuing and contemporary reality. It emphasizes our dependence upon God even at this moment. The danger of this view is, as Emil Brunner has pointed out, that creation becomes a co-deity with God: this view "defiles the world and despiritualizes God; inevitably it is pantheistic."[1]

In other words, we lose two very important ideas in the doctrine of creation with this notion of "continual creation":

---

1. Emil Brunner, *The Christian Doctrine of Creation and Redemption, Dogmatics:* vol. 3 (Philadelphia: The Westminster Press, 1952), 33.

(1) we lose the idea of the independence of creation, and (2) we lose the idea of the otherness of God.

Later we will see why these two ideas in a Christian doctrine of creation are so important to a balanced Christian theism.

Yet one can go too far in the other direction, making creation too independent of God. In that case, creation is so rigorously confined to "the beginning" that God no longer enters into the matter in any important way. In that case, the danger is just the opposite of pantheism; it is deism.

The doctrine of preservation, as distinct from creation, recognizes that without God's sustaining the universe, it collapses into nothing. Shortly after the first developments in human uses of atomic energy, Brunner wrote,

> In this age of Atomic Energy perhaps it is easier for us to understand how it is that the world is not, as a matter of course, able to go on its way, or to prevent itself from being destroyed. At every moment God "upholds" the world above an abyss of nothingness, into which it could fall, if God were not holding it. In any case this Biblical view [of preservation] seems to be in greater harmony with the present aspect of scientific knowledge (in the sphere of Natural Science) than with that view put forward [in the last century that understood nature] in a fully deistic sense as an Absolute.[2]

Preservation means that the creation not only began in full dependence upon God, but also it is at every moment dependent upon him. It means that creation not only began with God's free and willing act, but also it continues moment by moment, existing by the gracious and altogether free will of God.

The Independence of Creation

Creation is God's first step toward a self-humiliation that came into final expression with the cross of Jesus Christ. This must be the case since the creation is made "other" than God. The very idea of relationship implies limitation, even self-limitation.

---

2. Ibid., 153.

If the world were *only* an extension and a perfect reflection of the will of God, then we would have to ask in what sense it is other than God. The stronger the **monistic** view of God—that is, the belief in one ultimate reality—then the more the idea of creation comes into question. If the world, and every event of history, is only God's will being performed, then in what sense can there be a relationship or love? In what sense, indeed, can God love the world (John 3:16)?

The answer is that love requires separateness, otherness. When God created the world other than himself, he created the possibility of a world freely choosing and glorifying him. It is no wonder that elements of Islam (and here I am thinking of Sufism) come to resemble the pantheism of the early Indus Valley. The element of utter control of God over creation leads naturally to the assumption that reality resides in God and nowhere else, since nothing occurs outside of God's will. The strongly transcendent monism of Islam, in this case, merges with the radically immanent Hindu view of God. Monism of any kind can result in pantheistic conclusions. If only one will exists, then all reality is an extension of that will. Relationship, in that case, means nothing.

Yet the paradoxical position of Christianity—that is, that God has made his creation free, and yet it is purely dependent upon him—stands as the most fundamental of relationships. God loves the world in that he has created it good; and its goodness is crowned by the fact that it is capable of loving and choosing God. Without independence it could not have attained the highest of possibilities—that is, to participate in God's freedom to love. Yet even that is a reflection of its utter dependence upon God.

To fully appreciate that paradox within the Christian idea of creation, we must turn to the other side: from the independence of creation to its *dependence.*

The Dependence of Creation

Over against the understanding of an independent creation is one of a dependent creation. This side must also be acknowledged, lest we revert to an eighteenth-century deism. E. L. Mascall called the distinctive element of the idea

of creation, "dependent reality." This concept was viewed in
contrast to views of the world as "real and independent"—
views that would include atheism, naturalism, pantheism
and any monistic belief, including the philosophies of Hegel
and Spinoza. It also is seen in contrast to views of the world
as dependent and unreal—Platonism, Malebranche, and
perhaps Berkeley. Finally it contrasts with a somewhat
mixed concept in which the external world is dependent and
unreal, but the human soul is real and independent. The
chief example of this last type, thought Mascall, would be
Hinduism.[3]

The creation as a dependent reality is seen, for instance,
in the great Psalm 19, in which, "The heavens are telling
the glory of God; and the firmament proclaims his handiwork" (v. 1). We are nowadays often unaware of what was
so startling about these words. Among ancient peoples, nature was usually charged with divinity itself. Psalm 19 is an
ancient poem in which nature is not divine, but it is the
"handiwork" of the divinity, and it thus "reflects" his glory.
Nature is dependent and real, but it is not God.

The Book of Job witnesses to this same sense of the
world's dependence upon the deep mysteries of God. Creation cannot even be fathomed by the human mind:

> "Where were you when I laid the
> foundation of the earth?
> Tell me, if you have
> understanding.
> Who determined its
> measurements—surely you know!
> Or who stretched the line upon it?
> On what were its bases sunk,
> or who laid its cornerstone,
> when the morning stars sang together,
> and all the heavenly beings
> shouted for joy?"[4]

---

3. E. L. Mascall, *Via Media* (London: Longmans, Green, & Company,
1956), 3-4.
4. Job 38:4–7, NRSV.

Though creation is real, and not a mask of a deeper reality, it is nevertheless dependent upon the deep mysteries of God. It is dependent reality.

As a dependent reality, creation presents two important conditions, without which relationships cannot take place. First, because it is real, creation is an object apart from God; thus, his love for this world is not somehow a circular love for himself. Second, the dependence of creation means that the two sides of this relationship, creator and creature, could not be more unlike one another. Their condition of dependence emphasizes the separateness, the distinct condition, and the utter unlikeness of God and his creation.

Yet this fundamental distinction makes relationships possible. Pantheism—or monism of any kind—undermines the possibility of relationship, because it undermines the truth of any real distinction. Pantheism says that all things are God, but this is tantamount to saying that all things are the same. If all is the same, then the possibility of addressing an "other" becomes meaningless. Love becomes meaningless.

In Christian theism's understanding of dependent reality, however, the truth of the world's distinction from God accents the revealed truth of God's love for his creation.

The Problem of Evil

Theodicy, the problem of "justifying God," comes from the Greek terms *theos* (God) and *dike* (justice). It signifies a problem that occurs in an ethical monotheism, but does not necessarily occur in other theological or cosmological systems.

That is, because God (1) is all powerful, and because he is (2) altogether good, how does one explain the presence of evil? If he were all powerful, he *could* do something about evil. If he were altogether good, he *would* do something about evil. So, why is there evil? Why do terrible things happen to good people? Why does evil often seem to triumph? God and evil—why are these two not mutually exclusive realities?

Pagan dualism presents no such problem. Evil simply contends against good. Pagan polytheism can even assign responsibility for evil to some of the powers contending in the world of multifaceted powers and pluralistic values.

In monism, and especially in a very self-conscious pantheism, evil can be seen as a conditional, and perhaps even illusory, reality. It is evil only in that it represents a partial reality. The experience of evil is blotted out by the overwhelming wholeness of the one divine reality. Thus evil presents no problem, since, in effect, it is not ultimately real. Or, more likely, the whole idea of good and evil becomes meaningless. Everything is the same, and it is what it is; there is neither a good to oppose evil, nor an evil to oppose good. Reality is beyond good and evil.

But in a monotheism that claims both the reality of creation and the good of the Creator, we are inevitably presented with a dilemma. Must we choose between God's omnipotence and his goodness? Do we deny the reality of evil? If so, do we actually call into question the reality of a creation that has independent existence?

Augustine (354–430), a leading thinker of Western Christendom, dealt with the problem of theodicy. He approached the problem of theodicy in three ways: (1) evil serves the interests of good (we'll call this the "aesthetic answer"); (2) evil unwittingly serves the purposes of God (the "utilitarian answer"); and (3) evil essentially has no independent existence (*privatio boni*).

1. The *aesthetic answer* of Augustine sees evil as that which puts into strong relief the desirability of good. In his *Confessions*, he exclaims: "Far be it from me, then, to say, 'These things should not be! For should I see nothing but these, I should indeed desire better; but yet, if only for these, ought I to praise Thee; . . . and with a sounder judgment I reflected that the things above were better than those below, but that all [together] were better than those above [by themselves]."[5]

2. Augustine's *utilitarian* argument asserts that even what is evil might be used by God for a greater purpose. Thus all things ultimately lead to good, even though they are not good in themselves. This principle is strongly

---

5. Augustine, *Confessions*, VII. 13, *The Nicene and Post-Nicene Fathers*, vol. 1, ed., Philip Schaff (Grand Rapids: Wm. B. Eerdmans Publishing Co., 1988), 110.

related to Paul's words that "all things work together for good for those who love God, who are called according to his purpose" (Rom. 8:28). In regard to political evil, Augustine argues, for instance, "But God, as He is the supremely good creator of good natures, so is He of evil wills the most just Ruler; so that, while they make an ill use of good natures, He makes a good use of evil wills."[6]

3. The *ontological answer*, most basic of Augustine's replies to the problem of theodicy, lies in his strong adherence to the clear biblical doctrine of the goodness of God's creation. Evil cannot be something in and of itself. It cannot possess existence like that which is made good by God. Rather it is the privation of good (*privatio boni*). It is a distortion or a diminishing of that which is given as good.

The comparison is not unlike that of sickness over against health. If someone visits the doctor for a checkup, the doctor might well say (with perhaps a better bedside manner than this abrupt statement reveals): "You have a diseased heart." The problem is not that the patient *has* a heart, but that the heart he has—and that he depends upon—has gone bad. What qualifies the doctor to make such a diagnosis is that he is supposed to have a fair knowledge of the normal signs of a perfectly healthy heart. A diagnosis of illness makes no sense apart from the idea of health.

Evil, therefore, is not something in itself; it is something gone wrong. It is a spoiled relationship, a misguided love, a destructive hatred, an unhealthy desire, a defective faith, a distortion of the truth.

All of these I have mentioned are evils born of sins. Yet there is also what might be called natural evil or gratuitous evil. These are seen in a similar light, since the evil they represent is seen only in light of the incompleteness of God's redemptive work. Jesus commented on this kind of evil when he answered his disciples' question about the cause of a man's blindness (John 9:1–3), and about the death of those eighteen killed by a falling tower of Siloam (Luke 13:4). The most recent disaster can only be seen as evil be-

6. Augustine, *The City of God*, XI. 17, trans., Marcus Dods, *The Nicene and Post Nicene Fathers*, vol. 2, ed., Philip Schaff (Grand Rapids: Wm. B. Eerdmans Publishing Company, 1988), 214.

cause it must always be seen without its ultimate results. Thus evil results from disaster that, in the midst of history, is deprived of its providential and ultimate results. It is seen in terms of *privatio boni*. And since sinful human beings are deprived of their perspective from eternity, since we are then deprived of seeing matters in light of their ultimate result (and since that loss of relationship to eternity or to God is what it means to be fallen or sinful), then nature itself becomes for us accursed. Its mortality is not, in itself, evil; but since we experience only mortality (or a mortality that in our experience is severed from providence), then, for us, it becomes a fallen world. It is evil because it is deprived of its good.

Since all was created good (Gen. 1), then Augustine reasons that its existence is necessarily tied to its goodness. Therefore if things "shall be deprived of all good, they shall no longer be . . . whatsoever is, is good."[7] For something to be evil, it is deprived of existence. Nothing therefore can be completely evil, for then it would be deprived of all existence. Evil must borrow from, and exist by virtue of, that which is good, for it is the deprivation and perversion of that which is good.

Providence

Unlike **preservation,** which implies the maintenance of something given in creation, **providence** is oriented toward the future. The term is derived from the Latin *providere,* which means "to foresee." God foresees and therefore provides for the future.

The Bible can be seen as a series of assurances of God's providence. In the Old Testament it seems that the people of Israel meet one disaster after another—from slavery in Egypt, to near-annihilation in the wilderness, to oppression by Philistines, Assyrians, and Babylonians. Yet with each crisis, they are promised not only that they will survive, but also that their destiny will be fulfilled even beyond human imagination. So each turn of history, each new oppression,

---

7. Augustine, *Confessions* VII. 12, 110.

each new Davidic generation, each delivery from the oppressor, gave evidence of God's direction in history.

The New Testament focuses upon the life of Jesus, whose work was accomplished despite of the efforts of his enemies, first to discredit and then to kill him. In fact, their efforts became the means by which the Son of God triumphed. Yet his prayer was, "Your kingdom come, your will be done" (Matt. 6:10). His witness was that "I can do nothing on my own. As I hear, I judge; and my judgment is just, because I seek to do not my own will but the will of him who sent me" (John 5:30). Claiming no credit for himself, he depended perfectly on the providence of his Father.

Furthermore God's providence includes using the evil that opposes God as an instrument in accomplishing redemption. The big stick of evil is taken out of the devil's hand and used by Providence to give that enemy of God a thorough thrashing. Jesus' words to the Emmaus disciples after the Resurrection include, "Oh, how foolish you are, and how slow of heart to believe all that the prophets have declared! Was it not necessary that the Messiah should suffer these things and then enter into his glory?" (Luke 24: 25–26). The underlying view of the gospel is that God uses every occasion, whether good or evil, to pursue his ultimate goal of redemption. Nothing escapes the ceaseless divine pursuit of the ultimate good.

Providence, therefore, is the perfect reflection of the doctrine of creation. In creation, all things are created good, showing that God's intention toward his creation is altogether good. Providence is the assurance that when all is said and done, in spite of the intervention of evil, God's will is going to be accomplished. Good will ultimately triumph. All things—all events, all people, all intentions, all good works, and all evil works—ultimately will be turned to that purpose.

For that reason the psalmist—typical of the biblical writer on this point—shows trust in God in the midst of the most unwelcome circumstances. Psalm 3, for instance, recalls the crisis David underwent when his own son, Absalom, led a rebellion against him:

O Lord, how many are my foes!
Many are rising against me;
many are saying to me,
"There is no help for you in God."
But you, O Lord, are a shield
around me,
my glory, and the one who
lifts up my head.
I lie down and sleep;
I wake again, for the Lord
sustains me.
I am not afraid of ten thousands
of people
who have set themselves
against me all around.
Deliverance belongs to the Lord;
may your blessing be on your
people! (Ps. 3:1–3, 5–6, 8)

Heaven and Earth

Almost every time creation is mentioned in the Bible, it is called by the double reference to "heaven and earth" or "the heavens and the earth." The linguistic background of these terms tells us that the double reference to heaven and earth probably means "the heights" and "what is below."

Heaven, therefore, refers in the first instance to the skies, to the place of the sun, moon, and stars. But it also refers in a more general way to that which is inaccessible to humankind. Therefore, we are given dominion over the earth, but there is always that which is inaccessible to us. The more we explore the little space around the earth, the more we become aware of how vast are those inaccessible spaces beyond us. Ancient men and women certainly were aware of the division between a created order in which they lived and that other part of creation that far exceeds their reach. Naturally, therefore, heaven becomes a way of conceptualizing the abode of God and his angels, as well as the destiny of those who die and have their continued life in God.

In his Gifford lectures, Jürgen Moltmann asks, "Why is creation a dual world?" He notes the Bible's consistent use of this dual language in reference to the created order. The principal effect, he points out, is to conceive of the world in such a way that the visible created order does not center in itself. The world, in other words, is not complete in itself. There is that inaccessible and unknowable realm of creation that keeps us from knowing the world in its fullness. The world, "as God's creation," Moltmann said, "does not have its unity within itself; so it cannot be a unified, self-contained universe." Furthermore:

> If God is its Creator, then his creation has its unity in him, not in itself. . . . At the same time . . . heaven is neither God nor is it divine; it is a part of the created world. But as part of the created world it has to be distinguished from the visible world; for it is only if we make this distinction that the visible world can be understood as a created world existing from God, and open for him who dwells in heaven. "He who dwells in heaven" is the Creator who indwells his creation. The world-immanence of God therefore makes the world an eccentric world, and divides it into heaven and earth.[8]

The "eccentric world" is an apt way of expressing what is distinctive in Hebrew and Christian *cosmology*. The world that is created by God, but other than God, and for purposes that transcend the world, is a world that does not center in itself. We were expressing this earlier using the term, "dependent reality." It is eccentric because it centers in God and his kingdom or his will. In contrast to this view, the Greek understanding of *cosmos* is one of well-balanced completeness. The *cosmos* is understood as something whole, something that stands in perfect harmony because of its completeness. The Hebrew "heaven and earth" envisions a world whose wholeness and harmony is yet to be disclosed. It exists in terms of the *eschaton*, in which God's purposes are fully disclosed. Yet when it attempts to find its center in itself, it is in rebellion against its Maker.

That is why ideologies that attempt to find harmony and peace without God (e.g., the Communist ideology) inevitably live by continued violence, not only against God and his

---

8. Jürgen Moltmann, *God in Creation* (San Francisco: Harper & Row, 1985), 159.

people, but even against themselves. They represent, in Emil Brunner's words, "Man in revolt."

The biblical view of creation as heaven and earth, however, makes it clear that true peace can only be found in God. For, without God, the world is always partial and fragmented, alienated from its true home.[9]

Summary of the Doctrine of Creation

Now that we have touched upon the major aspects of the doctrine of creation, let me summarize the points we have covered. Each of these points is important for understanding the others. Together they comprise a vitally important grounding for the proper understanding of Christian theology:

1. God created *ex nihilo*, "out of nothing"—a way of expressing his absolute responsibility for all that exists.

2. God created everything "good." The flaws and the tragic circumstances in life are not the reflection of a flawed creation. Rather, creation reflects the unambiguous love and goodness of God.

3. The necessary next question, then, is "whence evil?" If God created everything, and everything reflects his character as the Good Creator, then how can we explain the reality of evil. The principal answer, since Augustine, has been that evil is not *of creation;* it is a distortion of the good. It is *privatio boni.*

4. This means that evil has no positive existence. Instead it derives its reality from the existence of good. Thus, the fault is not in the thing created, but in things wrongly related. Evil consists of relationships gone wrong.

5. Creation consists of "heaven and earth"; that is, earth is incomplete without heaven, or, again, the visible creation is incomplete without the invisible.

---

9. For a fuller discussion of modern culture and how it is affected by a belief or disbelief in heaven, see my volume, *The Eclipse of Heaven: Rediscovering the Hope of a World Beyond* (Downers Grove: InterVarsity Press, 1992).

Therefore the world we know can only find its completeness and its center, or central purpose, in that which transcends it. The world is "eccentric." It finds its center outside of itself.

Questions for Review and Reflection

1. In our understanding of the human appetites and the human passions, what difference does it make that God created everything *ex nihilo*?
2. What is the significance of the doctrine of *creatio ex nihilo* in one's treatment of environmental responsibilities?
3. What is the significance of the repeated words in Genesis: "And God saw that it was good"?
4. What is theodicy?
5. How did Augustine of Hippo justify the existence of evil in a world created by a good God?
6. What is the significance of the Bible's reference to creation as "heaven and earth" or "the heavens and the earth"?

■ ─────────────────────────── ■

SIN AND THE HUMAN CONDITION

Is there a basic explanation for the evil, the pain, and the injustice that men and women experience in the world? What are the options? Once we look at these, we'll be better able to note the distinctive features of a Christian doctrine of sin and evil. Here are four general possibilities.

1. The world is so ordered that human suffering and injustice, alienation and moral guilt, are inevitable. The problem is in the *system,* and the blame belongs to whoever has made the system. Blame it on the Creator! That is the ancient **gnostic** option.

2. Evil results from the moral failure of men and women who are either incapable of moral judgment (because of their ignorance) or incapable of moral action (because of their weakness). The gods are stronger than we; therefore we are caught in the tragic circumstances of desiring to overcome evil (both in ourselves and in the world) but being outwitted or overpowered by fates that are either indifferent or hostile to human aspirations. That was the option of Mediterranean paganism, the Graeco-Roman humanism of myth and drama.

3. Human suffering and inequities are natural circumstances and have no moral basis. No one is to blame, and good and bad experiences are matters of random chance. The world is neither just nor unjust; it is only painful or pleasurable. That is the option of *naturalism*, the neo-paganism of modern Europe and North America.

4. The world is created by a God who desires to love and be loved by his creation. Therefore his acts of creation, preservation, and providence are articulations of moral value. Evil is fundamentally the result of the disruption of that relationship, and is therefore a result of the moral failure of humanity.

This last option, of course, is unmistakably the biblical option. The root problem in the human experience is sin. It is not natural frailty that has undone us, nor ignorance, nor the fates, nor is it human mortality. The problem does not lie outside of us, but inside us and among us. The problem lies in humanity's failure to do that which everyone knows is right.

Some years ago the psychotherapist Karl Menninger was telling us that Western society was losing a grip on this very strong sense of personal responsibility for moral action. In *Whatever Became of Sin?* he argued that we believe in failure, illness, bad luck, a bad environment, and evil as a general result of circumstances, but not—evidently—in sin. The result is that people struggle with a vague sense of guilt for which there seems to be no relief. Without personal responsibility, without the admission of guilt, one cannot ask for or receive forgiveness. Indeed, there is nothing to forgive!

This dilemma occurs once we divest ourselves of the idea of sin. It is one that has been overcome by what has seemed to Christians, all these years, as the right answer. The other options are limited, and each has its definite negative features. We can explain bad behavior and evil consequences by resorting to *dualism* (as options 1 and 2), for dualism pits humanity's noble spirit against an impossible system. Yet if we accept dualism, we resign ourselves to the belief that evil is a necessary part of reality, and we cannot fully take responsibility even for our own actions.

If we accept option 3, we deny that moral values exist. Good and evil become conventions and arbitrary choices. But with every new Holocaust or social atrocity, we find ourselves unable to weather the storms of society that occur under the influence of moral nihilism.

Things simply do not seem to work with options 1, 2, and 3. The human being seems to be irrevocably a creature with moral aspirations who cannot help making moral judgments; and whenever that moral sense becomes defective, or is denied for whatever reason, the human being seems no longer human. The dualist at least has the advantage of sensing that his or her human impulses are frustrated by a tragically hostile side of reality. Neither the dualist nor the **nihilist**, however, can sufficiently motivate a human being, or a human society, to change behavior for the better to any significant degree.

In fact, throughout history there are only two interrelated movements that seem to have accomplished historic leaps in moral consciousness and provided the social and psychological motivation to live on a new moral plane. One was the Hebrew prophetic movement; and the other, much larger and affecting more diverse kinds of people, was the church of Jesus Christ, especially in its early stages but also in remarkable times of renewal throughout history.

The Central Issue in the Doctrine of Sin

You will recognize, as in the doctrine of creation, the element of *gospel* (that is, "good news") in the concern the church has expressed over its teaching on sin. The fundamental issue is whether or not we live in a world that is congenial to the human being's sense of moral vocation. Throughout all populations, for all of history, we find abundant witness to the human being's longing to love, to act with kindness and justice. (Even at times when people are occupied with slaughtering one another, it seems that they find nothing so important as justifying their actions—which is, of course, a perverse tribute to justice, but nevertheless a true one.) But the question is, "Do we live in a world that rewards and cultivates kindness rather than brutality? love rather than betrayal? justice rather than raw power?"

There is no lack of evidence that the coarser and more self-serving method is quickly successful in reaching limited material or political goals. Yet somehow the human spirit and human society seem never to give up entirely on the other. The Christian response to this underlying human longing, this undying sense of what is good, is that this indeed is of the very nature of God. That is why we never quite give up on the quest for what is best in human aspirations. The God who created us and all that exists is a God who created us "for good works" (Eph. 2:10).

The doctrine of sin, therefore, has this point of departure: God is not the cause or the author of sin. *Deus non est causa, auctor peccati*.

Instead, any biblical definition of sin takes into account that God has created all things good. Sin, therefore, is fundamentally a rejection of what is good. Sin is not a part of creation, or a part of the system that God began. It is like a computer virus that infects the entire system by corrupting the code. It is a confusion of relationships, in which that which is highest and best in human life is not honored and loved as such. And that which is less than God is loved more than God. Sin is, in a word, a disorder in our love life.

The fact that sin is a disorder, a perversion of the good in creation—caused by the human *response* to what has been given, and *not* in the thing that God has given—will be basic to our understanding of how the Bible approaches the idea of sin. With that fundamental approach to the issue of sin and evil in mind, we can now draw out a certain definition of sin that is based upon the multifaceted biblical vocabulary for the human rebellion against God.

What Is Sin?

The Old Testament Definition

The Old Testament concept of sin often centers in the idea of transgression, of going against the grain of things, or against the law. The Hebrew word >avaappears over two hundred times. They carry the implication of not recognizing limits, or crossing over or passing by the boundaries of the legal code. When this family of words is carried over into the New Testament it is rendered *parabasis*. For instance, in Romans 5:14 Paul writes of the "transgression" of Adam. Here he is using the term in a typically Hebrew and Old Testament sense as a crossing over (and thereby losing the sense of) limits set up by God.

A related term, used more frequently than transgression, is *chat'a,* which means "missing the mark." In the Septuagint and the New Testament we find the same concept appearing frequently as *hamartia.* This term renders remarkably well the Hebrew idea that what God has given in creation is good, but that human beings have missed or failed to live by their own true nature. The sinner has sinned against God and nature. That is not to say that nature informs us of how we should respond to the life God has given; but it is God, through his law, who informs us how to respond to nature. To mistake that appropriate response is to "miss the mark," offending God's intention for human life.

The whole story of the idea of sin in the Old Testament cannot be told in terms of vocabulary. The underlying common theme in the Old Testament seems to be a sense of alienation or estrangement from those with whom we should enjoy fellowship. Terms such as "rebellion"—*pesha'* or *marâ*—denote conflict with authority and active estrangement from God. Treachery [*mar'al*], is an even stronger word, implying not only acting against someone whose authority should be recognized, but also against someone who has related to you in love and loyalty. It is "breaking faith" against a covenant relationship.

The significance of the idea of estrangement or alienation comes through strongly in the Genesis story of Cain and Abel. There we see the human family set within a world of interrelatedness where God sustains the life and happiness of those made in his image through the fruit of the ground. They are related to one another, to God, and to the natural world. Cain, the farmer, envies his brother and slays him. The curse comes upon him, and he bewails his misfortune in these words: "My punishment is greater than I can bear! Today you have driven me away from the soil, and I shall be hidden from your face; I shall be a fugitive and a wanderer

on the earth, and anyone who meets me may kill me" (Gen.
4:13–14).

Cain is alienated in every way possible. He is separated
from "the soil" (the earth), from God, and from other people.
His sin has made him a stranger in the world; it has broken
every conceivable relationship. Seen in this light, the transgression is more than an offense against the law; it is that
which isolates the self. The ultimate meaning of this self-
isolation is death. For to die is to no longer exist in relationship to anything—to God, to nature, to fellow human beings.

The New Testament Refinement

What was implied in the Old Testament becomes much
more explicit in the New Testament. The New Testament
vocabulary for sin reflects much the same thought found in
the Old Testament. Sin is still spoken of as transgression or
lawlessness or "missing the mark." The idea of rebellion
also is carried over from the prophetic to the apostolic writings.

When we give attention to what is distinctive in the New
Testament treatment of sin, we find ourselves referring to
what some call the "effects" of sin. As we look at the ideas of
sin that come to the forefront in the New Testament, I am
not distinguishing these from what are often called sin's effects. The reason is simply that students of Christian theology often fail to see clearly what is distinctive and
compelling about the New Testament understanding of sin
when the causes and effects of sin are discussed as if they
are phenomena separate from sin.

There is no cause of sin that is not itself sin, and there are
no effects of sin that reach beyond sin itself. We can see this
in three New Testament ideas of sin: alienation, bondage,
and unbelief. Unbelief, for instance, is not a cause of sin—it
is sin. Bondage is not the effect of sin—it is a description of
sin itself. Each of these three important ideas of sin de-
serves special attention.

1. *Alienation.* The idea of alienation or estrangement,
   which was alluded to even in the text of Genesis, becomes a visually powerful image in the New Testament. The one who is out of fellowship with God is

"lost." Jesus came to "seek out and save the lost." We find numerous examples from the teachings of Jesus, illustrating those who are alone, alienated, in need of restoration to fellowship. The Pharisee exalts himself so that his sin denies him a common human sympathy with the publican, and the publican is alone and feels his alienation, yet is finding a way back (Luke 18:9–14). The rich man in Hades looks "far away" to where Lazarus is by the side of Abraham; the rich man is beyond help and beyond hope (Luke 16:19–31). The shepherd risks danger to save the one lost sheep (Luke 15:3–7). The woman rejoices over finding one lost coin (Luke 15: 8–10). The father recovers the one lost son, and the lost son has come back from his life in a distant land in which he was a stranger (Luke 15:11–32).

Tennessee Williams was once asked in an interview what was the theme of his play, *The Glass Menagerie.* He replied, "It's that one needs to cut the tender bonds of affection that bind you in order to realize oneself." That statement easily finds a sympathetic chord in the twentieth-century Western mind. Yet the truth is that the great distress of modern life seems to be not from the strength of many "tender bonds of affection" in family and community, but from the hollow sensation of being lost, a stranger, alienated even in the midst of those packed close together, crowded into cities and suburbs. The image of estrangement as a central meaning of sin (not just its effect, but the very act of cutting loose relationships: "Am I my brother's keeper?") ought to communicate effectively to contemporary people, for that is the source of much modern pain.

2. *Bondage.* The second New Testament image of sin seems at first to be the opposite of alienation. It is actually the image of the same thing, but from another point of view. Paul stressed that one can either belong as a bond servant to God—in which case one is free to live as one deep down really wishes to—or else one is in bondage to sin. "Therefore," he said, "do not let sin exercise dominion in your mortal bodies,

to make you obey their passions" (Rom. 6:12). He
speaks to those who know the power of sin to prevent
them from exercising freely the will to do what is
right. "I do not understand my own actions," said
Paul, "For I do not do what I want, but I do the very
thing I hate" (Rom. 7:15). His Christian readers of
the first century could understand that they once
"presented (their) members as slaves to impurity
and to greater and greater iniquity" (Rom. 6:19).
That was the experience of sin, an experience that
they had not entirely escaped, but that they had put
behind them in hopes of deliverance.

3. *Unbelief.* Sin also can be seen as the refusal to receive what is given, to see what is there, to love what
is worthy of love, or to hear what is true. This block-
ade against reality is what the Fourth Gospel, for instance, summarizes as "unbelief." Not believing
what God has given comes as a general predisposition toward "evil deeds"; but to believe in Christ is to
acknowledge what is true. So, John writes, "Those
who believe in him are not condemned; but those
who do not believe are condemned already.... And
this is the judgment, that the light has come into the
world, and people loved darkness rather than light
because their deeds were evil. For all who do evil
hate the light and do not come to the light, so that
their deeds may not be exposed. But those who do
what is true come to the light, so that it may be clearly seen that their deeds have been done in God"
(John 3:18–21).

There is a continuity here from belief to truthfulness to
deed, and from unbelief to falsehood to evil deeds. Unbelief
has not caused sin, and belief has not compensated for sin—
rather belief and unbelief is of the very essence of sin. That
is why Paul could be so condensed in his statement that
"whatever does not proceed from faith is sin" (Rom. 14:23).

Sin as unbelief *(apistis)* and as a general state of unrecep-
tivity and distrust certainly has roots in Old Testament
thought, and it is a concept that Jesus turned to frequently.
When asked why he used parables, Jesus quoted the words
of Isaiah,

You will indeed listen, but never
understand,
and you will indeed look, but
never perceive.
For this people's heart has
grown dull,
and their ears are hard of hearing,
and they have shut their eyes;
so that they might not look
with their eyes,
and listen with their ears,
and understand with their heart
and turn—
and I would heal them
(Matt. 13:14–15; quoting Isa. 6:9–10).

To believe, to trust *(pistis)* is to be open to the good that God intends, and to receive it as the acknowledged truth of reality. All things are created good. God intends good, and all things will end as God intends. To participate in evil signifies, to one degree or another, that one expects evil has a place in the world—it is to distrust what God has done. To believe that hatred, violence, lust, greed, and ambition are legitimate routes to accomplish some good is to *disbelieve;* it is to distrust God. It is to reject the way of Jesus Christ and to adopt the way of Satan, the one who accuses (Satan means "the Accuser") because he is the one who believes in the substantiality of evil. Satan is the one who says that you sin because you cannot help it, that it is natural and inevitable. To believe in the Son of God, however, is to believe that the good will ultimately succeed, and evil will finally give up its parasitic existence, its capacity for falsely presenting itself as substantial by perverting the good.

Sin and Temptation

Reinhold Niebuhr regarded temptation as a problem emerging from the contradiction between human finiteness and human freedom. The biblical basis of this point is that human beings are both part of nature and yet exercise dominion over nature. The temptation comes from both sides of this contradiction. As a part of nature, the human being finds the impulses of appetite and passions (sensuality) an

irrevocable aspect of personality and a limitation upon freedom. As one who conceives oneself as free to act in spite of,
or contrary to, natural impulses, one is tempted to deny
one's creatureliness and one's natural limitation.

On one side, the human being is tempted to give in to nature and thereby become guilty of sloth. On the other side,
the man or woman is tempted to set himself or herself in the
place of God, who alone is able to act without creaturely limitations. In that case, the human being is tempted to pride.

Both sides of this condition of sin, whether pride or sloth,
are rooted in self-centeredness. The prideful person has
sought to replace God with themself. The slothful person
has neglected to properly value what God has given—especially the self. Out of disappointment or the wish to escape
the pain of effort, he denies the gift of God by giving up.

Temptation to sin, therefore, operates out of two centers:

1. Nature: giving occasion to sensuality and thus
                     sloth.

2. Spirituality: giving occasion to pride out of our re-
                     latedness to God.

It is important to note that neither of these aspects of humanity is evil or sinful in itself. Instead, we can say that
they are very good; in fact, they are good precisely because
it is God who has created humanity in that way. Each of
these "goods," however, can be turned against God and
against the human being. The higher the good, the greater
the possibility and sometimes the temptation to evil. Hitler,
Lenin, and Mao were all talented, intelligent, energetic,
and self-disciplined; yet they used their good qualities to
serve monstrous intentions. Had these three been tempted
more by sensuality rather than pride, they might have destroyed themselves; but they might have done little or no
harm to the nations they devastated by their overweening
and compulsive pride.

Sin and Guilt

Sin must be distinguished from its objective results,
which we designate as "guilt." Even more so, must it be dis-

tinguished from the idea of "guilt feeling," which modern society seems to have relegated to the category of pathological disorders. Guilt is to guilt feelings as an injury is to pain. One person may feel the pain more intensely than another even when the injury is the same. The guilt feeling might be a perfectly healthy reaction to the objective harm being done by a person to his own character or to the life of another person. Or it might be an oversensitive conscience reacting on the basis of personal pride. The guilt feeling might be a reliable indicator of true guilt, leading the person to correct a wrong, or it might be an unreliable obsession based upon a disordered psychological sensitivity. Either can be the case.

Guilt itself is a concept based upon the objective harm done by sin. The word *guilt* derives from the idea of "debt." One has done an injury, and therefore a debt is owed: someone has been deprived of what is rightfully theirs, whether that be life, reputation, or just treatment.

Protestants, especially in modern times, have tended to differ with Catholics in distinguishing one sin from another in terms of degree of culpability. Catholic theology, following the analysis of Thomas Aquinas, has distinguished between levels of sin. Protestant theory has more often been impressed by the fact that any and all sin is rebellion against God. Protestants begin with the words of James's Epistle, "For whoever keeps the whole law but fails in one point has become accountable for all of it" (James 2:10).

Reinhold Niebuhr, for instance, argued that the higher religious truth is that all sin is equally rebellious against God: "Orthodox Protestantism, both Calvinistic and Lutheran, rightly discerned the perils of moralism and self-righteousness in the rigidities of natural law." However, he also warned that it was "mistaken for orthodox Protestantism to efface all moral distinction of history in the light of a religious conviction of the undifferentiated sinfulness of all men."[1]

What distinction, then, can be made? If all sin is equally disobedient, and if to disobey in part is to disobey all, is

1. Reinhold Niebuhr, *The Nature and Destiny of Man*, vol. 1 (New York: Charles Scribner's Sons, 1964), 221.

there yet any place for making a distinction? Yes, there is still a distinction in terms of the objective harm and real offense that is the result of sin. There is equality of sin, but inequality in guilt. The biblical truth that all men are sinners, says Neibuhr, needs to be balanced against the fact that, "There is nevertheless an ascertainable inequality of guilt among men in the activities of history."[2]

That the equality of sin does not affect the inequality of guilt, or objective harm, can be seen in two ways. First, some wrongdoing is simply more harmful than others. To hate is wrong, and so is killing—but the fact that either of these is participation in sin dare not blind us to the very unequal consequences. Second, the same sin might have unequal consequences when the degree of opportunity for sin is different. For instance, a poor person can be as greedy as a rich person. Yet a rich person's greed might work to the positive disruption of many other lives, while the poor person's greed may have few social consequences beyond his own small circle of acquaintances. A power-hungry postmaster is not likely to do as much harm as a U. S. district judge obsessed with the power he has over the lives of others. The opportunity and the potential for sin may be the same in any of these cases, but the consequences are far different. Therefore, while their sin remains sin—as much for one as for the other—there are great disparities in the guilt that results.

The idea of degree of guilt, furthermore, is not at all foreign to the Bible. The Old Testament requirements of a virtual hierarchy of sacrifices certainly implied varying degrees of guilt for which the sacrifices atoned. In the New Testament, the differing degree of guilt was the basic assumption when Jesus said, for instance, that the scribes who "devour widows houses and for the sake of appearance say long prayers . . . will receive the greater condemnation" (Luke 20:47). And when Jesus spoke of the commandment, "You shall not murder," he illustrated the guilt of those who do less than physical violence by saying: "If you are angry . . . you will be liable to judgment; and if you insult a brother

---

2. Ibid., 221–222.

or sister, you will be liable to the council; and if you say, 'You fool,' you will be liable to the hell of fire" (Matt. 5:22).

Clearly Jesus was teaching that all sin, even short of the physical act of murder, was an offense against God; but in doing so, he assumed a clear distinction in the degree of guilt.

Sin and Punishment

The idea of God's wrath or anger is offensive to some people and confusing to others. Undoubtedly that reaction to the notion of divine punishment, especially when it seems motivated by divine passion, comes from the very fact that the Christian concept of a God of love and mercy (which is also, by the way, rooted in a strong Hebrew prophetic idea of God) has so successfully engrafted itself into the human consciousness of what is characteristic or true about God.

Whether the idea is offensive and confusing or not, however, the serious student of the Bible must come to terms with two undeniable features of both the Old and New Testaments:

1. the gravity of sin;
2. the consistent opposition of God to sin.

Punishment, or wrath, is seen as a reaction on God's side to the reality of sin. It is his refusal to overlook or make compromises with that which destroys human life. While God appears to oppose humanity, he, in fact, allies himself to men and women in that he opposes their self-destruction.

In opposing human self-destruction, God allows the grave threat and reality of consequences for sin. In doing so, however, he does not oppose human freedom. It is paradoxical that God affirms human life by providing space and freedom for action, but in providing that space, he also insures the consequences of sin, which spells wrath and destruction.

Paul's analysis of God's reaction to sin in Romans 1 underlines this intimate relationship between human freedom and unwelcome consequences, or between the possibility of sin and the certainty of God's wrath against sin.

In this intimate connection between sin and wrath, we discover that sin is, in fact, its own consequence. God's love and wrath are revealed in one way: He allows men and women freedom to choose their own actions. In a series of statements about human sin and divine wrath, Paul uses the phrase, "God gave them up" to the sin they had chosen (Rom. 1:24, 26, 28). God's wrath is that he allows sin and does not prevent it. Or, he restrains sin, paradoxically, by allowing it along with its consequences.

Sin and Death

The connection between sin and punishment is seen perhaps even more clearly in the identity of sin with death. Already we have seen how the linguistic roots of the biblical terms for sin are found in the idea of separation, alienation, and estrangement. In "missing the mark" (*chatah* and *hamartia*), we fail even to be properly related to our own true identities. In lawlessness, disobedience, and rebellion, we have severed our relationship to God. With Cain, insisting we are not "our brother's keeper," we make ourselves independent of, and thus estranged from, all others.

The ultimate expression of this separation and estrangement is death. When we no longer relate to anything, we are dead. It could almost be the definition of death.

Therefore, when God said to the man in the garden that his rebellion meant "you shall die" (Gen. 2:17), this was not so much a prediction as it was a description of the nature of sin. The serpent's contradiction, "you will not die" (Gen. 3:4) was a refusal to recognize separation and alienation from God as the very essence of sin. When Paul said the "wages of sin is death" (Rom. 6:23), he was making a very apt analogy. It is not that death results eventually as a consequence of sin, any more than wages are paid at retirement! Instead, one works and is paid as the work is done, week by week, or month by month. Just so, death is the consistent daily payment for sin, because to sin *is* to die. Sin, separation, and death are interchangeable concepts; they partake of the same experience and reality.

Original Sin

The orthodox framing of an idea or theory of sin was not fully developed until the time of Augustine of Hippo (A.D. 354–430). As is frequently the case, this doctrine was developed in the throws of controversy over the nature of sin and its universal impact.

Pelagius, a British Christian and a contemporary of Augustine, was alarmed during his time in Rome (383–409) at the lack of moral discipline among Christians there. Along with Augustine, he was strongly critical of the libertine lifestyle of the Manichees and those they influenced. Especially among Christians, he said, such ought not to happen. Christians as well as anyone else, he argued, are to be held absolutely accountable for their sins. If they are not responsible, then how could anyone possibly say it is sin? We are not acting rebelliously against God if God has so made us that we cannot help but sin. We are only following our nature, and God is the author of nature.

To be perfectly consistent, argued Pelagius, we must assume that we are judged and condemned for sin only because we *can* do good, and we *can* resist sin. "The essential characteristic of Pelagianism," wrote Reinhold Niebuhr, "is its insistence that actual sins cannot be regarded as sinful or as involving guilt if they do not proceed from a will that is essentially free."[3]

What follows from this theory of sin is a conviction of personal responsibility for sin. In fact, there is a large element of common sense in this, and many Christians before Augustine were probably at least somewhat Pelagian in their outlook. The problems with Pelagianism, however, gradually came into view. They consisted of two main points:

1. The Pelagian idea of sin does not take into account the inertia of sin in the whole of the human race, a propensity that appears irresistible on the individual level. Paul spoke of this when he said he is "sold into slavery under sin" (Rom. 7:14), and he confessed "I do not do the good I want, but the evil I do not want is what I do" (v.19).

2. The Pelagian idea of sin, in order to be consistent, would also assume that salvation from sin is a matter of individual responsibility.

Augustine saw the dangers in this argument and countered with the scriptural analysis of sin as something

---

3. Ibid., 245.

that—even while it remains the personal responsibility of each individual—is due to an original decision that is passed down upon the whole human race. So, while sin is the concrete actions, attitudes, and thoughts of the individual, it is also the corporate disposition of humanity as a whole. The individual cannot, therefore, entirely free himself or herself from this corporate responsibility. The individual is in bondage, and therefore needs help from God in order to be liberated from the bondage of sin.

This universal presence and influence of sin, and the manner in which each individual is bound by that corporate dimension, was the principle meaning and importance of Augustine's doctrine. Augustine argued that Pelagius was mistaken in assuming that each individual in each case is dealing with an equally weighted opportunity to sin against God or obey God. The scales are not equally weighted, Augustine argued, but are weighted against us by the sheer strength of the predisposition toward sin in our humanity. Many interpreters have rejected Augustine's explanation of human propensity toward sin by a biological inheritance from Adam. It is usually pointed out that his conclusion was based upon a mistranslation of Romans 5:12, which says that "sin came into the world through one man, and death came through sin, and so death spread to all because all have sinned." Augustine relied upon a Latin rendering of *eph ho pantes hamarton* as *in quo omnes peccaverant*, which would come into English as "in whom all have sinned." Augustine took this to mean that the sin of Adam is passed down biologically to all humanity. But it doesn't have to mean that. It also can mean that the human race is so much at *one* in its sin, that to be human—because of the fall or the sin of Adam—is to sin. No one questions that Romans 5:12 speaks of the solidarity of the human race in sin. It is the biological interpretation that has been challenged.

Furthermore, since Augustine read *eph ho pantes hamarton* to imply a biological link with sin, he could easily draw the conclusion that sin was bound up in the sexual act out of which we all come into our biological being. This interpretation brought about further confusion, a very unbiblical coloring of sex, which the church and the Bible had always affirmed as the good gift of God to be received within the discipline of the marriage covenant. Thus, out of a mistranslation, the doctrine of original sin became associated with issues that are hardly central to its theological burden.

Without the biological transmission of sin, and certainly without the unfounded implication that original sin has something to do with sex, there is still the need to recognize two important arguments of this doctrine. First, sin is not merely an individual rebellion that can be settled on the basis of private repentance and obedience. Instead there is a corporate dimension to sin from which we cannot separate ourselves; we are caught up in a great wave of humanity and history that rebels from God from the very beginning. The individuals are mere particles within that wave that will be washed to their death, except for the redemptive power of God.

Second, the power of sin in the life of the individual and community is such that—far from each temptation being subject to the free, willing response of the individual—there is the necessity of supernatural help to free the will from the bondage of sin and empower it for works of righteousness.

The doctrine of original sin, therefore, expresses a common experience of the human being, both Christians and non-Christians. It is the experience of deeply desiring to do what is right, and yet not finding the power to live out that conviction. It is the profound sense that who we would want to be is not quite who we are. We live in a gap between those two levels of conscious awareness, some more comfortably than others, but none without awareness at some point in their lives that they are not who they would be. God evidently has made us to live in a certain way; he has called us to live on that level, yet something prevents us. The gospel speaks to that universal sentiment; it offers us hope in the redemption of Jesus Christ, and help through the presence and power of the Holy Spirit.

Augustine saw more accurately than Pelagius the depth of the problem, and the extreme need of help from outside against the power of evil in the human community.

Questions for Review and Reflection

1. How do the "figures of speech" that became the common biblical terms for sin contribute to our understanding of the nature of sin?

2. In what sense is sin alienation or estrangement? What biblical treatments of sin contribute to the idea of sin as self-isolation or alienation?

3. How would you explain the logical relationship of sin and death in the biblical doctrine of sin?

4. What was the essence of Augustine's critique of Pelagius? What was Pelagius's concern in the Christian attitude toward moral behavior?

5. What is the central significance of the doctrine of original sin?

6. Why, in the Christian doctrine of sin, is God *not* responsible for sin?

PART II

God and His Redemptive Purpose

■ ─────────────────────── ■

GOD WITH US: THE PERSON OF CHRIST

Christian theology centers in Jesus Christ. Without Christ we can claim to know nothing of God.

Therefore, Christian theology is the very opposite of abstract philosophical speculation. What it says about God begins necessarily with the very concrete person of Jesus and the history of his life, death, and resurrection.

Traditionally, we think of the doctrine of Christ in two ways, or under two headings: (1) the person of Christ, and (2) the work of Christ. These two categories are, of course, interrelated and cannot easily be separated from each other as if you could consider one without the other. Nevertheless, thinking about Christ in one way helps us to understand the other. To know that Jesus Christ died on the cross, and why he died, sheds light on what it means to say that he is our High Priest, for instance. To understand what Scripture, and Christians through the ages, meant by saying that Jesus Christ is the Son of God tells us more than we could otherwise know about the meaning and costliness of his work of dying on a Roman cross.

The Person of Christ

When early Christians said, "Jesus Christ is 'Lord,'" they were giving witness to the deepest mystery of the Christian faith. He is, they were saying, a real human, historical figure, who was also "Lord"—in other words, God. This confession of the **incarnation** of God in Jesus Christ was so central to what the church gave witness to, yet it was so difficult to say exactly what was implied by this statement (and sometimes, even more importantly, what was *not* implied), that it took Christian theologians more than two centuries to work out even the rough perameters of such a confession. He is divine and human; yet in what way could they say this? What was certain is this: They did not want to compromise either the deity or the humanity of Jesus. The testimony of Scripture did not permit them to consider Christ anything less than true God, or anything less than true Man. He is the God/Man. He is God who had become human and was, as we are, in the flesh. Taking these truths together, he is the God/Man: God incarnate. Yet how does one say any more about the revealed character of Jesus Christ without reducing the mystery to a mere sophistry, or stating the mystery as a mere logical contradiction?

The Humanity of Jesus Christ

It is interesting that the first doctrine the followers of Jesus Christ found themselves defending was that of his true humanity. Many were willing to believe in his divinity; so much so that some were unwilling to believe in his true humanity. Tradition has it that Tertullian said, "The human blood of our Lord was still smoking on the hills of Judea when there were some among us who said, 'He is not human.'" The matter is critically important in two ways. Not only does it tell us something extremely important about the nature of God; but, if the incarnation and the full humanity of Jesus is true, then it also tells us something that we cannot know otherwise about humanity. Wolfhart Pannenberg emphasized the importance of this point when he wrote, "As God's revelation, Jesus is at the same time the revelation of the human nature and of the destiny of man."1

Even this truth, when taken without its complementary truth that Jesus Christ is God, can be terribly misleading. We will give attention later to those types of heresies that emphasized Jesus' humanity to the exclusion of his divinity. For now, however, it will suffice to stress that the church was simply refusing to compromise on a matter that it found uncompromised in Scripture. In the Gospels, for instance, we find no *docetic*, otherworldly figure who has nothing in common with the humanity all around him. Instead, we find him hungry, thirsty, tired, moved to pity, and moved to anger. The passages that illustrate this point are numerous. It would be tedious to mention all of them here. If we were to list a few of them we might begin with Matthew's account of Jesus' being hungry (Matt. 4:2), and of his sleeping while in a boat with some disciples (Matt. 8:42). Or we could recall John's mention that on a journey south from Galilee, when he reached Samaria he was so weary that he wished to sit by the well (John 4:6).

We can recognize in Mark 13:32 that Jesus never claimed to know everything. He did not know, in this case, the time of the *parousia* of the Son of Man and the end of the age. He was tempted even as we are (Heb. 2:18). He really died (Mark 15:37), and he was buried.

Yet perhaps the most remarkable statement of the humanity of Jesus is found in Luke's Gospel. Luke tells us of his birth, but then he says, "The child grew and became strong, filled with wisdom; and the favor of God was upon him" (Luke 2:40). When Luke writes of Jesus' development and growth in this way, he could have made no stronger statement of his humanity. For the experience of human life is not one of completeness (certainly not completeness from childhood), but one of learning and maturing in different areas of life. Luke wishes to make very clear that Jesus knew even this experience. He was no Minerva, sprung full-blown from the head of Zeus as in the Greek mythologies of Luke's day. The early church's thinkers, at least the ones

1. Wolfhart Pannenberg, *Jesus—God and Man* (Philadelphia: Westminster, 1976), 191.

who had the strongest and most long-lasting influence on the Christian movement, not only cared not to cover up this fact of Jesus' true humanity; but they even clung to it tenaciously, challenging every philosophy that wanted to compromise the Gospels' recollection that he was indeed fully human.

The Deity of Jesus Christ

Once the full humanity of Jesus is stated, protecting us from a docetic error on one side, we then need to understand what it means to say that this human being was also God. We have seen that if we remove the concept of the humanity of Jesus, we don't have divinity left; we have nothing left. On the other hand the doctrine of Christology as it was formulated by the early church tells us that if we remove the deity of Christ, we don't have humanity left; we have nothing left. He is, at one and the same time, fully human and fully divine—*vere Homo, vere Deus.*

How does Scripture establish his divinity?

The apostle Paul's statements on this matter are unequivocal. In Christ Jesus, he writes, "The whole fullness of deity dwells bodily" (Col. 2:9). In his letter to Titus, he refers to Jesus as "our great God and Savior" (Titus 2:13). To these very straightforward statements of Jesus' deity, we could add the prologue of John (John 1:1–18), which is as clear a statement of high Christology as we will find anywhere, and starts not at Bethlehem or with the Jordan baptism, but says, "In the beginning was the Word, and the Word was with God, and the Word was God" (1:1).

We have little doubt that the Fourth Gospel wished to establish beyond question the idea of Jesus' co-equality with God the Father, especially when we read of the controversy that erupted in Jerusalem concerning this very point in chapter 5 of John. Yet, to appreciate the full power and the incredible subtlety with which the deity of the Son is established, we must also take note of the fact that his claim to deity was paradoxical in the extreme. When he replied to his critics, who pointed accusing fingers at his act of healing on the Sabbath, he said simply, "My father is still working, and I also am working" (v. 17). This is not my work; he said, in effect, it is what the Father does. "The Son can do nothing on his own, but only what he sees the Father doing" (v. 19). The utter humility of Jesus, and his unwillingness to claim any act or intention as his own, can only mean that his work is a fundamentally pure reflection of God's will. As such, his life and actions faithfully reflect the mind and will of God. When, therefore, those who knew Christ in the flesh would give answer to the question, "Was this indeed a man?" they would have to say, "Yes! Of course." On the other hand, they could give witness to the reality of Jesus' work being only the work of God, with no remainder and no contradiction. In the presence of such a man, they knew themselves to be in the presence of God himself. Therefore his complete deity is established by virtue of his humble claim to do nothing but what the Father had given.

The Unity of Christ

The church fathers found that it was not enough to affirm, with Scripture, the full humanity and the full deity of Jesus Christ. One must also say something about how these two natures are related in Christ. Does he have a dual nature in which the divine rules the human—a human body and personality with a divine mind or *nous?* Or was his humanity a temporal *mode* of God's self-disclosure?

The church wrestled with these kinds of questions for close to four centuries. Always, however, they were brought back to the standard of Scripture that seemed to say that the person of Christ is *one,* not divided, either in ontology or in time. Jesus Christ is the "same yesterday today and forever" (Heb. 13:8).

The early twentieth-century Reformed theologian, Louis Berkhof, almost lapsed into a docetic expression of Christ's humanity when he said that Jesus "has both a divine and human consciousness, as well as a human and a divine will." We must be careful not to follow such expressions to the point that we have attributed to Jesus a divided personhood. Does he have two states of consciousness or two separate wills? One could hardly gather this from the New Testament witness.

Even Berkhof, I think, is a bit alarmed at his own language, because he immediately says about the divine/human consciousness and will, "This is a mystery which we cannot fathom." Then he goes straight to the point that, I believe, is more in keeping with a clear Christology than his original observation, and he states the points accurately and eloquently: "Scripture clearly points to the unity of the Person of Christ. It is always the same Person who speaks. . . . Human attributes and actions are sometimes ascribed to the Person designated by a divine title, Acts 20:28; 1 Cor. 2:8; Col. 1:13,14; and divine attributes and actions are sometimes ascribed to the Person designated by a human title, John 3:13; 6:62; Rom. 9:5."[2]

■ ———————————————— ■

P. T. FORSYTHE ON THE UNITY OF CHRIST

When Jesus says, "I and the Father are one," he uttered an experience which the author of the Fourth Gospel cannot have merely imagined . . . . If anything is sure to us about the mind of Christ we are sure that such was the relation he cherished and expressed towards his Father. The only question is, what did it mean for him? . . . The intimate relationship between them is not accessible to us. We can only say . . . that it is impossible for us to exaggerate that intimacy. And the most subtle speculations of the church, when they are interpreted with the insight of a sympathetic intelligence instead of sealed up by the dullness of a scornful [mind], are but the finest efforts of human thought to feel its way into that divinest mystery.

[From P.T. Forsythe, *The Person and Place of Jesus Christ* (Boston: The Pilgrim Press, 1907), 75.]

■ ———————————————— ■

Two Natures. Nevertheless, while strongly affirming the unity of the person of Christ, orthodoxy in Christian teaching has steadfastly held to the distinct natures that are united in that one person. In a word, the two natures are

---

2. Louis Berkhof, *Summary of Christian Doctrine* (Grand Rapids: Eerdmans, 1938), 95.

not unified into a *tertium quid*, a "third thing," but retain their complete deity and complete humanity.

The definition of Chalcedon (A.D. 451) states this matter most forcefully by saying that the distinction of natures is "in no way annulled by the union, but rather the characteristics of each nature (is) preserved . . . coming together to form one person and subsistence [hypostasis] not as parted or separated into two persons, but one and the same Son and Only begotten God the Word, Lord Jesus Christ."

A Summary of the Four Major Christological Issues. Thus, after four ecumenical councils stretching from A.D. 325 (Nicea) to 451 (Chalcedon), the church had generally settled upon four matters that were to be fundamental in their understanding of the person of Christ: (1) his full deity, (2) his full humanity, (3) his unity in person, and (4) the distinction of his two natures.

■ ———————————————————— ■

THE DEFINITION OF CHALCEDON, A.D. 451

Therefore, following the holy Fathers, we all with one accord teach men to acknowledge one and the same Son, our Lord Jesus Christ, at once complete in Godhead and complete in manhood, truly God and truly man, consisting also of a reasonable soul and body; of one substance with the Father as regards his Godhead, and at the same time of one substance with us as regards his manhood; like us in all respects, apart from sin; as regards his Godhead, begotten of the Father before the ages, but yet as regards his manhood begotten, for us men and for our salvation, of Mary the Virgin, the God bearer; one and the same Christ, Son, Lord Only-begotten, recognized *in two natures, without confusion, without change, without division, without separation;* the distinction of natures being in no way annulled by the union, but rather the characteristics of each nature being preserved and coming together to form one person and subsistence, not as parted or separated into two persons, but one and the same Son and Only-begotten God the Word, Lord

Jesus Christ; even as the prophets from earliest times spoke of him, and our Lord Jesus Christ himself taught us, and the creed of the Fathers has handed down to us.

[From *Documents of the Christian Church,* edited by Henry Bettenson (London: Oxford University Press, 1967), 51–52.]

■ ———————————————————— ■

The Offices of Christ

Associated with an understanding of the Person of Christ, and yet forming a bridge to our discussion of his works, is the topic of what has traditionally been called the "offices" of Christ. It is important to emphasize that an office is more than a function. That is the reason I include this topic under the Person, rather than the work, of Christ. An office emphasizes relationship (in this case, Jesus Christ and his relationship to us and to the world) even more than it does a particular kind of work.

The offices of Christ are three: prophet, priest, and king. In these offices we conceive of Christ standing with us, and before God the Father, in three distinct roles or relationships.

The Prophetic Office. The role of the prophet is to bring a message to the people from God. Among the clearest, strongest, and earliest of Hebrew messianic expectations was that of a prophet who would come as the prophets of old, and especially one who would come as a prophet like Moses. By the time of Jesus, we might well expect that every Jewish child might have heard the prophecy about a prophet like Moses; it was a prophecy that was, by this time, generally applied to the expected Messiah. The prophecy was found in the great Book of Deuteronomy: "The Lord your God will raise up for you a prophet like me [like Moses, that is] from among your own people; you shall heed such a prophet" (Deut. 18:15).

In Luke 13:33, Jesus refers to himself as a prophet. He regards his fate as foreshadowed in the treatment of prophets before him (Matt. 23:29–36). Also the people on many occasions recognize him as a prophet (Matt. 21:11, 46; Luke 7:16; 24:19; John 6:14; 7:40; and 9:17).

The Priestly Office. In contrast to the prophet who represents God before humanity, out of his capacity or calling to speak, "Thus saith the Lord," the priest's office is that of representing humanity before God.

It is probably true that during his life on earth, Jesus was readily known by many as prophet. It was not until his life's work was finished, and until the disciples reflected upon what had been done, that his office as priest came clearly into view. This recognition of his priestly office is most strongly expressed in the Book of Hebrews. Here Jesus is referred to as priest again and again—in 3:1; 4:14; 5:5; 6:20; 7:26; and 8:1. Yet here he is not seen as a continuation of the Israelite priestly tradition, but as a priest of a wholly different order. "It is ever more obvious," the author of Hebrews writes, showing the superiority of Jesus' priesthood, "when another priest arises, resembling Melchizedek, one who has become a priest, not through a legal requirement concerning physical descent, but through the power of an indestructible life. For it is attested of him, 'You are a priest forever, according to the order of Melchizedek'" (Heb. 7:15–17).

The priestly office of Christ is implied when New Testament writers made mention of Christ as "the Lamb of God" (John 1:29) and "our passover" (1 Cor. 5:7), in which the work of Christ on the cross is pictured as a priestly sacrifice. It is also suggested in numerous passages that describe Jesus' work as that of representing human interests before a just God, as when Mark recalls the words of Jesus that, "The Son of Man came not to be served but to serve, and to give his life a ransom for many" (Mark 10:45).

In the Old Testament sacrificial system, the worshiper who gave a lamb or a bull to be sacrificed customarily placed his hand on the head of the sacrificial animal. This gesture signified the giver's identity with his gift. In this small gesture, it was implied that it was not truly the animal, but the worshiper—the owner of the animal—who made restitution to God by giving of himself. In the case of Jesus, it is significant that we have here a perfect identity (a true identity, not an implied one), in that the one making the sacrifice *is* the one being sacrificed. In this case, the one who intercedes for us is also of us. That which the priests of the Old Testament and the priests of intertestamental times prefigured is accomplished directly and perfectly in Christ.[3]

The Kingly Office. What the title "Christ," messiah, or the "annointed one" conveyed most readily to the Jews of Jesus' day was the office and role of a king. The prophets and psalmists of the Hebrew people had long since prepared the nation for the expectation of a king who would recall the days of David, who would institute rule among the nations (cf. Pss. 2 , 132 as well as Isa. 9:6–7). These promises were reiterated even in days of imminent disaster (Mic. 7:8–10). In fact, they seem to have grown into promises that extended far beyond the usual political hopes of a downtrodden nation, growing more all-encompassing even as the disasters and devastation to national life grew more appalling.

It is difficult, for instance, to miss the irony of Ezekiel's words at a time when the land of Israel lay desolate, plundered by hostile neighbors, the cities largely abandoned, many of the people in exile. Despite all this, he prophesies that a son of David "shall be their prince forever" (Ezek. 37:25), and in their later days even the nations (Gentiles) will know that "I the Lord sanctify Israel" (v. 28).

By the time of the New Testament, messianic expectations were evidently developed to the point that Jesus could speak to the people about a "kingdom of God" that was multi-leveled in its significance to them. (In chapter 11 we will discuss the levels of meaning of this "kingdom" in the Gospels.)

After the death and resurrection of Jesus, and certainly after the destruction of Jerusalem in A.D. 70, the idea of a messianic kingdom was no longer confined to one of a mere earthly political reign. The hope of Christians within Israel, and later of a Christian Roman empire, outstripped such limited expectations and became the hope of a true and

---

3. An important recent study of the sacrificial system and its socio-psychological background has been done by Rene Girard, in *The Scapegoat* (Baltimore: Johns Hopkins Press, 1989). Much more remains to be done on this topic, but his works will be especially important to the future understanding of Christian roots in Hebrew patterns of thought, and in the reassessment of the "ransom" theory of atonement.

transcendent "prince of peace." They would have, by then, perfectly understood the words of the seer in Luke who said, "He will reign over the house of Jacob forever, and of his kingdom there will be no end" (Luke 1:33).

Christological Heresies

Most of the matters we have discussed with regard to the person of Christ were hammered out over a long period of time, and often in reference to errors that emphasized one aspect of the biblical witness to the exclusion of others that the church saw as also critically important. In the case of Christology, this is particularly evident. We have seen, for instance, that Christological doctrine has been formulated around four important centers of thought: (1) Jesus Christ is fully divine; (2) he is also fully human; (3) these two natures are centered in one person; (4) and the union compromises neither the humanity nor the divinity. Let me state that in four brief topic headings to make the matter perfectly clear:

- Fully divine

- Fully human

- One person

- Two natures

Now it is best to understand christological heresies as failing the test of orthodoxy, or even vigorously opposing orthodox Christianity, on one of those four points. They usually fell into error by trying over-zealously to defend one proposition (one established truth in orthodox thinking, that is) to the exclusion of its complementary truth. As we list and discuss briefly each of these, you will see that some Christians have so defended the divinity of Christ that they failed to affirm his humanity, or vice versa. Some have so insisted on the two natures that they denied the one person; and, likewise, the opposite error has also occurred.

As we look at the classical types of heresies (if one can use such a term!) we will see that, in each case, the heresy tends to *affirm* an important aspect of Christology, but does so by denying another sometimes equally important truth.

1. Heresy that affirmed the divinity of Christ, but denied his full humanity.

These heresies can usually be categorized as docetic heresies, although there are various types of docetism that have occurred historically. *Docetism* comes from the Greek term *dokei,* meaning "seem" or "appear." *Docetism* is therefore "seemism"; it is the idea that Christ appears to be a man, while in fact he is God.

Gnostic heresies of the second through the fifth centuries were strongly docetic. While there were important variations among the types of gnosticism, all of them incorporated a dualistic vision of the cosmos in which matter and flesh were linked with evil, and were the source of worldly problems. Therefore, with their concept of Christ being highly influenced by this metaphysical or cosmic *dualism,* they came to reject any suggestion that Christ—the real Christ, representing the real God—could be closely associated with flesh. Either Jesus was a phantom resembling a man, or else the man Jesus was only an instrument of the anointing Spirit of God, the true Christ. In any case, they firmly rejected the belief that God had come in the flesh, that he was incarnate, that he suffered and died, or that he was bodily raised from the dead.

Apollinarianism. Apollinarius (A.D. 310–390), bishop of Laodicea, was a strong opponent of the Arians, who had denied the true deity of Christ. (We will come to the case of the Arians and **arianism** shortly.) In making his case for the truth of a fully divine Christ, however, he fell into a mode of conceptualizing Christ that plainly denied Jesus' true humanity. Holding to the view that man is comprised of body, soul, and spirit, he understood Christ as being endowed with the *Logos,* the divine Word, in the place of a rational soul. This explanation, however, proved to fall somewhere between strict docetism and arianism. The incarnate Son would then be neither God nor man, but some third, unique entity, an incomparable admixture of God and man.

Apollianarius's several opponents, led by Basil, came to see how vital was the connection between the incarnation of Christ and the redemption of humanity. If Christ were only human in terms of his body and his senses, and not human in his intellect and will, then the human intellect and will were not redeemed in Christ. Yet these powers of intellect and will were, if anything, more seriously affected by sin than anything else. For man to be redeemed, Christ must have represented the whole of man.

2. Heresy that affirmed the humanity of Christ, but denied his full divinity: Ebionism.

This attempt to defend the dignity of God by refusing, essentially, the incarnation was promoted by heretical Jewish Christians early in the life of the church. They rejected the gospel witness of the virgin birth, preferring to believe Jesus was the son of Joseph and Mary. At baptism, they conjectured, Jesus became the Christ by virtue of receiving the Spirit of God. Before the crucifixion the Spirit abandoned Jesus. The work of Jesus was, therefore, the work of an extraordinary human being, the true Messiah, but not the divine Son of God.

Arianism. The fourth-century Alexandrian Christian named Arius authored one of the most serious and pervasive challenges to orthodox Christianity. Strictly speaking, his heresy was directed against the Trinity; but the heart of the matter was a christological issue. Defending monotheism, he rejected the idea of any uncreated reality other than the Godhead, whose simplicity and uniqueness must not be compromised. Therefore, he defined Christ as the unique and transcendent, but *created*, Son of God.

This error remains as the prime example of a Christian monotheism that is so loyal to the abstract principle of the oneness of God (it is almost, as some have suggested, the worship of the "number one"), that it loses sight of the very meaning of Christ as Immanuel, God with us. Had Arians succeeded in persuading the church, Christianity would have ended in a theology of ***monism*** such as we find in Islam today.

■ ──────────────────── ■

ARIUS' DENIAL OF CHRIST'S UNCREATED DEITY

The following words of Arius are quoted by Athanasius in Discourses Against the Arians *and* Encyclical Letter to the Bishops of Egypt and Libya :

God was not always a Father; indeed, there was a time when God was alone, and He was not yet a Father. Afterwards, however, He became a Father. The Son was not always; for inasmuch as all things were made out of what did not exist, the Son of God, too, was made out of what did not exist; and as all that are made do exist as creatures and works, He too is a creature and a work; and since formerly all things did not exist, but were afterwards made, so also there was a time when the Word of God did not Himself exist; and before He was begotten, He was not; rather, He has a beginning of existence.

[Cited in W. A. Jurgens, *The Faith of the Early Fathers* vol. 1 (Collegeville, Minn.: The Liturgical Press, 1970), 276.]

■ ──────────────────── ■

3. Heresy that affirmed the two natures, divine and human, but denied the unity of Christ's Person.

The Nestorian controversy began around A.D. 428 or 429, when Nestorius, bishop of Constantinople, objected to the practice of referring to Mary, mother of Jesus, as *Theotokos*, "mother of God." She was indeed the virginal mother of Christ, he argued, but not the mother of God. How could a mortal be the mother of him who is eternal?

The sensitivity to this rather shocking title, mother of God, was widely appreciated. Yet the larger question that came into view with the bishop's probing, however, was this: If Mary is *not* the God-bearer, then in what sense is Jesus God? Did he become God at a later time? Or, if he was God from the beginning, even from eternity, then how can one reasonably object to the title *Theotokos,* even though it jars the mind a bit. Perhaps that jarring is only a consequence of the jarring paradox of the incarnation. It reflects the scandal of a God who can be both everywhere and here, whose general presence and particular presence are not contradictory.

Nestorius answered this question in a way that seemed to relate Christ to God the Father only in the sense of this moral connection. Jesus was in God and of God; he is truly identified with God in the sense that he did the will of the Father. In this line of reasoning, Nestorius did, in fact, attempt to preserve the true humanity of Jesus and also his true divinity. Yet was this God becoming man? Or was it man becoming God? Was the incarnation the action of God upon human history; or was it merely the response of man to God?

What was at stake was the *unity* of God and man in Christ. To say that the Jesus Mary gave birth to is other than the God who created Mary is to make a distinction between the essential deity of God the Father and his Son. Slowly, and in halting steps, the church came to articulate the fundamental limits of Christology so as not to confuse the persons of Father and Son, for the witness of Scripture distinguished them: the Son, for instance, prays to the Father, but neither did the church want to separate the natures, denying the prior deity of Christ that goes back to the very beginning, or we might say, extends to the very core and essence of all reality.

Sometimes a heresy will seem, at first, to be altogether reasonable, or even a good defense of Christian truth. On closer inspection, however, we cannot help but admire the steady insistence of the church, speaking by a far-reaching consensus, upon issues that turn out to be truly foundational in the sense that they set the course for further thinking about both the nature of God and the life of the Christian.

Here in the Nestorian error we find an example of how the church considered the weightiness of this implication in the gospel: that God became man in history because he included humanity in his own nature from the beginning. If Jesus' divinity were only ***accidental***—that is, something added to his humanity—then the good news of the God-Man would be lost. To put the matter quite bluntly, God understands us because he is also one with us. God is among us, not as a divine doctor among wounded patients, but as one of the wounded who willingly (as opposed to necessarily) shares our predicament. He is, in Henri Nouwen's words, the "wounded healer."

4. Heresy that affirmed the unity of Christ's Person but denied the dual nature of Christ.

The heresy that took this approach was *Eutychianism*. As you might imagine, it was a reaction to Nestorianism. Once the importance of the unity of Christ's Person was discovered or affirmed in the Nestorian crisis, there were those—first of all, Eutyches, archmandrite of a monastery in Constantinople—who so vigorously defended against that error that they, so to speak, fell off the horse on the other side.

Eutyches wanted to say that Christ was not two natures after the incarnational union of God and man. He argued that Christ was "*of* two natures, but not *in* two natures." He was still fighting the fight against Nestorianism, and he was so intent upon avoiding the error of dividing the person of Christ that he made an equally grievous mistake in losing the whole point of the incarnation. "I admit that our Lord was of two natures before the union," Eutyches is quoted as saying at his hearing in Constantinople in 448, "but after the union one nature . . . I follow the doctrine of the blessed Cyril and the holy fathers and the holy Athanasius. They speak of two natures before the union, but after the union and incarnation they speak of one nature not two."[4]

The story of how the church reacted to Eutychianism is a long one. At first it seemed that Eutyches and his defenders had won. Eventually, however, after this controversy had been raging for three years, a new ecumenical council was called at Chalcedon (near Constantinople) in October 451. Out of this council came the famous christological statement, known as the Chalcedon definition, declaring Jesus Christ to be . . .

---

4. "The Admissions of Eutyches" in *Documents of the Christian Church*, 49.

one and the same (Person), and we all teach this with one voice, the same perfect in Godhead, the same perfect in manhood, truly God and truly man, the same of a reasonable soul and a body, of one substance with the Father as touching His Godhead and the same of one substance with us as touching his manhood, in all respects like us apart from sin; begotten of the Father before the ages as touching the Godhead, the same in the last days for us and for our salvation born of the Virgin Mary, the Mother of God, as touching the manhood; one and the same Christ, Son, Lord, only begotten, acknowledged in two natures without confusion, without change, without division, without separation; and that by no means taking away the distinction of the natures through the union but rather preserving the special property of each nature, and bringing them together into one Person and one hypostasis, not separated or divided into two persons, but one and the same Son and only begotten God the Word, the Lord Jesus Christ.

The Cornerstone of Christian Theology

It is hardly possible to overestimate the importance of these developments that we see coming to a final formulation in the Chalcedon statement. All of the implications of the incarnation of God in Christ were not self-evident in the first century. The witness of Scripture concerning the deity and the humanity of Christ, concerning the unity of his Person and the integrity of his two natures, appeared either logically inconsistent or partaking of a very deep mystery. Yet all of these marks of Christology were evidently vital to a full understanding of the nature of God's work in Christ.

These points of reference about the person of Christ proved to be the essential cornerstone of Christian theology. From Chalcedon on, the thinking of the church would take its measure from these critical principles. It represented an enormous leap forward, not only in the Christian church's capacity for building its understanding of God, its theology, but also its understanding of humanity, the human situation with regard to sin and salvation, and its understanding of what God had done for them in Christ.

In the next chapter, we will see how the principles discovered about the person of Christ bear fruit in the understanding of Christ's work.

Questions for Review and Reflection

1. What are the four basic concerns of a doctrine of the Person of Christ?
2. Name and define one heretical school that arose in opposition to each of these four points of orthodox Christology.
3. In your view, does it make a practical difference for a Christian living today that Christ was fully human, that is, that he had a human mind and will as well as a human body?
4. Why do you think it was important for the church to establish a careful statement of orthodox Christology such as was done at Chalcedon?
5. What are the pitfalls for Christian thinking and Christian living inherent in docetism?
6. Which of the heretical tendencies do you think are found today, either in popular religious talk or modern theology?

CHAPTER   SIX

■ —————————————————————— ■

GOD FOR US:
THE WORK OF CHRIST

We gave attention first to the doctrine of the Person of
Christ. Yet, historically, the church was giving witness to
the work or the function of Christ long before the full implications concerning his humanity and divinity became clear
to them.

At our own point in history, however, after we have seen
the importance of avoiding some of the earlier pitfalls in
Christology—pitfalls that believers of a much earlier day
worked strenuously to point out—we can see how all that
the earliest Christians claimed for the *work* of Christ presupposed what the church later insisted upon with regard
to his *person*. As *prophet*, for instance, Jesus not only proclaimed the Word of God, but also he *was* and is that word.
In his person, he represented the Word of God as no other
prophet ever could. As *priest* he presented upon the altar a
perfect sacrifice, only this time the offering was not a lamb
representing man, but it was the man, the perfect represen-
tative of all humanity. As *king* he was the *anointed*, the
Messiah; yet his anointing signaled the rule not of an earthly delegate of God, but also of God himself. Consequently,

105

Christians quite early thought of Christ as *prophet, priest,* and *king,* filling the three messianic offices of Israel. And this came to be a way of speaking that strongly articulated both his person and his work.

By the Middle Ages, however, the priestly function of Christ, as one who perfectly **atoned** for believers in his death and came to intercede for them in his resurrection and ascension, began to be the focus of theological discussion. It was in the work of **atonement** that the meaning of Christ's life is most fully expressed. At the same time, it is this work and its value for us that raise some of the most difficult questions for the Christian faith.

The Idea of Atonement

Practically the only technical theological term that derives from English is this term **atonement**. It means, of course, that God and the believer become one—thus: atonement. Even though the term we use is relatively modern, however, the idea of atonement goes back to the earliest practices of Israel and among the earliest lines of the Old Testament.

It occurs to me that I began writing these lines on atonement during the Jewish *Yom Kippur,* Day of Atonement. This day commemorates a religious ritual of the Hebrew people that was instituted as the most comprehensive sacrifice to atone for the sins of the people and to cleanse the sanctuary. All of the atoning sacrifices involved the shedding of blood, which represented the shedding, we might say, of *life.* A rabbinic saying to that effect is quoted in Hebrews 9:22, "There is no atonement except with blood."[1] In this shedding of the blood of sacrificial animals, the lives of the people were cleansed of the guilt they bore and the sanctuary was made a fit "dwelling place" for the *Shekinah,* or "presence," of God.

---

1. Leighton Pullen commented that "the only exception proves the rule. It is to be found in Leviticus where a vegetable offering was allowed as a substitute for the usual sin offering, when the offerer was too poor to give the ordinary sacrifice." *The Atonement* (London: Longmans, Green, and Co., 1906), 74–75.

Now, in view of the interrelationship of those elements—
blood, life, and the cleansing of the sanctuary, all represen-
tative of the need to remove sin, or, in other words, to take
away the barrier between God and the worshiper, so that
they might be "at one"—we can see the great significance of
the sacrifice that was prescribed on the Day of Atonement.

All of the atoning sacrifices involved the shedding of
blood. That was true of the peace offering, the burnt offering
(the '*ola*, from which we derive the term *holocaust*), the sin
offering, and the guilt offering. In such cases the blood was
either thrown against the altar of burnt offering, outside
the sanctuary, or sprinkled outside the veil of the sanctuary
upon the altar of incense, or smeared upon the horns of the
altar of burnt offering. In the case of the sacrifice of the bull
and the goat on the Day of Atonement, however, the blood
was not presented merely outside the sanctuary, or even inside the outer room of the sanctuary where only the priests
could minister, but it was taken into the Holy of Holies,
within the veil, that sacred space that was excluded to everyone except to the high priest, who was allowed to enter
for this one purpose on this one day. There the high priest
dipped his fingers into the blood of the bull and thereafter
into the blood of the goat, and sprinkled the blood on the
mercy seat of the ark of the covenant and before the mercy
seat. This event was repeated each year and signaled the re-
mission, or the sending-away, of the sins of the community.

Why was this so important? Why was so much of early Israelite culture invested in these rites of atonement? Surely
much of the answer is hidden in the mystery of God's inef-
fable nature and purpose. We do see that the idea of a community whose life derives from its *oneness* with God, a
community that is chosen or elected for that purpose and
that lives in covenant with God, continued to express this
self-awareness through the atoning sacrifices.

The covenant of an elect, or chosen people, was the defining experience of Israel. The Israelites were saved out of
Egypt for the one purpose of being a people of God's own
possession (Deut. 4:20). God nurtured them as his own child
(Hos. 11:1). Because God has delivered his people in the
past, he will do so in the future (Isa. 43:14–19). Their identity with the God who chose them, entered into covenant

with them, and sustained them through every trial, imposed also some peculiar obligations upon them: "Now therefore, if you will obey my voice and keep my covenant, you shall be my own possession among all peoples; for all the earth is mine, and you shall be to me a kingdom of priests and a holy nation" (Exod. 19:5–6, RSV).

Atonement was expressed in the covenant relationship of God with his people. And the meaning of that covenant, and thus of that identity or atonement, would have to be expressed in national obedience to God's call and God's law. The atonement for Israel came to mean more than a cultic purity; it had strong implications for the moral life of the people.

Atonement in the New Testament

Against this Old Testament background, we see that the New Testament concern for atonement is parallel in certain important ways: (1) The life of a community (this time the church) depends upon the accomplished atonement. (2) The atonement is effected by means of sacrifice. And (3) the priestly intercession for the community, made possible by the work of the high priest (who is also, this time, the prophet and the king) operates to bring salvation to the world at large.

Yet the differences in the New Testament idea of atoning sacrifice also are important. (1) The community of priests is not a nation but is gathered out of all the nations. (2) The atonement is accomplished once for all rather than a repetitious offering of annual sacrifice; it is final in the sense that it is ultimate, and thus the effective atonement for all time. And (3) the High Priest, Christ, presents not the symbolic blood of animal sacrifices, but his own blood; in other words, his own life as an offering to God.

So the theology of atonement is hardly one that originated with medieval discussions of discrete theological interpretations. It is true that the kind of sorting out of alternative views of the meaning of Christ's atoning work took place late in the history of theological development. This is where we go to find what has now become the classic theological statements of the meaning of reconciliation, following the lead of Anselm, Abelard, and others. But the idea that something radically new has taken place in the divine-human relationship was born with the advent of Christianity and has its strongest and deepest roots in the covenant theology and the cultic practices of ancient Israel.

A survey of some of the critical New Testament passages will show that a number of themes come into play with any effort to reduce this idea of atonement to a theological teaching. Is the reality of atonement best understood as a satisfaction of God's determined goal of righteousness? Is it the payment of a moral debt? If so, to whom is the debt owed? Or is it the beginning of a moral movement, fueled by the imitation of a godly life, that ends in satisfying God's requirement?

We can see elements in the relevant New Testament passages that seem to answer rather specifically each one of these questions.

Atonement in the Synoptic Gospels

In the Synoptic Gospels, two passages appear to be central to the question of atonement. The first occurs as Jesus is teaching his disciples about the meaning of greatness or leadership in the community of his disciples. It would not be, as among the Gentiles, that the leaders would lord it over their followers; instead they would imitate Jesus' example as a servant who came "not to be served but to serve, and to give his life a ransom for many" (Mark 10:45). Here we find an intimation that Jesus is an example to be followed, and also that his sacrifice is a ransom, implying that his form of service would free others from a bondage.

The other passage is found in Mark 14, where Jesus institutes the Lord's Supper. He says to his disciples, "This is my blood of the covenant, which is poured out for many" (v. 24). The idea of substitution and of penalty is strongly suggested here, and perhaps the idea of ransom can be argued here as well.

Atonement in the Fourth Gospel

The Gospel of John sheds a rather different light upon atonement by suggesting that the accomplishment of Jesus' work transcends time. His death and resurrection cast bright shadows of ultimate reality back upon the events of Jesus' earthly life. Jesus prayed that, after his resurrection and glory, his disciples might be included in the oneness that he showed with his Father (John 17:22–24).

Furthermore, the Gospel of John speaks of atonement more at the level of a contemplative relationship with God, rather than as a condition apart from the believer's experience. John's Gospel would radiate, for instance, Jesus' words: "I am the way, and the truth, and the life. No one comes to the Father except through me. If you know me, you will know my Father also. From now on you do know him and have seen him" (14:6–7).

Atonement in this fourth Gospel tends to be understood as the standing of the Son with the Father. It is a relationship that the believer becomes a part of, for "those who love me will be loved by my Father" (14:21).

John's presentation of atonement, since it is more abstract and more related to psychological experience, probably appeals more to modern minds. It is important to remember, however, that even here the whole matter of human relationship to God rests upon following Jesus in solidarity with his act of sacrifice. To Simon Peter, in chapter 21, Jesus says not simply "know me" or "love me," but "follow me" (vv. 19, 22). The implication was clear. Jesus had been to the cross, and Peter had failed to follow him, instead denying him three times. Even in John, the idea of atonement is strongly based upon the cross of Christ.

Atonement in the Pauline Writings

Since the subject of atonement is so clearly central to the thinking of Paul, it is not surprising that the avenues to his thought on the subject are too varied to summarize easily. An attempt to touch upon aspects of his thought, however, will help us see the full range of New Testament concerns in expressing what has happened in the work of Christ for humanity.

Paul is found, for instance, frequently expressing Christ's work as a victory over the enemies of humanity. The enemies are sin and death, from which we must be set free (Rom. 8:2). Also the enemy includes the demonic powers: "Our struggle is not against enemies of blood and flesh, but against the rulers, against the authorities, against the cosmic powers of this present darkness, against the spiritual forces of evil in the heavenly places" (Eph. 6:12).

The atonement involves more than the psychological and social reconciliation of God and humanity; Paul says it embraces even the physical cosmos. The whole of creation "waits with eager longing for the revealing of the children of God," at which time all of nature will be "set free from its bondage to decay and will obtain the freedom of the glory of the children of God" (Rom. 8:19, 21).

Finally it is difficult to miss the strong **eschatological** note in Paul's teaching on reconciliation. The dying of Christ on a cross has implications for the ultimate destiny of the believer. "For if we have been united with him in a death like his, we will certainly be united with him in a resurrection like his" (Rom. 6:5). In nineteenth-century theology, especially among the inheritors of Schleiermacher's system of interpretation, the **eschatological** note had almost been lost. Early twentieth-century American Protestants often worried that the emphasis on eschatology would weaken resolve to make a difference in present society. By the late 1960s, however, theologians such as Jurgen Moltmann and Wolfhart Pannenberg were reminding their colleagues of the inescapably strong element of eschatology in the New Testament. Furthermore, they were showing how the concern for justice in the present really *requires* that note of future redemption.

Three Theories of Atonement

The church did, however, come to the point that the cultic language of the early church and the allusions to Old Testament practices no longer sufficed in explaining the Christian doctrine of atonement. As the subtle differences in the way Christians appropriated this mystery of reconciliation came to light, it became necessary to interpret the reality of atonement in ways that satisfied the questions of a later age, a much more metaphysical age. This necessity has remained in our own modern times.

Though the effort to post these theories under different headings has sometimes resulted in five or six different theories of atonement, we can satisfactorily reduce these to three principal theories:

1. The ransom theory
2. The satisfaction theory
3. The exemplar theory.

Let's take a brief look at each of these and then draw some general conclusions about the atoning work of Christ, especially as this can be made understandable in today's world.

The Ransom Theory

Called by Bishop Gustaf Aulén the "classic theory" or the "Christus Victor" theme, this explanation of the atonement probably embodies most consistently the real sentiment and proclamation of the early church. In this theory, God engages not merely the mind or the soul of humanity, and is not merely engaged in a transaction with individuals who either believe or disbelieve, but he has overcome the enemies of humanity; particularly he has defeated Satan by giving as ransom his Son in exchange for the release of believers from bondage. Christ entered into a conflict with sin, death, and the devil, and has emerged victorious. In a sense, his entire life was a contest against that which held humankind in bondage, but it was his death that was the final victory.

The metaphor of ransom is expressed in various ways by the church fathers. Irenaeus undoubtedly had in mind the practice of paying an enemy to release prisoners of war or to set free a captive city. Gregory of Nyssa spoke of Satan as a greedy fish that took the bait, namely the life of Christ, and consequently was captured by the fishhook of God's intention to redeem sinners from their bondage and to raise Christ and his church from the dead. Augustine spoke of the cross as a mousetrap. "What did our redeemer do to our captor? As our prize, He held out His cross as a mousetrap and set as bait upon it His own blood."[2]

In a persuasive modern revival of this doctrine—a doctrine that was routinely rejected by orthodox Protestants

---

2. Augustine, Sermon CXXX, 2; cited by Robert H. Culpepper, *Interpreting the Atonement* (Grand Rapids, Mich.: Eerdmans, 1966), 77.

and disparaged by liberal theologians of the nineteenth and twentieth centuries—Aulén reminded theological readers that this theory was the dominant view of Christian writers from Irenaeus to John of Damascus, and was a major element in the thinking of Athanasius, Ambrose, Augustine, and Gregory the Great.

In setting forth a case for clarifying the historical misconceptions with regard to the "Christus Victor" ransom theory, Aulén suggests a number of reasons that post-Enlightenment theologians have either ignored or strongly resisted this theory. Perhaps the most important reason is the modern rejection of **dualism,** or any explanation that sees a power contending with God, or indeed, even pitting itself against humankind. Aulén makes clear that this dualism, which is consistently detected in the Fathers, is not a metaphysical dualism like that of the Gnostics, in which flesh and spirit are opposed to one another or matter is opposed to the realm of divinity. Rather, this is a limited dualism in which man is not merely reduced to his present condition by his own sin, but he is also caught in a condition of rebellion against God that surpasses his strength to oppose it. Therefore, the human being requires help. Redemption is, then, not only an appeal to humanity; it is a struggle and a conflict with that which holds mankind in thrall. Redemption holds in view mankind, God, *and* a world ruined by sin.

The Enlightenment period in modern Europe was marked by its high estimation of nature and reason. One can deduce from this that such intellectual tastes were not likely to value super-nature and the trans-rational mystery of a world that exists in an essential conflict. The language of the New Testament, however, and the consistent language of most church fathers reminds us that the idea of conflict, and the conviction that God has rescued humanity from an overwhelming condition of spiritual oppression, is difficult to escape in any consistent reading of Scripture.

The Satisfaction Theory

Adolph Harnack called Anselm the first theologian to frame a theory of atonement. Gustav Aulén notes that, for most of this century and the last, the ransom picture of atonement was rarely dignified with the label of a coherent theory, and theologians habitually spoke as if the "satisfaction theory" of Anselm and the "moral influence" or "exemplar" theory of Peter Abelard were the only two valid alternatives. The theory framed by Anselm in his classic *Cur Deus Homo?* (Why the God/Man?) is often characterized as the objective idea of the atonement, and the Abelardian theory is called, in contrast, the subjective idea of atonement.

Another way of distinguishing these two is to say that in Anselm's theory, the change that takes place with regard to human guilt is a change in God. In Abelard's, the change that takes place is in the human being.

In *Cur Deus Homo?* Anselm attempts to give a reasoned explanation for the necessity of the incarnation and the atonement. Written somewhat in the form of a Platonic dialogue, Anselm's student, Boso, raises questions that might be raised by uncultured unbelievers.

While Boso serves as the foil to Anselm, he is yet clever enough to discredit the idea that God paid a ransom to Satan. The idea, he says, that "God should have proceeded against the devil to release man, rather by right of equity than by His own sufferings, since the devil by slaying Him in who was no cause of death, and who was God, had justly lost the power which he had over sinners . . . all this, to my mind is of no force whatever." He continues:

> For did the devil or man belong to himself or to any other save God, or were in the power of any but God, this perchance might justly be asserted; but seeing that neither devil nor man exists but by God, and that neither subsists outside His power, what claim should God urge with his own, concerning His own, upon his own, except to punish him.[3]

Thus, in Anselm's view, a debt was owed for sin, and Christ indeed paid the price for sin; but it was paid to God, not to the devil. The debt, furthermore, is owed to God because of the supreme worth of God's purpose for humankind. It is not an overlooking of the gravity of sin, but in fact

---

3. St. Anselm, *Cur Deus Homo?* I. VII. (London: Griffith Farran, Okeden & Welsh, 1885), 9–10.

it is precisely in taking the seriousness of sin into account that brings to light the necessity of reimbursing God for the loss due to sin.

In this theory two impressions come forcibly to the forefront: the supreme importance of God's intention for man, and the seriousness of human rebellion against that divine goal. Thus the debt and its satisfaction represent changes that take place in God himself, through his incarnation, on behalf of humankind. For the reason that the effective change takes place in God, this theory is often called an objective theory of atonement; that is, the operation of atonement is one that takes place apart from the human will or consciousness.

The Exemplar Theory

It is quite certain that Abelard had little effect upon the theology of the atonement in his day, just as it is certain that later theologians (especially in the nineteenth and early twentieth centuries) could find much to sympathize with in him. Abelard's view of the atonement was, in contrast to Anselm's earlier "classic" view, subjective in its effect. The change that took place with Christ's death had to do with the change in the heart of the believer, rather than in God. Christ was the example, inspiring the imitative love of the follower. He quotes, in support of his argument, Luke 7:47: "Her sins, which were many, have been forgiven; [for] hence she has shown great love." Abelard did not leave out the sacrificial component of the atonement. Instead, he saw this as a basis for considering Christ's work as meritorious, and therefore effective for salvation. But the consequence of his work was its power to incite love in those who follow in imitation of Christ: whether they die literally in response to faith, they are impelled to give up their lives of devotion to the way of life Christ had pioneered.

The lasting value of Abelard's view was his use of a very important and powerful element in the New Testament understanding of Christ's work. Paul, for instance, never tires of calling upon believers to imitate Christ in thought and deed. He points to himself and others as examples leading them closer to the pattern of life found in Christ (cf. Phil. 3:17). Both Paul and most notable writers of the early church saw the church as a fellowship devoted to participating in the life of God by following the example of Christ. The power of imitation, and the strong impulse toward imitation in human society (an impulse without which we would have neither language nor common manners—in a word, no culture) is often overlooked by modern thinkers. Abelard, while hardly satisfying the objective aspect of atonement, at least brought into view a subjective and imitative element that does justice to an important part of the biblical witness and makes sense of many of the earliest teachings of the Christian church.

■ —————————————————————— ■

E. Y. MULLINS ON ATONEMENT

We ask: What attribute or quality in God controls in the atonement? Is it righteousness, or is it love, or is it merely the divine sovereignty, which conditions the saving work of Christ? The reply is that it is not one of these alone, but all in combination. The atonement was not the mere appointment of the divine sovereignty, as some have claimed, without reference to other qualities in God. Nor was it a provision of his righteousness to which love was subordinate, nor of his love to which righteousness was secondary. The atonement was not the product of any mere attribute of God. It was the expression rather of the inner being of the righteous and loving God who was sovereign.

God drew the world back to himself by a cord which was made up of two strands, righteousness and love. The atonement then was not a mere utilitarian expedient for accomplishing an end which might have been otherwise achieved. It was rather a divine enterprise in which the requirements of righteousness and of love were met at every stage.

[From: E. Y. Mullins, *The Christian Religion in Its Doctrinal Expression* (Philadelphia: Roger Williams Press, 1917), 335.]

■ —————————————————————— ■

For Whom Did Christ Die?

How to formulate a theory of the atonement is not the only issue, and perhaps not even the most divisive issue, regarding this doctrine. It is the scope of the atonement effected by Christ that has created at least an equal amount of debate. The question is: Did Christ die for all humans, regardless of their initial belief or response? Did he die rather for all people, but his death is effective for those who believe? Or did he die for the elect of God, and only those chosen will be saved and not those who were born and remain outside the number God intended to save? In modern times these alternatives are referred to as (1) universalism, (2) general atonement, and (3) limited atonement. Briefly, we might state the argument for each of these.

Universalism

While traditional Christian teachings have rejected the idea that all people would be saved, whether they had heard the gospel or responded to it in belief, universalism is a recurrent theme among a variety of theologians from the early days of the church until now. That fact should not be surprising. There is a strong thrust in Christian thinking and in the Bible itself that emphasizes the power of God to overcome all opposition. What does it mean for God to win, these thinkers reason, other than to say that he wins everyone and every enemy over to his side?

The biblical roots of this universalism are quite striking in their emphasis upon the ultimate triumph of God. One passage frequently cited is Philippians 2:9–11:

> Therefore God also highly exalted him
> and gave him a name
> that is above every name,
> so that at the name of Jesus
> every knee should bend,
> in heaven and on earth and
> under the earth,
> and every tongue should confess
> that Jesus Christ is Lord,
> to the glory of God the Father.

Universalists can even find strong evidence in the Book of Revelation, with its apocalyptic emphasis upon struggle with the power of evil. In chapter 19, when the one who is called "faithful and true" appears on a white horse, he slays his enemies with a "sharp sword" that is depicted as coming from his mouth—i.e., the gospel. If the gospel slays the enemies of Christ, does it not mean that it turns them into friends and followers of Christ? Ultimately, the universalist would argue, God cries out, and the world with all its inhabitants cannot resist his grace.

It is not without some scriptural justification, therefore, that the great Origen defended the idea that all would inevitably and ultimately be saved. Even Satan could not finally escape God's all-powerful purpose of redemption. In modern times, Karl Barth (among many others) argued that the rejection of sinners applies now only in the condemnation of Jesus Christ on the cross.

The difficulty the universalist faces is in arguing consistently from the evidence of Scripture. That is especially true when Jesus, himself, spoke often and forthrightly—too often and too typically for the matter to be ignored. He warned his hearers that they might be utterly shut out of the blessings of God and condemned to punishment for sin.

General Atonement

The mediating position might be stated in this way: Christ died for all; and those who believe in him, confessing him as Savior, will be saved (while those who do not, will not). This is the idea of "general atonement."

The support for such a position in Scripture is impressive. In John 3:16 the provision for salvation is clearly held out to "everyone who believes." Hebrews 2:9 states that Christ suffered death "so that by the grace of God he might taste death for everyone." First John promises that "If anyone does sin, we have an advocate with the Father, Jesus Christ the righteous," who is the "atoning sacrifice for our sin." So far, we might read that to apply to the atonement of a limited number, to the elect. But then we read, "And not for ours only but also for the sins of the whole world" (2:1 and 2).

Limited Atonement

The teaching that Christ died only for the elect of God, in other words that it is foreordained who would or would not be saved, is known as "limited atonement." This doctrine is usually thought to receive its most prominent form in the theology of John Calvin and his theological heirs in the Reformed movement. The corollary of the doctrine of predestination is this idea of limited atonement. Romans 9 is usually cited as the classical text in support of this doctrine.

The scriptural argument is supported by the appeal to rational consistency in this way: If Christ died for *all*, does not the rejection of Christ by *some* mean that, to that extent, his death was to no effect? So, on the basis of the efficacy of Christ's death, he must have died only for those who are chosen and foreordained (or some would rather say, foreknown) to be among the saved.

The importance of these alternatives becomes more strongly focused as we approach the meaning of salvation in the life of the individual and the church.

Questions for Review and Reflection

1. What prevents us from being "at one" with God apart from Christ?
2. What are the three general theories in explanation of the cross of Christ—the theories of atonement?
3. Which of these appears to you stronger on the basis of scriptural evidences?
4. What are the implications for evangelism and missions if one adopts the view of limited atonement?
5. What ethical argument might be made either for or against universalism?
6. Why do you think modern people have difficulty understanding the patristic preference for the ransom theory of atonement?

CHAPTER SEVEN

■ ———————————————————— ■

GOD WITH US STILL:
THE HOLY SPIRIT

I had an interesting exchange recently with two friends at a committee meeting. One friend was more apt to speak in terms of intimate give and take with God. She was of a decidedly charismatic bent. Returning from the copier with handouts for the group, she said, "God's good! The copier's working."

My other friend was much more of a reformed type. She was more impressed with the sovereign majesty of an almighty God and a little suspicious of those who claim to know this Great Mystery too well. She leaned over to me and whispered: "God's good, even if the copier doesn't work!"

In Christian theology we are always aware of a certain tension in our understanding of God. On the one hand, we understand God as one who really cares for us personally and individually, even to the point of looking after our smallest needs. Yet on the other hand, we know that we can trivialize God's actions into mere magic, losing sight of the awe-ful greatness of a sovereign God.

121

The doctrine of the Holy Spirit hinges on this question of the greatness of a God who can still be present among us. Jesus compared the coming of the Holy Spirit, the *Paraclete*, with his own presence among the disciples. "I will not leave you orphaned" (John 14:18). "I will ask the Father, and he will give you another Advocate [*allon paracleton*]" (v.16). When he said this, he could have used the term *heteron*, which also means another. But it means another "of a different kind." Instead he used *allon*, meaning "another of the same kind." This is significant. The intimate presence, guidance, and friendship of Jesus would be continued. The *Paraclete,* or the Holy Spirit, is God present and abiding among his people. He is also referred to in the New Testament, especially in the writings of Paul, as the Spirit of Christ.

Who Is the Holy Spirit?

The first difficulty we encounter in teaching about the Holy Spirit, or in understanding the traditional Christian teachings, is simply in knowing how we might think of the Spirit in relationship to, yet distinct from, the other persons of the Trinity.

The Holy Spirit and the Father

Early references to the Spirit of God in the Old Testament help us understand the New Testament background. We find the term *Holy Spirit* in the Old Testament only in Isaiah 63:10–11 and in Psalm 51:11.

Two metaphors are used in the Old Testament to describe the presence of God or Spirit. One is *neshemah*, meaning "breath." The other is *ruach*, meaning "wind." These terms imply a number of things about the Spirit of God. He is invisible to the eye; yet his presence is felt, like the wind. Like the wind, he can be gentle or destructive. Like breath, his presence means life and his absence means death.

These terms are translated in the New Testament with the Greek term *pneuma*, "air." Thus the doctrine of the Spirit is called *pneumatology*. Whether "breath," "wind," or "air," we know that the words we use for spirit imply a certain connection of intimacy and mystery. Recall the way Jesus brought out these implied aspects when he said, "The wind blows where it chooses, and you hear the sound of it, but you do not know where it comes from or where it goes. So it is with everyone who is born of the Spirit" (John 3:8).

In the Old Testament, we can detect three distinct levels of understanding with regard to the effects of the Spirit. One has been called an *ecstatic* understanding, the second is *messianic* in nature, and the third relates the Spirit of God to creation—the *creator* spirit.[1]

Ecstatic experience of the Spirit relies wholly on an outward, visible, sometimes dramatic manifestation of the Spirit. Examples are found in the early cultic prophets, whose experiences of the Spirit of God consisted of ecstatic utterances, trances, and dancing (c.f., 1 Sam. 10:9–13), and also among the judges whose actions are described simply in terms of the Lord's "possession" of them for the sake of slaying the enemy (Judg. 6:34).

When we move from the ecstatic to the *messianic* Spirit, we must first notice the degree to which the work of the Spirit is understood in both subtle and inward terms. It is manifested not so much in outward dramatic works as in an inward disposition of the heart. It is a demonstration of the Spirit that might become known in terms of *words*—the words, for instance, of the classical writing prophets, who appear in Israel between the eighth century and the fifth century B.C.

The third idea of the Spirit of God emerging in the Old Testament is that of the *creator* Spirit. Here and there in the Old Testament, and in certain very powerful texts, we draw the connection between the work of God in human experience (which is being referred to as ecstatic or messianic) and the work of God throughout the created order. It is the Spirit of God who was "moving over the face of the waters" in the creation story (Gen. 1:2). The Spirit (*neshemah*) is also implied in the creation of man, whom God formed "from dust from the ground, and breathed into his nostrils the breath of life" (Gen. 2:7). Everything depends upon the Spirit of God for its continual existence:

---

1. Dale Moody used these categories in *The Spirit of the Living God* (Philadelphia: Westminster Press, 1968), 14–32.

These all look to you,
to give them their food in due season;
when you give to them,
they gather it up,
when you open your
hand, they are filled with
good things.
When you hide your face,
they are dismayed;
when you take away
their breath, they die
and return to their dust.
When you send forth
your spirit [*ruach*], they
are created; and you
renew the face of the
ground. (Ps. 104:27–30)

The prophetic movement in Israel set up such a powerful expectation of the Spirit of God that the prophecies of the final days (or of the messianic kingdom) were often described as the coming of the Spirit with great power. "The Spirit of the Lord God is upon me," announced Isaiah, "because the Lord has anointed me; he has sent me to bring good news to the oppressed . . . to proclaim the year of the Lord's favor, and the day of vengeance of our God." (Isa. 61:1–2). Joel proclaims: "Then afterward, I will pour out my spirit" (Joel 2:28).

The expectations of the Spirit that tend to build up in the prophets are, in the New Testament, found at full force. John the Baptist comes announcing that his baptism (of mere water) will be superseded by one who comes to "baptize you with the Holy Spirit and fire" (Matt. 3:11).

When we move into the language and thought of the New Testament, we find references to the Spirit of God—now more often called the Holy Spirit—more prevalent and more personal. In the first three Gospels, Luke is the one who makes the work of the Holy Spirit central. He continues this outlook in Acts. One might say that the Gospel of Luke is about the Anointed One ("Messiah" means the "anointed one") and Acts is about the "anointed people." The anointing, of course, refers to the presence and empowerment of the Holy Spirit.

The Gospel of John is preeminently the Gospel of the Spirit of God in Christ. Here we find the teachings on the *parakletos*, Paraclete (chaps. 15–16). The Holy Spirit—the comforter, or counselor—is also seen as teacher (14:26), witness (15:26), judge (16:8–11), and guide (16:12–15).

The Letters of Paul fill out our understanding of the Holy Spirit with their references to the regenerating and sanctifying power of the Spirit. The writings of Paul carry through the idea of the Spirit that was seen in the Gospels, that the Holy Spirit is neither an impersonal power nor a personality that can be considered apart from Christ. The Holy Spirit is the Spirit of Christ. As George S. Hendry said, "The Spirit continues the presence of Christ beyond the brief span of his historical appearance and completes it by affecting its inward appearance among men."[2]

Principles of Christian Pneumatology

The earliest issues that arrested the attention of church theologians were those concerning the nature and role of Christ in relation to God the Father. It was some time, into the fourth century in fact, before the doctrine of the Holy Spirit came fully into the discussion. Naturally some of the same questions that had surfaced in formulating the teachings about Christ also would occur in regard to the Spirit. The issues centered upon how Christians would understand the deity and personhood of the Holy Spirit. Like the earlier Arian controversy in Christology, there were those who denied the deity of the Spirit. Like the earlier Sabellian controversy, there were attempts to deny the distinct personhood of the Spirit. So the division of natures (Arianism) and the confusion of persons (Sabellianism) were once more at issue for trinitarian Christian theology.

Gregory Nazianzus was a major figure in the fourth-century controversy over the Spirit. As bishop of Constantinople when the great ecumenical council was convened, Gregory helped define the person and deity of the Spirit. He argued that when the full teaching of Scripture concerning the Spirit is taken into account, one must conclude that it

---

2. George S. Hendry, *The Holy Spirit in Christian Theology* (Philadelphia: Westminster Press, 1965), 26.

bears witness, not to an impersonal power or energy, but to God himself. Further, the Spirit must be understood not as God in a modalistic fashion, but as distinctively God the Holy Spirit.

■ ——————————————————— ■

GREGORY NAZIANZUS ON THE DEITY
OF THE HOLY SPIRIT

You see lights breaking upon us, gradually; and the order of Theology, which it is better for us to keep, neither proclaiming things too suddenly, nor yet keeping them hidden to the end. For the former course would be unscientific, the latter atheistical; and the former would be calculated to startle outsiders, the latter to alienate our own people. I will add another point to what I have said; one which may readily have come into the mind of some others, but which I think a fruit of my own thought. Our Savior had some things which, He said, could not be borne at that time by His disciples (though they were filled with many teachings), perhaps for the reasons I have mentioned; and therefore they were hidden. And again He said that all things should be taught us by the Spirit when He should come to dwell amongst us. Of these things one, I take it, was the Deity of the Spirit Himself, made clear later on when such knowledge should be seasonable and capable of being received after our Savior's restoration, when it would no longer be received with incredulity because of its marvelous character. For what greater thing than this did either He promise, or the Spirit teach. If indeed anything is to be considered great and worthy of the Majesty of God, which was either promised or taught.

[Gregory Nazianzus, *Theological Orations 5, The Nicene and Post-Nicene Fathers*, vol. 7 (Edinburgh: T&T Clark Publishers), 326.]

■ ——————————————————— ■

The Holy Spirit and the Son

The second great controversy regarding the Holy Spirit had to do with what was called in the West, the "dual procession of the Spirit." At issue was the relationship of the Holy Spirit to the Son. Bishops in the West had begun to attach the phrase "and the son" (*filioque*) to the Nicene Creed, which originally stated, "[We believe] . . . in the Holy Spirit, the Lord and Life-giver, that proceedeth from the Father." The Western bishops were attempting to forestall any Arian tendencies if people should read into the creed subordination of the Son to the Father. So they tried to clarify by saying the Spirit proceeds from the Father *and the Son.*

Furthermore they were attempting to discourage teachings that implied that the experience of the Spirit of God is different from the experience of Christ. The church had seen, often enough, the dangers of *enthusiasm,* that is, a religion based almost exclusively on highly emotional experiences. The experience of the Spirit easily could lead to teachings and behavior out of keeping with the teachings and the moral example of Christ. The safeguard was always that the Spirit does nothing, as far as the New Testament is concerned, without reference to the Son. Theologians pointed to John 15:26: "When the Advocate comes, whom I will send to you from the Father, the Spirit of truth who comes from the Father, he will testify on my behalf."

Eastern churches, on the other hand, were more concerned to preserve the traditional idea of the Father as *monarchia*. This concept of Father maintained the underlying theological premise that God is one, and from him alone all things receive their being. It was no denial of the Son, they argued, to say that the expression "God the Father" articulates the belief in God as One. Therefore, the Spirit ought to be seen as proceeding from the Father, *through* the Son, and not "from" the Son, as though the Son's operation is independent of the Father.

There are evidences that the Eastern and Western churches are finding areas of agreement that may bring some accord in this millennium-old doctrinal division. Both East and West want to preserve the oneness of God (the East's principal concern), and both want to preserve a clear statement of the Son's equal status with the Father (the West's concern).

How to articulate both of these without compromising either of these remains the chief difficulty in reaching some accord in the theological division of East and West.

The Holy Spirit and Scripture

The third major development in the doctrine of the Holy Spirit paralleled, and came out of, the Protestant Reformation. The Reformation was a reaction, in part, to the loss of confidence in a morally corrupt and doctrinally unreliable church. The church, however, was seen as, (1) the instrument by which the grace of God is mediated, and (2) the authority in matters of doctrine. Luther's idea of the Holy Spirit's "infusion of love" into the heart of the believer fortified and guaranteed the work of the church, a work that otherwise was in serious disrepute.

The even further-revealing development in Protestant doctrine, however, occurred in reference to the church's decline as a source of doctrinal authority. Luther had, of course, elevated Scripture to the place of authority more recently claimed by the church. The church had not created Scripture, he said; it was the Word of God that created the church. Therefore, doctrine and practice must rest upon Scripture alone—*sola scriptura*.

Calvin, however, saw to it that the Scriptures did not simply become a "paper pope," and even worse, one that was subject to unreliable vagaries of private interpretation. Since Scripture was produced by the work of the Spirit, the Spirit also illuminated the meaning of those same words. Their internal witness, or **testimonium**, corresponds to the outward witness of the written Word. One confirms and testifies to the other. The heart liberated by the Spirit responds to the Word with a lively recognition of truth. The Word, on the other hand, awakens the mind and opens the heart to the operation of the Spirit. That is why Jacques Pannier would say the Reformers "never said at any time that man was justified by freedom nor by authority nor by reason nor by anything exterior or human, but by the action of the Holy Spirit, by the acceptance of the sacrifice of Jesus Christ, by the communion of the heart with God."[3] The Holy

---

3. Cited in Bernard Ramm, *The Witness of the Spirit* (Grand Rapids: Eerdmans, 1959), 10.

Spirit mediates the outward and the inward, the Word written with the Word experienced, the word assimilated by reason and the word confirmed by conscience.

The Works of the Holy Spirit

Now we are ready briefly to survey the scriptural witnesses to the works of the Spirit. Those works deserve much more treatment than we have space to give them here. We can, however, broadly categorize these works as creation, redemption, revelation, remembrance, guidance, unification, and consummation.

Creation. The first mention of the Spirit regards the act of creation. The Spirit of God hovering over the waters expresses the act of bringing order out of chaos. Ambrose (339–397) said that, "When the Spirit was moving upon the water the creation was without grace; but after this world being created underwent the operation of the Spirit, it gained the beauty of that grace, wherewith the world is illuminated." Without that grace, the world comes to nothing. This "grace" means that creation is not simply an event of primal history, but it is a realty of each moment and is carried forward to the end. Therefore, says Ambrose,

> And that the grace of the universe cannot abide without the Holy Spirit the prophet declared when he said: "Thou wilt take away thy spirit, and they will fail and be turned again into their dust. Send forth thy spirit, and they shall be made, and thou wilt renew all the face of the earth." Not only, then, did he teach that no creature can stand without the Holy Spirit, but also that the Spirit is the creator of the whole creation.[4]

While the church fathers, including Ambrose, emphasized that the creative works of the Spirit are no different from that of the Father and the Son, it is also true that because of the ministry of the Spirit, we recognize creation as a contemporary gift, as an event that is granted moment by moment. It is the Holy Spirit who allows us not to take creation for granted.

---

4. Ambrose, "Of the Holy Spirit II.V." *Nicene and Post-Nicene Fathers*, 2nd series, volume X (Grand Rapids: William B. Eerdmans, 1989), 119.

Redemption. Jesus said to Nicodemus, "Very truly, I tell you, no one can enter the kingdom of God without being born from above" (John 3:5). Just as God creates by the Spirit, so he also redeems to a new life. The doctrine of redemption mirrors the doctrine of creation in that the perfect work of the Spirit of God is presupposed in each. That which God has done in the beginning through the Spirit is altogether good. (Recall the importance of that point in the doctrine of creation, chapter 3.) Likewise, that which God will accomplish in the end will be altogether good.

In connection with this idea, the Creed of Constaninople (A.D. 381) calls the Holy Spirit the "Giver-of-Life." Ambrose wrote that the "more excellent regeneration [that is, being born again, being brought to life again] is then the work of the Holy Spirit; and the Spirit is the Author of that new man which is created after the image of God."[5]

Revelation. Both the Old and New Testaments attribute the work of the prophets and the production of Scripture to the inspiration of the Spirit of God. "Many years you were patient with them, and warned them by your spirit through your prophets; yet they would not listen" (Neh. 9:30), gives very accurately the sense in which Jews understood the words of prophesy that came to them in Scripture. In the New Testament, these words are unsurpassed: "First of all you must understand this, that no prophecy of scripture is a matter of one's own interpretation, because no prophecy ever came by human will, but men and women moved by the Holy Spirit spoke from God" (2 Pet. 1:20–21).

Consequently, the accurate understanding of what is revealed may come only by the aid of the Spirit; for, as Paul wrote, "No one comprehends what is truly God's except the spirit of God" (1 Cor. 2:11).

Remembrance. The New Testament church came to understand its experience not as a continual discovery of novelties. Instead they were discovering new levels of meaning and purpose in the words and deeds of Jesus. These events in the life of Jesus, moreover, fulfilled what had been given in Old Testament prophecy. Therefore, the Holy Spirit, the Paraclete, would come to them and help them remember

---

5. Ibid., 123.

these things. "But the Advocate, the Holy Spirit, whom the Father will send in my name, will teach you everything, and remind you of all that I have said to you" (John 14:26).

Guidance. This remembrance is also a part of the Spirit's work in guiding the believer. "When the Spirit of truth comes," Jesus said, "he will guide you into all the truth; . . . and he will declare to you the things that are to come" (John 16:13).

One must be careful not to take this promise of guidance in the sense of fortunetellers and soothsayers. The early Christians, as well as the Hebrew prophets, took a dim view of simply foretelling the future, or attempting to read the future in a speculative sense. Instead, this concept of the Spirit's work is tied to the need for wisdom, or guidance to know what is right and wrong—to have this knowledge powerfully impressed upon the Christian so that the believer's judgment will be illuminated regarding the certain future of obedience and the future of certain judgment. When the Paraclete comes, he will "prove the world wrong about sin and righteousness and judgment" because the outcome of things is already determined: "The ruler of this world has been condemned" (John 16:8, 11).

Unification. The topic of spiritual gifts draws much interest, and it is indeed an important aspect of our understanding of the works of the Holy Spirit. In the New Testament, however, we find that these gifts are always taught within the context of the oneness of the Spirit and the unity of the church. "Now there are varieties of gifts," Paul wrote, "but the same spirit. To each is given the manifestation of the Spirit for the common good" (1 Cor. 12:4, 7).

The gifts of the Spirit—utterance of wisdom, knowledge, faith, healing, miracles, prophecy, discernment, or tongues and the interpretation of tongues—are always subordinate to the good of the whole body of believers. Paul likens it to the human body with its distinct members: each hand, foot, or ear contributes to the wholeness of the entire body. They are intended to serve the coordinated working of the entire organism and have no function apart from that. The individual, distinct, and quite separate gifts function for the sake of the one body. Their distinct works enhance the wholeness and oneness of the body.

At the same time, we must see clearly that the Spirit does not promote unity by overcoming distinction and diversity, but instead by enhancing each difference as a contributor to the unity of humanity in the church. This is not the unity of pantheism, where everything is reduced to undifferentiated sameness. It is the unity of *community,* and thus a unity in which differences are valued.

Thus, while sin makes distinction an occasion for conflict, the Spirit makes diversity an occasion for unity. To the Ephesians, Paul wrote that "In him the whole structure is joined together and grows into a holy temple in the Lord; in whom you also are built together spiritually into a dwelling place for God" (Eph. 2:21–22).

Consummation. The Christian's confidence in a personal and cosmic destiny is no abstract ideology and not a speculation about the future. It is grounded in a living experience of God. Therefore, Paul would write to the Corinthians, "What no eye has seen, nor ear heard, nor the human heart conceived, what God has prepared for those who love him— these things God has revealed to us through the Spirit; for the Spirit searches everything, even the depths of God" (1 Cor. 2:9–10).

The Holy Spirit spans the gap between current experience and the promised consummation. Thus the power of the Spirit to call Christians into service and to strengthen them for enduring hardships merges with his power to make the future present. In the Spirit we are enabled to be faithful, for the Spirit assures us that the victory is at hand.

The Holy Spirit After the Coming of Christ

Since the nature of the Spirit of God is obviously revealed to us through Old Testament witness as well as New Testament, the question often arises as to what is different about the Spirit after the coming of Christ. This question is all the more important since the Gospels impress us with the idea that the presence of the risen Christ has brought believers into a new relationship with the Spirit. In fact, Luke summarizes this anticipation of the Gospels with these words in Acts from the time of Jesus' resurrection appearances: "While staying with them, he ordered them not to leave Jerusalem, but to wait there for the promise of the Father.

'This,' he said, 'is what you have heard from me; for John baptized with water, but you will be baptized with the Holy Spirit not many days from now'" (Acts 1:4–5).

It is often thought that the distinctively Christian aspect of the doctrine of the Holy Spirit after the advent of Christ relates to the miraculous and ecstatic manifestations of the Spirit that we find in the Book of Acts. Here the signs, the healings, and especially the speaking in tongues seem to be prominent evidences of a new dispensation with regard to the Spirit of God. They are indeed signs of the new presence of the Spirit in the church.

There is little doubt that Luke intended to demonstrate this point as part of his accounting of the new work of God. Whether one believes that these ecstatic and miraculous powers of the Spirit are valid today as in the first days of the church (and that question is debated with some vigor by evangelical theologians especially), it is quite certain that Luke identified these events as assurances that God was present in a new and powerful way in the church. Luke takes us from an account of the messianic person (in the Gospel) to the messianic people (in Acts), and they are seen to be messianic by virtue of their anointing by the Spirit.

At the time of his ascension, Jesus promises his disciples that they "will receive power when the Holy Spirit has come upon you" (Acts 1:8a). This entire history of the early church is then a working out of that promise as the disciples become Christ's witnesses "in Jerusalem, in all Judea and Samaria, and to the ends of the earth" (v. 8b).

Yet here we must ask a question. Because these are signs of the new presence of the Spirit in the world, does this necessarily mean that the signs themselves are *what* is new about the Spirit after Christ? Have Christians sometimes confused sign with substance? In other words, do the ecstatic manifestations of the Spirit, such as speaking in tongues, constitute the distinctive New Testament and Christian experience of the Spirit?

The answer to that question, I think, is no. They are signs of a new presence of the Spirit; but as signs they are not truly different from the Old Testament experience of the Spirit, even as far back as the judges and the early monarchy. The ecstatic experience of the Spirit was the earliest concept of the Spirit, and it remains as a part of the understanding of the Spirit right up into the New Testament. I personally have no objection to the idea that the Spirit can be known among us in much the same way even in modern times.

It is important to say, however, that this is *not* the New Testament distinctive. What is distinctive, then, about the Christian experience of the Spirit? The clearest statement of what is *new* in the New Testament experience of the Spirit is found in the Gospel of John: "If you love me, you will keep my commandments. And I will ask the Father, and he will give you another Advocate, to be with you forever. You know him, because he abides with you, and he will be in you" (John 14:15–16, 17b).

The *new* in the New Testament experience of the Spirit is the fact that believers will be given the power to "keep my commandments" because of the abiding presence of the Spirit. It is not the occasional manifestation of the Spirit in ecstatic visitation (however valid and important these may be) that distinguishes the church's experience of God. It is the fact that now God is known as a constant presence who operates in us to do the works he wants us to do. The church will know of God's Spirit because, now, "he abides with you, and he will be in you" (v. 17). The abiding presence of the Holy Spirit, rather than the occasional and spectacular, is also consistently emphasized by Paul (cf. Rom. 8:5–11; 1 Cor. 6:19; Gal. 5:16–26). This then is what is new: That which men and women had deeply and desperately longed for is made available to them—reconciliation with God in their everyday works, their profoundest desires, and their constant striving.

Questions for Review and Reflection

1. What are the common Old Testament and New Testament names for the Spirit of God or the Holy Spirit?
2. Why do you think it was important for the early church theologians to establish the deity and personhood of the Holy Spirit?
3. What was the central issue in the *filioque* controversy between East and West?

4. Name and define the importance of each of the works of the Spirit.
5. What is different, do you think, in the classic Christian attitude toward distinctions among people from that of the pantheist or monist view of the world? Why is this important?
6. How can the Christian doctrine of the Spirit overcome difficulties presented by distinctions of gender, race, language, and heritage in the human community?
7. How do spiritual gifts contribute toward the unity of believers in the church?
8. What important distinctions would you make between Old Testament and New Testament perspectives on the Spirit of God?

GOD AMONG US: THE CHURCH

Suppose you were to travel the world and inspect the great variety of forms and styles of life and worship that go by the name "church." In the course of your travels you visit a Roman Catholic church in Germany, an Orthodox church in Greece, a Baptist church in Romania, and finally return home to visit Methodist, Episcopalian, and Pentecostal congregations in the United States. After such a survey, you might well be hard-pressed to find a strong common description for them all.

Yet there are definite characteristics of the church that traditionally have been held to by Christians around the world and in every major denomination. However distinct their buildings and customs, practically all Christians, from the early centuries of the Christian experience, seem to have agreed upon certain essential attributes of the church. Even though the frequent use of these terms, in many of our churches, may be in eclipse, no church body among any of the broad categories of Christians has ever rescinded the language of the Nicene Creed that gives us four attributes, or "marks," of the church. According to the creed, the Church is *one, holy, catholic,* and *apostolic.*

The ways in which Christians define these four attributes, and the ways in which they apply them concretely to the church are varied. Many denominational distinctions, ironically, can be traced back to disputes over just how the church should be *one.* And often those matters that keep the visible church from presenting a unified witness to the world have much to do with disagreements over what it means for the church to be *holy.* Moreover, the catholicity of the church—that is, the claim of its relevance to all times and all people—is often disputed between groups on the basis of *apostolic* authority. By its catholicity it claims relevance to the world, and by its apostolic identity it claims a distinction from the world. Thus the relevance and the identity of the church often stand in tense opposition to each other, and while one side or the other threatens to take over, only when both characterize the church can we say it is truly the church. Or at least we must do so unless we are prepared to abandon the historic Christian understanding of what the church is, an understanding that is rooted in the Bible.

The claims made concerning these four attributes are often further confused by three distinct ways of interpreting them. Are the claims to be one, holy, apostolic, and catholic to be understood:

- *historically,* that is, as a tradition of order and authority, handed down in unbroken succession from the beginning of the church?

- *sacramentally,* that is, as a mystery hidden with God that can only be approximately realized in the church we see—the church we know historically and as a group of living yet sinful human beings?

- *eschatologically,* that is, as a reality promised by God and as an identity provisionally claimed by those whose pilgrimage leads to the full disclosure of the kingdom of Christ and his church?

One interpretation is focused upon the past, one upon the present, and one upon the future. As in the understanding of atonement and salvation, all three can shed some important light on the meaning of the doctrinal subject, in this

case the church. However, since the Protestant Reformation, less reliance has been placed upon history or tradition
as the basis for understanding the church and more reliance has been placed upon the latter two. For those in the
so-called "Free Church" tradition, such as Baptists, the emphasis tended to be placed on the eschatological dimension
of the four attributes. The way in which we see these characteristics applied to the life of the church—whether as historical heritage, as present in sacrament, or as present in
terms of a promise—will have an impact upon such matters
as how we view the clergy and their role, how we understand membership and initiation into the church, and how
the church is to be organized as a polity. It will also, in
many ways, affect the nature of the church's proclamation
and mission.

Defining the Church

It is important that we return to these four attributes, for
they, more than anything else that might be stated about
the church in various theological systems, tie us to the
Scripture. First, however, let's start out with the basic idea
of the word "church." *Ekklesia* is the Greek term used by
New Testament writers. The term is used outside the New
Testament, and prior to the New Testament, to refer to
gatherings of citizens called together for political or business purposes. The implication of the historical usage of the
term includes the idea that the collective mind and action of
the people is important. It is, in fact, of the very nature of
the assembly; it is a consultation of the people for some collective action. Basically, the word means an assembly or a
congregation. One can easily see the relationship between
this term and the Jewish use of "synagogue," which also
means an assembly or congregation.

The term *ekklesia* is used in the Gospels only in Matthew
(16:18–17). This leaves us with the impression that the existence of the church as a movement separate from Israel was
not clearly established in the minds of the apostles during
the lifetime of Jesus. We do have an account, however, of
Jesus' instruction to his disciples concerning the church in
Matthew 16. The Epistles, of course, deal much more

frequently and fully with the church. Paul's letters to Ephesians and Colossians are particularly important in this regard. The fact that nine of the thirteen Pauline Epistles (fully one-third of the titles in the New Testament) are addressed to the church in various places is significant. It tells us, at the least, that the church was the focus of New Testament thinking, and the nature and proper ordering of the life of the church was uppermost in the minds of these writers. If we were reading these documents for the first time, we would certainly get the strong impression that the way the church was conducted, and the way members making up the church lived in relation to one another, was seen by them as strong validation of the gospel. "Conduct yourselves honorably among the Gentiles," Peter said, "so that, though they malign you as evildoers, they may see your honorable deeds and glorify God when he comes to judge" (1 Pet. 2:12).

By contrast, modern writers have often either assumed, or entirely neglected, thinking about the nature of the church. Even Karl Barth, who wrote a protracted theological work by the title *Church Dogmatics,* once wrote that it is advisable not to use the word "church" in theology because the word is "overshadowed and overburdened" in such a way that it is easily misunderstood.[1]

The definition given by A. H. Strong, the great nineteenth- and early twentieth-century Baptist theologian, shows less reluctance to deal with a term that may, on some counts, be overburdened, but is necessarily a part of what must be understood in the New Testament if Christian theology and the Christian way are to be understood at all. He defined the church, in part, as, "the whole company of regenerate persons in all times and ages, in heaven and on earth."[2]

The Church Is One

When we were considering the Trinity, we noted that the language of God's oneness is not that of a **monism,** such as

1. Karl Barth, *Evangelical Theology* (Grand Rapids: Eerdmans, 1963), 37.

2. A. H. Strong, *Systematic Theology* (Philadelphia: Judson Press, 1907), 887.

one finds in Islam or in classic Hinduism and Buddhism. These examples of oneness have much to do with the mathematical preference for the "number one" and for the fundamental principle of absolute simplicity. This kind of **monotheism** is the philosopher's preference for fundamental principles reduced to stark simplicity, but they have little to do with Israel's or the church's preference for the unity of God. They also lose completely the Christian idea of God's unity in the three persons of the Trinity because the idea of the **triunity** of God expresses the oneness of God as a *unity of community.*

The church reflects this same language when considering herself *one.* It is not the oneness of an administrative unit; nor is it one in the sense of an imposed monolithic identity. Instead it is the oneness of hearts drawn together in mutual love, and the oneness of people sharing in community because of their willing devotion to God through Christ. It is a unity not based upon obligation but upon kindred desire. It is a unity not based upon tradition (not that this does not play an important part in the historical and visible church), but based essentially upon a common hope. It is a unity that ties together those of disparate pasts in a united destiny; so that while the differences of our pasts often separate people and cause them to fail in understanding one another, the common point of reference in the future for those who are in Christ binds believers together in mutual sympathies and growing common desires. The values of historically separate communities begin to conform to the higher values of a community anticipating the ultimate reign of Christ.

A. H. Strong noted that the unity of the church, "since it is a unity of the Spirit, is not enforced, but an intelligent and willing, unity." This concept, for Strong and for others in Baptist and kindred groups, became a basis for a democratic, congregational polity: "While Christ is sole king . . . the government of the church, so far as regards the interpretation and execution of his will by the body, is an absolute democracy."[3]

It should be stressed that the unity of the church does not imply uniformity. Nor does it even argue for equality, ex-

---

3. Ibid., 903.

cept in the sense that all are equally loved by Christ, or all are equally indicted by the Law. Yet the unity of the church exists along with the diversity of the members. It does not negate that diversity; on the contrary, it uses it to build and strengthen the unity.

Paul writes to the Ephesians about the unity of Jews and Gentiles in Christ. "For he is our peace; in his flesh he has made both groups into one and has broken down the dividing wall, that is, the hostility between us" (Eph. 2:14). Paul speaks of hostility between Jews and Gentiles that certainly existed in his own day, and the intensity of their mutual hostility would come to be seen in the violent eruptions of the Jewish Wars a short time later. This kind of hostility has erupted with particular virulence and with massive bloodshed in the pogroms, the mob actions, and ideological "final solutions" of later times, right on down to the twentieth century. But Paul's words can be taken as instructive with regard to all ethnic distinctions and all kinds of national rivalries. Even further, it can be taken as illustrative of the fact that any important distinction is potentially one source of hostility.

But if these groups are "in Christ" (a phrase Paul uses liberally, especially in Ephesians), then that which formally was the occasion for "dividing walls" (as in the temple) and an occasion for hostility and suspicion, becomes now the very way the oneness of new larger association is expressed. The diversity contributes now to a new identity and a new oneness. Those who formerly were at one another's throats, because of their differences, are now able to see those same differences as gifts.

Those in Christ are "one" in that they receive differences as gifts in the overall unity. They are not "the same" in the sense of a democratic leveling that instinctively fears the effects that differences inspire when they incite envy or suspicion. Yet they are one in that they all have a transcendent loyalty. They are each called to a higher destiny, and that is altogether different from finding unity in a lower common denomination. That is why it is frequently observed that the gospel calls us to an equality that levels us "up" and is not strongly related to the civil idea of equality that looks to the minimal rights and desires of citizens.

Therefore, Paul begs the Ephesians to lead lives worthy of this high calling, "With all humility and gentleness, with patience, bearing with one another in love." These are words that call for looking to one another with gratitude, not protecting one's own interests, so that the whole body with the full power of the will can "maintain the unity of the Spirit in the bond of peace," thus expressing the reality of "one body and one Spirit . . . one Lord, one faith, one baptism, one God and Father of all, who is above all and through all and in all" (4:2–5).

The differences within the church then are transformed into gifts (v. 11), while in the fallen world they are the sources of envy, fear, power over others, and conflict, giving occasion for "every kind of doctrine" to justify evil, "trickery" to gain advantage over others along with "craftiness and deceitful scheming"(v. 14). The body unified in Christ is a body in which each distinctive part is "working properly" and "promotes the body's growth in building itself up in love" (v. 16).

The unity of the church is ideal and not visible. A strong thesis in Christian **ecclesiology** extending from Augustine to Calvin and down to the present, especially along the Protestant line, has emphasized the distinction between the church as unity in its essential mystery, and the church as a visible institution that is manifestly fragmented and partial. The unity lies with God and not with the human institution. Another way of expressing this, perhaps, is to say that the world will recognize this unity only in the eschatological full disclosure of the church, not in the time-bound institution that now struggles with sin and is limited and beset on all sides with its own human frailty.

For most Baptists, the unity of the church, expressed in the visible institutions, best remains an informal and not a formal reality, because sin inevitably takes the occasion of a formal and bureaucratic unity to assert power and worldly ambition in a way that informal unity, that comes from united hearts and minds, does not allow. George Truett, in his famous 1920 speech from the steps of the nation's capitol, expressed this idea of unity quite forcefully:

> The spiritual union of all true believers in Christ is now and ever will be a blessed reality, and such union is deeper and higher and more enduring than any and

all forms and rituals and organizations. Whoever believes in Christ as his personal Savior is our brother in
the common salvation, whether he be a member of one
communion or of another, or of no communion at all.[4]

The Church Is Holy

The idea of the "holy" is found throughout the Old and
New Testaments. The term generally describes a category
of things in life. It refers to something or someone "set
aside" and "distinct" from ordinary or "profane" things. In
the Book of Leviticus, for instance, one can detect that ancient Israelites categorized things as (1) sacred or holy, (2)
profane (a word that means before or outside the altar), and
(3) "unclean." The holy must be approached with caution
and with ceremony because it is of a higher order than the
profane things of ordinary life. The unclean things must be
left alone, or made clean, because they are too far removed
from the holy. Generally speaking, all primitive cultures observed these kinds of distinctions and the ritual practices
they involve. It is a way of organizing the world conceptually, especially as the world relates to its highest values and
its most fundamental fears. There were, therefore, holy offices—such as priests—and holy days, as well as holy things
and holy places, such as those associated with the temple.

In the New Testament, however, we can detect a strong
tendency to use the word "holy" in referring to persons, and
not to things or places. Therefore the church is made up of
"saints" or "holy ones," the *hagioi.* What is holy concerning
the church is never its location or its furnishings but its
saints who are equipped "for the work of ministry, for building up the body of Christ" (Eph. 4:12). Christ chose those
who are in the church "to be holy and blameless before him
in love" (Eph. 1:4). One can speak of the Holy Spirit of God
(for instance, Acts 11:16), and of the saints who make up the
church, wherever that church might appear, whether in
Jerusalem or Corinth, whether in Rome or Galatia. Yet we
see a distinct moment in the New Testament away from re-

---

4. "Baptists and Religious Liberty" in *A Baptist Treasury*, Sydnor L.
Stealey, ed. (New York: Crowell, 1958), 264.

ferring to things or places as either holy or unclean and defiled.

The Reformation, and even more so the Radical Reformation and the Free Church movement, tended to see in the
New Testament no justification for a "sacramental" understanding of either the things associated with the church or
the church as an institution. The church is holy in that its
communion of set-aside believers is holy. The term *holy* by
now was always referring to *proper,* not to common nouns,
always personal matters, not impersonal even where the
impersonal thing is considered something that mediates the
personal.

What was being called holy or defiled in the Old Testament (often categories of things, places, and so on), is transformed into language about the people of God in the New
Testament. Notice, for instance, how Paul uses the language of the Old Testament, in reference to the temple, to
refer to the church. No longer is the temple a place, or even
an institution; it is a living fellowship: "For we are the temple of the living God; as God said, 'I will live in them and
dwell among them, and I will be their God, and they shall
be my people'" (2 Cor. 6:16).

On the other hand, that which stands at the other end of
the scale from holy things is reinterpreted in the New Testament to refer not only to a thing, but also to the deepest
matters of human will and behavior. Jesus teaches, "It is
not what goes into the mouth that defiles a person, but it is
what comes out of the mouth that defiles. What comes out
of the mouth proceeds from the heart, and this is what defiles. For out of the heart come evil intentions, murder,
adultery, fornication, theft, false witness, slander. These
are what defile a person" (Matt. 15:11, 18–20).

The reinterpretation of these categories of clean and unclean, holy and profane, are seen in Peter's revelation concerning the formerly forbidden association with Gentiles. In
the vision he was told to eat from the "unclean" animals he
saw, and protested that he had "never eaten anything that
is profane or unclean." And then, "The voice said to him . . .
'What God has made clean, you must not call profane'" (Acts
10:14–15). Paul takes these lines of thought further when
he writes to the Colossians: "Therefore do not let anyone

condemn you in matters of food and drink or of observing festivals, new moons, or sabbaths. These are only a shadow of what is to come, but the substance belongs to Christ" (Col. 2:16–17).

To say that the church is holy, therefore, takes on something other than a **sacramental** meaning. In other words, it is not in things, events, places, and so on, that the mystery of God lies. The reality of God in the church comes from the faithful hearts and faithful lives of believing disciples of Christ. In Colossians, Paul makes this point to the nth degree. In submitting to "holiness" regulations, Christians missed the point of what is holy and what is defiled. Instead, Paul says, "If you have been raised with Christ, seek the things that are above, set your minds on things that are above . . ." so that when Christ is revealed, "You also will be revealed with him in glory" (3:1–2a, 4). The holiness of your life with Christ consists not of things, but of holy living: "As God's chosen ones, holy and beloved, clothe yourselves with compassion, kindness, humility, meekness, and patience. Bear with one another . . . forgive each other. . . . Above all, clothe yourselves with love, which binds everything together in perfect harmony" (Col. 3:12–14).

The Church Is Catholic

Since the word *catholic* is so commonly associated with the Roman Catholic Church, it is necessary, most of the time, to remind ourselves that the creeds of early Christendom were not referring to a distinct organization, but rather to the convictions that if the church is indeed Christian, then it is necessarily "catholic." That is, it is a reality that exists for the whole world. It pertains to the world, explains the world, and calls the world to salvation. It is universal not in the sense that it is everywhere, but in the sense that no people and no subjects are excluded from its prayers, its intellectual investigation, its redemptive purpose, and its proclamation of good news. That is why it was so fitting and natural for the Christianization of the world in antiquity and the Middle Ages to be followed by the springing up of great universities in places like Paris and Oxford.

That is also why, even when the Protestant reformers were drawing back from and criticizing the church, they still considered that their reforms were for the "catholic" church, for the church in its universal dimension. Luther never considered himself *not* a catholic. His criticism of the pope and the papal institutions of his day might very well be expressed this way: that they were not nearly catholic enough. They were too provincial and narrow in their interests, forgetting that the whole life of humanity, and not simply the good of institutions, is the real object of the church. That is what makes it "catholic."

Most Christians in the Free Church tradition have shared in the ancient *credo* to the effect that the church is "universal" in scope, or "catholic." The Philadelphia Confession of Faith (1742), a Baptist statement that had wide influence in America, said: "The catholic or universal church, which, with respect to the internal work of the Spirit and truth of grace, may be called invisible, consists of the whole number of the elect that have been, are, or shall be gathered into one under God, the head thereof, and is the spouse, the body, the fullness of him that filleth all in all."[5]

Baptists bore the brunt of the Campbell controversy in the United States in the early nineteenth century, and this should have been a real opportunity to strengthen Baptist ecclesiology by thinking through the issue of what is the nature of the church. The controversy at that time revolved around the idea of the church and the interpretation of the sacraments or ordinances. The thorough airing of these issues, however, was not to happen. The nation was, by about 1845, awash with the issues of slavery and sectional rivalry, and the Baptist churches were caught up in the winds of controversy that would soon rip the nation apart and plunge it into the bloodiest four years in American history.

Out of that painful time came the tendency *not* to deal with the doctrine of the church at all. Perhaps this was because the churches, taken collectively, were too badly broken by the strife and controversy of war. Paradoxically, however, the business of private religion, and the associa-

5. "The Philadelphia Confession of Faith" in *A Baptist Treasury*, ed. Sydnor L. Stealey (New York: Crowell, 1958), 51.

tion of individuals with the claim of Christianity, was more vigorous than ever. It may well be, as in other painful times in history, corporate religion suffers and the faithful seek comfort in a privatized form of religion. Dietrich Bonhoeffer and Jürgen Moltmann both noticed that such a phenomenon had gripped the German churches during the painful period between the wars and especially during World War II.

At any rate, Baptists seem to have gone in two directions. On the one hand, the movement known as Landmarkism, led by J. R. Graves and J. M. Pendleton, rejected the whole idea of a universal church except as an eschatological prophecy. The ablest theologians among Baptists, however, failed to deal with the issue in any prominent way. John A. Broadus (1827–1895) could write a "Catechism of Bible Teaching" and deal with everything from "God," "Providence," "The Word of God," "Man," "The Savior," to "The Trinity," "Atonement," and "Regeneration," as well as "Some Duties of the Christian Life," without devoting a single lesson to the church. E. Y. Mullins (1880–1928) wrote his great systematic theology, *The Christian Religion in Its Doctrinal Expression,* and scarcely mentioned the church in a dozen brief passages, much less develop that doctrine in a major section of his work. The same could be said of W. T. Conner, who spoke lucidly of the church in a couple of statements out of the 576 pages of his work, *A System of Christian Doctrine,* but devoted no major heading to the topic of the *ekklesia.*

W. T. CONNER ON THE CHURCH

You may have a religious organization composed of men and women not regenerated, but you cannot have a Christian church. This shows that the center of the life of a church must be Jesus Christ. Men are drawn together because they are drawn to him. He is the central magnet.

The active agent in bringing the church into being is the Holy Spirit. A church of Jesus Christ is a product of the activity of the Spirit. As the Spirit constitutes the individual a Christian by bringing him into right relation with Christ, so he constitutes a company of individuals a church by bringing them into Christian fellowship. A church, then, is not simply an organization, it is an organism. It is a church by virtue of the fact that all the members possess a common life. The Christ who dwells in the church through his Spirit animates the whole body.

[From W. T. Conner *A System of Christian Doctrine* (Nashville: Sunday School Board of the Southern Baptist Convention, 1924), 257.]

Only A. H. Strong, among the post-Civil War Baptists, dealt positively and intentionally with a doctrine of the church, but even then he did not deal with the idea of the church's catholicity in any complete sense. He wrote of the "universal" church as a body that includes all believers, but catholicity implies much more than that. It implies the applicability of the church to all people and to all things. It speaks not simply of the inclusiveness of the church, but of the broadest possible concern of the church.

The Church Is Apostolic

To say that the church is apostolic is to say that the tradition coming down to the present time comes from the original witness to the life and teachings of Jesus. Apologists for the Roman Catholic Church and the non-Roman, but "catholic" tradition of the Anglican church have, in modern times, defended the view that apostolic authority is handed down from the apostles through episcopal succession, that is, through the consecration of each generation of bishops in a direct line from the apostles. This line of descent from the apostles through the bishops by the laying on of hands is called **apostolic succession.** Catholics tend to identify this succession of bishops with the idea of the church's apostolic authority.

We must admit that the image of such a visible succession of church authority is very appealing. Perhaps, for some of us, it is also very important. But I think the twentieth-century theologian Emil Brunner put this matter in a most helpful light when he called to mind Martin Luther's statement, "What is true to Christ, that is apostolic." Brunner goes on to comment, "The apostolic character of the church rests primarily upon the fact that 'it is concerned with Christ,' that is, upon its essential spiritual conformity with the fact of Christ, as it is handed down to us in the apostolic witness."[6]

The point that Brunner raises here necessarily poses a very important question: Which is the true meaning of the apostolic character of the church? Is that church apostolic that traces the succession of bishops? Or is it the one that listens to, and is informed by, the witness of the apostles? Is it a sacrament that makes a church truly apostolic; or is it the words of the apostles themselves, contained in the New Testament, that mold and form the life of the church?

Brunner argues, and I would agree, that, "There is in the original idea of the ekklesia as we find it in Paul not the slightest trace of the thought of guaranteeing the fidelity of tradition by the legitimacy of episcopal succession."[7] We

6. Emil Brunner, *The Christian Doctrine of the Church, Faith, and the Consummation.* Dogmatics: vol. 3, trans. David Cairns (Philadelphia: Westminster, 1962), 117.

7. Ibid., 119–120.

could, of course, easily recall from history a dozen or more examples of apostate or heretical Christian leaders who were doubtless ordained in proper apostolic line of succession. Doesn't it stand to reason, and isn't it more consistent with the spirit of the New Testament, that the church is apostolic when it has been faithful to a witness from the apostles?

This does not mean, necessarily, that the church ought to be some kind of reconstitution of the "primitive" first–century church. What it does mean is that the church orders itself, and conducts its life, under the influence of the gospel as that gospel was first given and as the gospel is faithfully passed on. Nor does this mean that the thinking of the church does not develop and unfold over the ages, anymore than a mountain stream and a major river must remain the very picture of the springs that were their source. But the church is apostolic where its life and its thought still retain the purity of its ancient origin in the apostolic witness of Christ—when its teaching and practice still lead to the reality of God, and when its life still guides us reliably to faith, hope, and love.

Questions for Review and Reflection

1. Interpret Paul's statement in Ephesians 2:20 to the effect that the church is "built upon the foundation of the apostles and prophets, with Christ Jesus himself as the cornerstone."
2. Can the church change to meet new social and cultural conditions and still be a reliable witness to the apostolic faith? Explain.
3. Distinguish the idea of the "unity" of the church from the idea of the "catholicity" of the church.
4. What is the basic meaning of "catholic"?
5. What relevance do the four Nicene attributes of the church have to a local congregation?
6. What are these four attributes?
7. What makes a church "apostolic"?
8. Does the existence of denominations, in your view, destroy the fundamental unity or oneness of the church?

PART III

God and His Kingdom

BELONGING TO THE KINGDOM: SALVATION

Salvation as Justification

What is the best that might be hoped for in human life? That is perhaps a dangerously ambiguous question. But it is undoubtedly one that you and I deal with every day.

Even if we do not deal with that question on a philosophical level, we do on a practical level. After all, we make choices. We take one course of action rather than another. We choose the pleasure of watching a football game on television today over the satisfaction of having done our lesson well tomorrow. We choose the comfort of the couch over the rigors of a workout at the gym. We choose to save money today instead of spending it on a movie and eating out. We make choices, and in these we reflect a rather complicated set of values, values that are often not held too consistently, but that are always in our minds and are worked out on the level of the will and the affections. They are worked out in how we work and play, what we buy and sell (and for how much), what we love, and what, if anything, we are willing to die for.

In order to make such choices, we are constantly working against the mental background of a sense that some things we can choose are better than others. That idea of what is better or worse may reflect no more than "what I prefer," or "what causes me least pain or the most pleasure," or it may reflect values held to even when I don't especially think I would personally gain from the choice, yet I feel it is the only honorable choice to make.

If there is a "better" and a "worse" choice among the things we decide for or against, we have almost assumed (even without thinking about it) that *something* we might choose would be better than anything else. The Christian assumption is that there is a *summum bonum*, a greatest good. That greatest good—the best that might be hoped for in human life—is the knowledge or the love of God. Further, that greatest good is not only something that exists as a possibility for us; but we are actually attracted to that good; we are drawn to it in the way Augustine described in his *Confessions*, when he said, "You made us for yourself [Lord] and our hearts find no peace until they rest in you."[1]

Now I want to make one further point about this *summum bonum,* this great good of knowing and loving God. Not only is this an option for us and a possibility, and not only are we drawn to it with a powerful attraction, but we are actually intended for this end and purpose. We are intended to live in fellowship with God.

A couple of tables away at a campus eating establishment, I could not help overhearing a conversation among three women students, earnestly engaged in conversation about how, for one of them at least, many attempts to find a satisfactory course in life all ended in disappointment and frustration. The others were listening intently, sympathetically and sharing with her in a sincere and intelligent way, how Christ can become a Way in life and that the resources of this Way never fail and never disappoint.

I was, first of all, impressed by the sincerity and wisdom with which these young adults were talking about their faith and their own search. In the second place, however, I was impressed with how their story is the story in which we all share; we each look, in many different ways, for that

---

1. Augustine, *Confessions,* trans. R. S. Pine-Coffin (London: Penguin Books, 1961), 21.

which gives life meaning and vitality. The search inevitably leads to God, unless a stubborn rebellion persistently interferes. In fact, life might well be understood as a continuing drama, emerging from the conflict of this deep and intuitive search of the soul for God, and the stubborn rebellion of every human heart that inevitably tries to deny and divert the underlying human quest for God.

Stated in another way, experience tells us that a great gap lies between one's inner longing and one's daily experience. When we dealt with the doctrine of sin, we were talking directly of this reality. When the discussion turns to a doctrine of salvation, Christian theology addresses the questions: "Must human life always fall short of its true goal?" "Are we created with an inner longing for that which can never be attained; or is there a way?" Another way of putting this question, using a bona fide theological term, is, "Can I be justified before God?" Or, in the time-honored language of evangelical Christianity, "Can I be saved?" Often when evangelicals use that question, they are not thinking of the whole range of experiences that fall under the idea of salvation, or of the many aspects of salvation; they are thinking of what is perhaps better called "justification." Martin Luther did most to bring the term justification into the center of theological discussion, but it is also a word firmly rooted in the biblical way of thinking about the human predicament and the way out.

Justification and the Law

In Protestant Christianity, we have put special emphasis upon the doctrine of salvation by grace through faith; and along with this idea, we have emphasized the futility of attempting to achieve salvation by works. The **soteriology** of the church, or its doctrine of salvation, is especially indebted to the writings of the apostle Paul. The development of soteriological thought in Protestantism, in fact, can be followed in a fairly direct way from Paul to Augustine to Martin Luther. A concise statement of Paul's counsel under the general topic of salvation would consist of his words to the Galatians: "We know that a person is justified not by the works of the law but through faith in Jesus Christ" (Gal. 2:16). He added, with even greater stress, "I do not nullify the grace of God; for if justification comes through the law, then Christ died for nothing" (Gal. 2:21). These are basic principles in the soteriology of Paul.

If we are not careful, however, we'll misjudge this argument of Paul's to mean that faith and works are two *contrary* ways to relate to God. Paul does not say that. Instead, faith is a way of realizing what works intend. That is, the problem with good works and obedience to the Law is not that they are irrelevant to true religion, but that we lack the purity of heart and the strength of mind and will to actually do what is required. We fall short; we miss the mark. Therefore Paul is more likely to bring faith and works into a relationship such as this, when he wrote: "Work out your own salvation with fear and trembling; for it is God who is at work in you, enabling you both to will and to work for his good pleasure" (Phil. 2:12–13).

This means that a person's works, on their own, cannot measure up to the high standard of God's righteousness. But God will work in us (that's grace) to accomplish his purpose in our obedience. Are we trusting in our works in this case? No. Are we obedient, then, if we do not work? No.

In a real sense, the aim of our work is already accomplished even before we begin. The absence of obedient works is not just a deficiency in work, but it is shown to be a deficiency in faith! Faith anticipates the accomplished work of God in the believer; and it empowers that divine work, allowing Christians to live in obedience to their calling to righteousness. The words of James cannot be left out of any consideration of faith, when he wrote, "So faith by itself, if it has no works, is dead" (Jas. 2:17).

Old Testament Background for the Doctrine of Justification

This positive relationship between faith and works is essential to understanding the Christian doctrine of justification. In order to see this clearly, let's look first at how the Old Testament concept of justice or righteousness stands in the background of this whole discussion. Of all the important features of the Hebrew religion, the most remarkable, and in many ways the most fruitful, was their understanding of Israel's covenant relationship with God.

This Hebrew understanding was quite distinct from that of the other religious communities surrounding Israel. Israel's neighbors practiced religion as a powerful resource for the needs of the people and to assuage the fears of individuals. The gods were seen as the sources of power: power to live, power to kill, power to grow crops, and power to avoid disasters. A people's relationship to the divine often degenerated to the level of *quid pro quo;* in other words, they gave to the unknown powers, and these powers responded in their favor. Religion often found its highest expression in fear; and then it declined in a daily habitual practice to the level of what might be called "pragmatic superstition."

Now, while considering this *quid pro quo* form of religion, this religion with a practical design, it must also be said that often the religion of Israel became degenerate in precisely the same way. It became the means to an end. It was motivated by the desire for self-serving good.

Israel's great contribution, and the central insight of the Hebrew prophets, however, was a thundering denial that this pragmatic and superstitious practice, based upon a dread of the unknown, is a true and valid relationship to God. The prophets introduced a *critique* of religion. The principle by which they criticized the religion of Israel embodied an insight that rose to such prominence and such power of expression in Israel that it virtually became the hallmark of Hebrew religion. This insight also powerfully distinguished the Hebrew prophetic religion from all other religious communities in the world. In an important sense, a new idea of God—indeed, a new experience of God—was breaking into the world in the form of Hebrew prophetism. After the germ of this faith spread to the world through Christianity, the world would never be the same again; and it could never successfully turn its back on this truth.

That insight, revealed to these prophets, stood in contrast to a *quid pro quo* religion. It included the conviction that God desired the obedience of righteous or just words and deeds. Up until this point, throughout most of the world, the moral laws that governed a community were not always strongly related to religion. In fact, within the sphere of religion, one might even break these laws of human decency and honor, because the necessity of power in religion might well require the breaking up of the usual order of the community life. Laws and customs follow their own logic, compelling loyalty within the tribe and family, keeping peace within the city, protecting the rights of some and the privileges of others. Nevertheless, breaking the laws and customs also presented some compelling possibilities: Who knows but what such practices, done at the right time for the right reason and devoted to the right god, could be very strong medicine! So, while a nation certainly has laws against murder, their priests might on occasion sacrifice human beings, as the Carthagenians and other Phoenician people did. While the sanctity and loyalty of marriage was normally held to be a strong covenant binding both the couple and the nation, in the name of certain fertility practices found throughout Canaan and in other parts of the Mediterranean world, the worshiper might be drawn to the temple in order to visit a cult prostitute.

For the Hebrew prophets, however, a certain insight into the ethical nature of God came to be increasingly clear, especially after the eighth century. For them, the impulse to do what is *right*, and to require what is right in both individuals and the community, was not something other than religion; it was the very heart of religion. That human beings desire to do what is right and resist wrong (not perfectly but very imperfectly, and where they do so at all they do so feebly and inconstantly, with many vacillations and doubts) is relevant to the worship of God. If one God created all things, then he must also have created within us the desire for what is good and honorable and just (at least for ourselves). Even those who rebel against the maxims of righteous living bear witness to the power of righteousness. They invariably attempt to justify themselves to themselves or to others, or they rebel with such mindless and self-destructive ferocity that the existence of a standard of right and wrong can hardly be doubted. If God has placed within us the desire for good, and instructed us with a revealed Law, supporting the good and punishing the evil, then that righteousness or justice (i.e., the right and just way) must be of the very nature of God.

Knowledge of What Is Right Is Not Enough

By the first century and the emergence of Christianity, this identification of God as one who required ethical righteousness was highly refined and pervaded the entire range of Israel's religious expression. It was especially sophisticated in the Pharisaic movement, which had been the most enthusiastic supporter of Hebrew prophetism and had thought deeply and consistently about the implications of the prophets' insights. It is difficult now for us to imagine that the close association of religion and morality was ever a rare thing, but the *ethical* monotheism of Israel was something of a new phenomenon in the world of religion, even though other peoples had briefly and partially anticipated such a thing. Apart from Judaism and the nascent Christianity, religion had little evident power to affect the moral life of the individual or the moral order of a community. From Isaiah to Ezra, and from Jeremiah to Jesus, we see something new and powerful coming into the world, the conviction that a people can only worship God truly by doing what is good and just, and that the power of the religious life consists in learning to love that which is kind, merciful, beautiful, and just.

"With what shall I come before the Lord, and bow myself before God on high?" Micah asks. Is God pleased with burnt offerings? with year-old calves? even with a libation of oil? perhaps "ten thousands rivers of oil"? If a calf, and oil, and burnt offerings are not enough, what if I sacrifice my first-born child? Finally he writes what is the heart of Israel's prophetic religion:

> He has told you . . . what is good;
> and what does the Lord require of you
> but to do justice, and to love kindness,
> and to walk humbly with your
> God? (Mic. 6:6–8).

As the consciousness of this way of relating to God became more and more of the very character of Israel's religion, another matter also became more apparent than ever. It was that human beings will never measure up to the standard of a *holy, righteous* God. Paul, in the New Testament, was one who made much of this Old Testament insight. It was he who understood and proclaimed what is implied by the great distance between humanity, with its sin, and God, in his righteousness. Human beings inevitably fall short (cf. Rom. 3:23).

Paul then bears down upon the point (especially in Romans and Galatians) that the good news is that, although men and women cannot rely upon their own righteousness, they can rely upon God's righteousness. If they trust in him who has revealed himself in Christ, his righteous nature will be accounted as theirs. It is a matter of trusting that God will unfailingly accomplish what he has intended for a human life.

There is, however, an easy miscalculation that I am likely to fall into when I appropriate into my thinking what God promises. I can go wrong in either of two directions. One involves trying to live without the Law. The other involves relying altogether on the Law. Let me describe each of these briefly, calling attention also to the technical terms that are usually associated with these alternative extremist views with regard to the Law.

1. I can say that since God fulfills the requirement for my righteousness, on my behalf, without relying on my own efforts, then I am no longer bothered with the necessity of living a just or righteous life. This comes to be **antinomianism;** that is, the law *(nomos)* no longer applies to me. Since my righteousness is granted apart from the law, then it exists without reference to the law.

2. I can say that since it is a change in behavior that God is requiring and that he intends, it is by my own careful and even fastidious attention to the law that the requirement of righteousness is satisfied. This becomes *legalism*, and comes into the formal lists of theological errors as **Pelagianism** (about which we will say more later).

For generations the church charted its course between these extremes. By choosing the first, Christians risked giving up the great central insight of Old Testament religion— that true religion issued in right thinking and right behavior, a righteous life. By choosing the second course, they missed the point of what was good news about the gospel;

and they failed to see why Christ's life, death, and resurrection were ever needed.

Antinomianism

The first great crisis in the life, and especially the intellectual and moral life, of the church was over antinomianism, and it was a protracted crisis. It involved the "gnostic" varieties of Christianity. Gnostics believed in salvation as a kind of transcendental "rescue" from this world, with all its material and physical concerns. Thus, the gnostic's concern with the just order of a life, or of communities, definitely fell far below their concern for escaping the claims that this life had upon believers. Their philosophy tended toward antinomianism, for any law regulating life in this world had nothing to do with the "other" world to which they belonged.

Irenaeus (c.130–c.200) described the theory of gnostic antinomianism, or **libertinism,** in which they view themselves as holding a view superior to ordinary Christians. Irenaeus wrote:

> To us [in the Church] . . . a moral life is necessary for salvation. They themselves, however, according to their teaching, would be saved absolutely and under all circumstances, not through works but through the mere fact of their being by nature "spiritual." For, as it is impossible for the earthly element to partake in salvation, not being susceptible of it, so it is impossible for the spiritual element (which they pretend to be themselves) to suffer corruption, whatever actions they may have indulged in. As gold sunk in filth will not lose its beauty but preserve its own nature, and the filth will be unable to impair the gold, so nothing can injure them, even if their deeds immerse them in matter, and nothing can change their spiritual essence. Therefore, "the most perfect" among them do unabashed all the forbidden things of which Scripture assures us "that they which do such things shall not inherit the kingdom of God."[2]

---

2. *Adv. Haer. I.6. 2–3;* cited in Hans Jonas, *The Gnostic Religion* (Boston: Beacon Press, 1963), 270–271.

Pelagianism

The second crisis over this issue came from the other direction. A Christian from Britain named Pelagius (died in 418) was so scandalized by the conduct of Christians he found in Rome that he began to urge reform along lines of ascetic practices and stringent moral guidelines. There was nothing wrong with this, of course, and it is doubtless true that Christians in Rome appeared to have lost their moral rigor, especially to a country cleric from the outskirts of the empire. The problem came in his theological defense of such measures. In his urgent exhortation toward good works and right conduct, he made the case that no one could escape condemnation for evil conduct when, in fact, the opportunity for good equaled the opportunity for sin. The human being can choose either, he said, and the Christian had the advantage of being enlightened as to which choice is right.

If men and women had no choice but to sin, he argued, God could hardly hold them accountable. Since God does condemn sin, however, that must mean the sinner is fully responsible for the sin. If we are truly accountable for our actions, it stands to reason that the Christian has an equal choice between good and evil. That person needs only to be enlightened as to the truth of what is the right choice. It is that enlightenment that constitutes grace.

Augustine was the great opponent of this Pelagian analysis. He denied, first of all, that human beings have a free and equal choice between good and evil. In fact, the matter is weighted heavily in favor of sin because of the **original sin** of Adam. From Adam, Augustine argued, we all inherit the guilt as well as the inclination toward sin. Augustine, of course, was an astute observer of the human personality; and what was perhaps most important about his use of the doctrine of original sin is that this biblical disclosure of man's entrapment in his own sin, an entrapment that involved not only individuals but also the entire race, was difficult to deny from the standpoint of the observable human predicament. He knew that, while every person can choose against sin and for righteousness, the battle is not an equal one. To choose against sin in a world system that denies God is to swim upstream in a strong current. It requires more than a sense of direction; it requires more stamina than a person is likely to have on their own.

So, for Augustine, while the Christian may know to confess error, repent of sin, and turn to follow Christ in the ways of righteousness, without divine aid none of these things will be done, and the best efforts of the human being will be futile. That is why the efficacy of Christ's death and the power of his resurrection are needed. That is why the Holy Spirit is given. That is why Paul argued the necessity of God's grace, for salvation does not depend "on human will or exertion, but on God who shows mercy" (Rom. 9:16).

What we must see here is that two great principles are held together in the Christian faith. While one threatens to be lost when the other is held in isolation, both must be included in a full presentation of the Christian case for salvation. These two principles are:

1. God calls men and women to righteousness, having created them for this purpose (cf. Eph. 2:10).
2. He also provides the way of fulfilling his requirement out of his own gracious dealing with us (Eph. 2:8–9).

Both Augustine and Pelagius would agree to both of these principles. But the way in which they used these in their doctrines of salvation was remarkably different. Let me briefly describe the differences by noting the distinct arguments of Pelagius and then Augustine.

Pelagius built his doctrine of salvation on these three principles:

1. Human beings have a free will, and they are accountable because God would not command what men and women cannot obey. To do so would not be just, and God is a just God.
2. Sin is not an innate condition of the human life but is caused by the presence of sensuality, which in itself is innocent but gives occasion for sin, and by the presence of evil examples.
3. Grace is God's enlightenment of the human reason, allowing the will to be exercised for good.

As you can see, these tenets of Pelagianism offer a rather optimistic view of the human being's power over sin and the capacity to choose what is right. All that is required is clear insight (provided by grace) and a willing heart. Natural reason, as long as it is supernaturally illuminated, can then overcome the tendency toward evil.

Now, in drawing the contrast which we find in Augustine, we will necessarily be simplifying the picture somewhat, but only for the sake of emphasizing a feature of traditional theology that we dare not overlook: If hope were to be a dominant note of the Christian heart and mind, which in fact it was, it would henceforth always be framed as a hope in God, not a hope in humanity. In this way the Christian, following Augustine, could be seriously optimistic, yet take the predicament of human sinfulness with utter seriousness. Pelagius could hold on to one of these truths, but not the other.

Augustine, on the other hand, built his doctrine of salvation on the following three principles:

1. The will of human beings is not free, but is in bondage. The guilt and propensity toward sin that each individual bears in solidarity with the human race weighs heavily in the balance on the side of sin.

2. Sin is conditioned by its origin, passed down to the whole of the human race, inherited from Adam, and is a condition that does not allow complete freedom in the choice of individuals.

3. Grace is more than the enlightenment of human reason. It is the forgiveness of sin and the strengthening of the human will to do good and turn away from evil. "Give me the grace to do as you command," Augustine wrote, "and command me to do what you will!"[3] Therefore, grace both heals and strengthens.

The church has historically rejected Pelagianism. The Reformation might be seen as an example of how strongly Christians have rejected this error. The Reformers' critique of their contemporary church was that it had allowed to take root a new form of Pelagian theology and had spread among the people a doctrine of salvation by works. The danger of Pelagianism in all its forms is that it loses sight of the absolute necessity of Christ's death and demeans the power of his resurrection. It fails to take into account that, without

---

3. Augustine, *Confessions,* (Book 10, section 29) 233.

God's intervention on our behalf, we are soon overpowered by the sheer inertia of sin that has its center not simply in the heart of the individual, but in the human race as a whole. The Pelagian weakness is exposed in that it fails to take into account the depth and weight of the power of sin in the human situation.

Therefore, any adequate doctrine of salvation must include, at the least, all of the following:

1. A proper assessment of the guilt (or the objective debt incurred by sin) that already lays claim to the human race and to each individual.
2. A realistic view of the power that sin, and the propensity toward evil, has in the course of human life, in the circumstances of the human community, and in the experience of individual lives.
3. An appreciation of the need for God's intervening power, not only to pardon for sin and open the eyes toward what is right, but also to strengthen the will for repentance, faith, and obedience.

Turning to God: Conversion

Both A. H. Strong and William W. Stevens have included the ideas, or experiences, of repentance and faith under the heading of **conversion**. Christian conversion involves both a turning away from something and a turning toward something. It is both turning away from the created things of the world as the goal of life, or more broadly turning away from sin as the character of thought and action; and it is turning toward God in confidence that he answers the longing of the human heart. In a sense, it is not two things—repentance and faith—but one. We cannot truly repent of sin without turning to God, as Jesus' parable of the "return of the unclean spirit" shows (Luke 11:24–26). Nevertheless, we can still consider these two separately even if they are, in reality, one turning of the soul toward God.

Repentance. Without repentance, the Christian idea of salvation is meaningless. In the Old Testament the call for repentance (*shub*, to turn around) was most often directed to the nation or community. It implied that a radical redirection of life, a mid-journey course correction, was needed because the alternative was destruction (see, for instance, 2 Chron. 7:14).

In the New Testament, we find the terms *metanoia* and *epistrophe* expressing an equivalent idea, a mid-course correction. Yet in the New Testament the idea focuses more on the individual and implies a soul-deep change taking place that radically alters the mind and the heart.

We can consider repentance in two ways. On the one hand, repentance is a revolution that takes place in the life of an individual who starts out in the Christian life. It describes the results of a crisis (even though the individual might not recognize it as such, perhaps until sometime later) in which a choice is made between continuing in sin and turning away from it and forsaking that way in favor of the way God has provided through Christ. This call for an immediate decision is the basis for Paul's appeal to King Agrippa in Acts (26:29).

It is important, on the other hand, to notice how Paul moved in this appeal from his own experience of early preparation and seeking after God (vv. 4–8), to active resistance to the will of God (vv. 9–11), to his own critical confrontation with Christ (vv. 12–18), and to his personal declaration of faith: "After that, King Agrippa, I was not disobedient to the heavenly vision, but declared (the gospel)" (v.19). Repentance also involves a long-term, one might say life-long, turning of the will and affection and mind toward God. It is then seen as a continuous process. The idea of repentance as a training in Christianity is implied in such instruction of the apostle as we find in Romans 12:2 and Ephesians 4:23, where he speaks of the continual renewing of the mind. This is also what Paul expresses in Philippians 3, where he writes, "I want to know Christ and the power of his resurrection and the sharing of his sufferings by becoming like him in his death. . . . Not that I have already obtained this or have already reached the goal; but I press on to make it my own, because Christ Jesus had made me his own" (vv. 10–12).

It is undoubtedly the case that some believers experience conversion as a "crisis" and an immediate change in heart and mind with a dramatically new outlook on life, while others see their conversion as gradual, or at least involving a number of decisions and experiences of God contributing toward a maturing faith. It is also likely that many see their conversion as involving both a crisis and a gradual maturing awareness. The idea of **prevenient grace** argues for the possibility that one can see conversion as both a maturing of events set in motion long before one came consciously to Christ, and as the crisis of arriving at a fork in the way and having to make a decision about one's ultimate destiny.

Christians today have become so accustomed to the word "repentance" that the weightiness of this turning away from sin and turning toward God is frequently overlooked or, at least, underestimated. Ambrose (A.D. 340–397), bishop of Milan wrote that repentance should reflect the attitude of a true debtor, requesting forgiveness with humility and not asking presumptuously as if it were a right. Ambrose describes repentance as strong medicine indeed:

> Does any one think that that is penitence where there still exists the striving after earthly honors, where wine flows, and even conjugal connection takes place? The world must be renounced; less sleep must be indulged in than nature demands; it must be broken by groans, interrupted by sighs, put aside by prayers; the mode of life must be such that we die to the usual habits of life. Let the man deny himself and be wholly changed.[4]

Repentance is inseparable from faith. As we move to consider the topic of faith, we should continually keep in mind these two ways of expressing the same decision. Repentance emphasizes turning away from one's habitual affections and way of life; faith, on the other hand, suggests the positive side of this same decision, the decision now to trust in God and live in obedience. Both repentance and faith are essential to entering into the Christian life, and they are no less essential to the continuation of life in Christ. Now, let's turn to the other side of conversion.

Faith. The idea of faith as a term denoting what we believe (e.g., "I hold to the Christian faith") is not the most

---

4. Ambrose, *Concerning Repentance,* bk 2, chap. 10 in *Nicene and Post-Nicene Fathers,* ed. Philip Schaff & Henry Wace, vol. 10 (Grand Rapids: Eerdmans, 1955), 357.

common New Testament use of the term. Instead it most often signifies the act of believing. The words *pistis* or *pisteuein* are translated, respectively, "faith" ("belief") and "to believe." *Pistis* is used to denote the capacity to believe, as in Jesus' comment to the woman healed of her hemorrhages, "Daughter, your faith has made you well" (Luke 8:48). The verb form *pisteuein,* however, is more common and expresses the idea that faith is an active decision on the part of the believer. We find this form of the term, for instance, in John 5:24: "Very truly, I tell you, anyone who hears my word and believes him who sent me has eternal life, and does not come under judgment, but has passed from death to life." When we speak of faith or belief in the context of the Christian life, we must understand this idea of three levels.

The first level of faith is simply the *acceptance of revealed truth* about God in Christ. This involves more than an intellectual acceptance, although it certainly includes this element. It also involves receiving and trusting what God has made apparent to the mind.

The second level of faith involves the *trusting obedience* of what Christ has taught and commanded. The idea of faith is often correlated in the New Testament with the idea of active obedience on the part of the believer. For instance, in John 3:36, we find, "Whoever believes in the Son has eternal life; whoever disobeys the Son will not see life, but must endure God's wrath." In this sense, the intellectual assent and moral action are virtually inseparable; it is an apprehension of truth that is only meaningful in terms of real-life results. This idea of faith is distinct from Pelagianism in that one trusts not in the works themselves, but rather in God who calls forth the works. It is obedience that has no aim of bargaining with God, but an obedience prompted by God, and that trusts in God for the outcome.

On the third level of faith we find that the receiving of the truth (the passive first level) and the trusting obedience to Christ (the active second level) result in a *personal knowledge* of Christ. The Fourth Gospel refers to this as an "abiding" in Christ, the reality of Christ being focused in us through an intimate acquaintance with his ways. "You have already been cleansed by the word that I have spoken to you," Jesus said to his disciples, and then continued: "Abide

in me as I abide in you. Just as the branch cannot bear fruit
by itself unless it abides in the vine, neither can you unless
you abide in me" (John 15:3–4). In this sense, the faith of
the believer is altogether active: It is Christ who undergirds
the living, active fruit-bearing of the believer who has perfect freedom to "be" the person he or she is intended to be in
the world. In a larger sense, these actions and this life no
longer can be seen as that of the believer, but as that of
Christ.

I would refer to these aspects or levels of faith as *passive*,
active, and *synthetic* or *organic*.

The first level of faith alone is not enough to encompass
all of faith. It can be only an intellectual assent that fails to
come up to the level of active obedience. That level, left to
itself, would be deficient in the way that James spoke of a
belief without works. If this is what we call faith, James
said, "even the demons believe—and shudder" (Jas. 2:19).
Obviously, belief must amount to more than this.

The second level of faith, however, without the trusting
acceptance of what Christ has given, can short-circuit faith
by becoming a self-willed reliance upon good works. It can
be little more than a Pharisaic legalism, the sort that Jesus
condemned as observing the letter of the law but negating
the spirit. It is what Augustine condemned in Pelagianism,
in that the human being turns to self instead of turning to
God, seeking to find strength in one's own resources rather
than turning in reliance upon the gift of God. Thus faith will
be misguided (and in reality fail to be faith) if it is either entirely passive or entirely active in its mode of expression.

The third level of faith, however, grows out of an attitude
of trust, receiving with thanksgiving the gift of God, and
calling the believer to active obedience. It becomes a learning of the way of Christ from Christ and in the presence of
Christ. It creates in the believer a new heart and mind, re-
ceptive to the Word of God and active in trusting obedience.
It is organic in character because it is no longer merely a
passive observer, nor a self-willed activist, but a faith that
begins with God himself and manifests itself in the life of
the believer. It is a faith that reflects Jesus' own explanation of his life with the Father, when he said, "The Son can
do nothing on his own, but only what he sees the Father

doing; for whatever the Father does, the Son does likewise" (John 5:19).

Salvation as Redemption

As important as the idea of justification is, it is not the only way of thinking about salvation that the New Testament employs. To be "set right" or "declared righteous" is one thing, and it is a very important thing; but to be taken back into the family, to be forgiven, and to be received with open arms and warm words of restored affection is something else. So the idea of **redemption** relates to the way in which God receives a sinner who comes to him. While justification alludes to the justice of God, redemption refers to his mercy. While justification presupposes the holiness of God, redemption presupposes his intimate sympathy. The opening words of Jesus' model prayer are, "Our Father which art in heaven." Justification is a reminder that God's standards are heavenly, just as he is "in heaven," but redemption reminds us that he is "our Father."

In the Old Testament, the word *ga'al* refers to the redeeming of a member of the family from a debt that has caused that person to be taken into slavery. It was the responsibility of the next of kin to pay the price necessary for the redemption of the kinsman, restoring him to the family and releasing him from bondage.

This word was used in reference to God's delivering his people Israel from bondage in Egypt. In Exodus God spoke to Moses about recalling his covenant with Israel and hearing the cries of his people. Therefore: "I will redeem you with an outstretched arm and with mighty acts of judgment" (Exod. 6:6). When Isaiah used the term *ga'al* in reference to God's releasing the people from their exile in Babylon, the implication was quite clear: God is their "next of kin." The name that Isaiah frequently uses for God is "Redeemer," which is a name always formed from *ga'al* (cf. 44: 22–23).

Even though the terms, *redeemer* or *redemption* are not used frequently in the New Testament, the idea of redemption by a "kinsman" (someone bound in covenant relationship to a debtor) is indispensable to the New Testament understanding of what God has done in Christ. Jesus has paid a price, in his own blood, to redeem those in bondage. His payment amounts to a "ransom" so that "you were ransomed from the futile ways inherited from your ancestors" (1 Pet. 1:18).

To reflect a moment on the differences between the idea of redemption and our earlier glance at salvation as justification, it is well to begin with the simple observation that redemption is the more personal of the two terms for salvation. The term *justification* rings with forensic overtones, the language of the courtroom and criminal proceedings. Redemption, however, carries the idea of family, resided over by a kind but just patriarch. The picture that comes to mind is that of the father looking for the prodigal son, or David weeping over Absalom. The term justification was especially influential in the Latin West, where legal jurisprudence was an important tradition, and the idea of justice was most strongly associated with this system. It is not surprising, then, that the German Reformation under the influence of Martin Luther centered largely in a discussion of justification. Redemption, however, with its implied family setting and the duties related to the tender bonds of kinship, recalls the oriental family with its intricate code of mutual obligations, its more informal dispensing of justice, its value for harmony over abstract notions of justice, and its inevitable tendency to identify the family with the offender.

Forgiveness. One who has been redeemed is forgiven a debt. The next of kin has come and paid the price of the debt in order to set the kinsman free. The reason the debt was paid in the first place was that the debtor could not pay it himself. The meaning of this kind of analogy for the one who is redeemed by Christ is clear. It is precisely because the sinner was unable to extricate herself from the depth of her guilt that God provided for redemption. Even if someone else has paid the debt, it is nevertheless paid. If the debtor could have earned his way out of it, the intervention of the next of kin would not have been needed.

God's forgiveness is complete. It is not earned or merited. It comes from a source other than ourselves; yet it is a debt altogether forgiven, as if it had never existed.

In the New Testament, while the older idea of redemption fades into the background, the restatement of this idea as forgiveness comes into prominence. It becomes clear in the New Testament that *guilt*, a word rooted in the idea of debt, is essentially an indebtedness to God. It is, first of all, God who has been rejected, who is offended, and who is dishonored by sin. The idea of an offense against God is carried in the words of Psalm 51, which recalls David's lament of his adultery with Bathsheba and his causing the death of her husband: "Against you, you alone, have I sinned, and done what is evil in your sight, so that you are justified in your sentence" (v. 4).

Viewing the redemption of God in this light, God is not only the one who pays off the debt, he is also the one to whom the debt is owed. So, while paying the debt, he is also forgiving the debt. He is both the rescuer and the injured party.

Paul brings these two ideas together, that of redemption and forgiveness, in his letter to the Ephesians. "In him [Christ]," Paul wrote, "we have redemption through his blood, the forgiveness of our trespasses, according to the riches of his grace" (1:7).

The importance of this reality of forgiveness is perhaps something we realize more in the heart than in the mind. Yet it is universally understood what power resides in the capacity to forgive. The person forgives another for a wrong that was long remembered and a grudge nursed over time, and suddenly the bitter rivalry that separated them is dissolved. When true forgiveness takes place, often a stronger feeling of intimacy and mutual sympathy than ever existed before replaces the enmity.

Thus God reveals himself to men and women not simply as one powerful enough to create worlds and to give life and take it away; he comes as one with an infinite capacity to forgive. Therefore our standing with him rests on a new recognition of what lengths he will go to in order to advocate for us. As H. R. Mackintosh stated the matter, "It brings God Himself into a man's life in an immediate (yet not unmediated) way and establishes a new connection in which He and that life shall henceforth stand to one another."[5]

---

5. H. R. Mackintosh, *The Doctrine of the Person of Jesus Christ* (Edinburgh: T & T Clark, 1923), 358.

Reconciliation. Because of the affective power of forgiveness, then, we can understand why the idea of God's redemption of man was often expressed as reconciliation. Reconciliation recalls the condition of alienation: the alienation of man from God.

The theme of alienation is quite important in the Genesis story of the fall. After the intrusion of sin, we see that the human condition is marked by the experience of no longer being at home in the world, expelled from Eden. This idea is most compactly stated in the story of Cain, who kills his brother and then disclaims his responsibility for his brother ("Am I my brother's keeper?"). In a concise statement of the human condition of alienation, Cain protests his punishment from God, saying, "Today you have driven me away from the soil, and I shall be hidden from your face; I shall be a fugitive and a wanderer on the earth, and anyone who meets me may kill me" (Gen. 4:14). He is alienated in three ways: from nature, from God, and from society. This describes a comprehensive alienation, one that results in the isolation of the individual. It describes a condition in which sin, and its resultant guilt, has dissolved those ties that are the very matrix of life, leaving the individual without a world, without a God, without a companion. It is ultimately the isolation of death.

When Paul writes of the new life in Christ, he uses the language of reconciliation, a language that expresses the opposite of alienation. It is alienation overcome; the dividing wall of hostility has been broken down; the new humanity is unified, making peace so that among Jews and Gentiles Christ "might reconcile both groups to God in one body through the cross" (Eph. 2:16). The result, he says to the Gentile Ephesians, is that, "You are no longer strangers and aliens, but you are citizens with the saints and also members of the household of God" (v. 19). In Christ, isolated individuals have found their home, their world, and their God. He who was created for fellowship, and wandered alone in the land of Nod (the land of wandering, or the land of the stranger), is taken back into the household of God.

GENERAL DISTINCTIONS AMONG TERMS
IN SOTERIOLOGY

	Justification	Sanctification	Regeneration	Redemption
The vocabulary environment	The legal system	The Family	Parent/child	Community
Personal reference	More impersonal	More impersonal	Individual	Communal
Time reference	Historical past	Present progressive	Individual past, present, or future	Future
Primary biblical reference	Pre-exilic prophets, John and Paul	Pentateuch, post-exilic prophets, John and Paul	Ezekiel, John	Pentateuch, Isaiah 40–66, Synoptic Gospels

Salvation as Grace

One of the most intriguing and helpful explanations that the apostle Paul gives for salvation is found in Romans 10. In discussing the nature of salvation from the standpoint of grace, I want to focus on this passage in particular, since it vividly draws the connection between Old Testament and New Testament understandings of God's **salvific** work.

We have already reviewed the biblical disclosure of God's requirement for righteousness and how this requirement illustrates both the nature of God and the nature of human longings. We also noted, however, that this same insight into the requirement of righteousness (doing what is right, as well as desiring and loving what is right and what is the "greatest good") leaves us with the sobering realization that no one can truly accomplish what is required. No one is righteous, as Paul emphasized (Rom. 3:9–18). Paul Tillich emphasized the "tragic" element in the biblical understanding of humanity, in that the human soul longs for that which it can in no way achieve. It aspires to righteousness, to the good, but it is unfitted for the gaining of it. We are left with an enormous existential dilemma, a gaping chasm between the demands of a holy God and the capacities of frail and sinful humanity.

Paul makes clear, however, that God himself has given his own answer to this dilemma. He has bridged the chasm, not by depending upon our righteousness, but by inviting us to depend upon his.

Chapter 10 of the Roman Letter states the matter as a paraphrase of Deuteronomy 30. In that passage, Moses speaks of the law as that which everyone already possesses. It is not necessary to "go up to heaven for us, to get it for us so that we may hear it and observe it," nor to "cross to the other side of the sea." No, he says, this "word" of the law is already on the tip of your tongue, "in your mouth and in your heart." That is how close and how pervasive and how evident the law is to us.

Now Paul substitutes the name "Christ" for the idea of "law." Christ, being the "end" or fulfillment of the law, is one with this basic principle of reality. Therefore, in acknowledging Christ we acknowledge what we *recognize* as the word of God to us. In a sense, the gospel came to us as new—

178 A Basic Christian Theology

or good news. But in another sense, it called us back to our true home like the prodigal son who "came to himself." Thus the gospel is given to us, in one way, as a gift—something we never had before. But in another way we awaken to find what we had always possessed—namely, God's unending design to save us. It is a desire and a promise that he will fulfill. Yet we have it not because we deserve it, but because we no longer resist the gift. That is the Christian meaning of gospel.

Salvation as Regeneration

In 1976, when Jimmy Carter was running for President, much of the media professed to be surprised and puzzled by his allusion to being a "born-again" Christian. It is probable, of course, that the idea of being born again, of regeneration, is more common in some communions than in others, and may be a relatively foreign idea to the more unchurched part of a largely post-Christian America. But the idea of regeneration is thoroughly biblical. At heart, it expresses the doctrine that Christian conversion is not something that emerges out of nature, or out of this life, but it is supernatural. It is a life that comes upon us from God, giving us a new life and a new start in life.

The language is that of the Gospel of John. When Jesus says to Nicodemus, a rabbi and member of the Sanhedrin, that anyone entering the kingdom of God must be "born from above," Nicodemus expresses puzzlement. Jesus returns with the astonished reply that, after all, Nicodemus is a teacher of Israel, and "yet you do not understand these things?" (John 3:10). In the course of the passage, it becomes clear that to be "born from above" means the same as to be "born of the Spirit." Therefore entry into the kingdom of God is a matter that takes place, first, from the initiating will of God. It is not a human attainment, any more than the first birth is a matter of willing oneself to be born. It is God's desire to save and bring the sinner into a new life that makes it possible from the beginning.

The image of regeneration is especially important in our own times. It clearly depicts how the Christian message of salvation is distinguished from competing messages in the contemporary world. The prevailing popular philosophy of the modern West, for instance, is a kind of Romantic Pantheism. It is a philosophy that encourages the thought that a salvation of sorts can spring from the development of human nature, of those possibilities that lie within. Over against this dream of human fulfillment on the basis of psychological endowments, the Christian call to salvation emphasizes that the solution to our problems lies in turning to a Source outside of ourselves. It lies, therefore, in a new relationship. The Spirit of God does not come from within us, but comes to us from we know not where (John 3:8). We *receive* the Spirit of God and we receive salvation; we do not unlock it from within.

The salvation of the romantic pantheist only drives human beings further into isolation. They are convinced they are their own salvation, and all the time it is their self-reliance, their self-centeredness, that is the very form of their affliction and the cause of the individual living unto death. The only adequate answer to modern isolation and modern attempts to fortify the individual against the claims of a living and saving God is to be born from above and therefore to find the world a larger place than was ever dreamed of by the man or woman attempting to live independently.

The other style of modern philosophy that competes with the Christian call to regeneration might be termed "gnostic." It is an ideological predisposition toward believing that problems arise from the fact that the world is poorly organized. If circumstances, especially the circumstances of the larger society and the body politic, were changed, then the afflictions of life would be solved. Over against this idea, the idea of salvation as regeneration informs us that the solution does not lie in structures, the superficial organization of society and its institutions, or in the manipulation of powers. The answer, instead, lies in relationship, a renewed relationship with God and with the neighbor.

The third philosophy competing in the modern world is a kind of Pelagian reliance on works as the means toward the end of salvation. Typically this takes hold in Christian or quasi-religious communities that are convinced of the call to the discipline of good works. Their insight into the call of true religion is accurate, in that good works must always be in evidence where the will of God is known and obeyed. The weakness in this philosophy, however, is the weakness of Pelagians of all times: Good works simply do not flourish where there are unrepentant hearts and minds that are easily led astray. The church must never abandon evangelism, even while it presses for a better world on the level of works of righteousness.

All three of these modern options are not altogether modern. The Romantic Pantheism reflects the several ancient styles of thought that eminated from Stoicism, and they have much in common with Hindu philosophies as well as the Transcendentalists of New England more than a hundred years ago. The gnostic style of analysis of human problems reflects the Marcionites and Manichaeans of the early Christian centuries. The Pelagian style of salvation was rightly detected as a departure from Christianity in the fourth and fifth centuries.

But the options are always limited. And the same, or very similar, scenarios are played again and again in the course of history's search for the way to God. That is why the understanding that it is God who brings about new life must never be lost from the thinking of the Nicodemuses and the Johns of this age. It will always be true that the gospel is given so that everyone "who believes in him may not perish but may have eternal life" (John 3:16).

Questions for Review and Reflection

1. What terms express different aspects or models of salvation? Define each one.
2. Express in your own words the meaning of *salvation* in Christian theology?
3. What theological model of salvation would you use if you wanted to emphasize that salvation comes from the active work of God's Holy Spirit?
4. What biblical expression for salvation best conveys the understanding of God as a Father longing to restore an estranged son or daughter?
5. What biblical term best conveys the idea that God wills to restore the individual to his or her lawful status as member of the community under God?

6. What is the meaning of *conversion?* What examples outside of the Christian or religious experience can you give of the idea of conversion?
7. What is the relationship between repentance and faith?
8. Define *grace.* What is *prevenient grace?*
9. How would you begin to discuss the relationship of faith and obedient works in the economy of God's salvation?
10. How would you explain what it means to become a Christian or how anyone can come to Christ?

LIVING AS KINGDOM CITIZENS: SANCTIFICATION

The Meaning of Sanctification

"In reality there has been only one Christian," Friedrich Nietzsche said, "and he died on the Cross."[1]

What might have surprised this philosopher of "The Anti-Christ" is that most Christians who understand their faith well would partly agree with him. They would partly agree because they know that the standard set by the Man who died on a cross indicts every one of them. But they would *only partly* agree because they understand that the reason they are Christians is not that they are righteous, but because he is. They are therefore justified on the ground of his righteousness and not their own.

So, they are both already Christian and not yet Christian. What we will be, John writes, "has not yet been revealed." Yet we know that, on the day he is revealed, "We will be like him, for we will see him as he is" (1 John 3:2). In the meantime we confess the distance that remains

---

1. Friedrich Nietzsche, *The Anti-Christ*, trans. R. J. Hollingdale (New York: Penguin Books, 1968), 151.

between who we are and the one by whose name we are called if we are Christians.

When we begin to think about the tension, this unresolvable gap that Nietzsche wanted to use as a glove in the face of Christians, between what we experience and what is promised in the Christian life, we are likely to use the term **sanctification** instead of **justification**, which was the way we began to talk about salvation in the last chapter. In reality, however, it is sometimes difficult to talk about the differences between these two because they are so closely related. Let's first outline the similarities between justification and sanctification, and then we more nearly will be able to focus on the distinction:

- Sanctification, like justification, is a work performed by the Spirit of God and cannot be claimed by special merit or works.
- Sanctification, like justification, can be thought of in terms of an altogether accomplished reality (cf. 1 Cor. 1:30) in which the reality of sanctification is already possessed by the believer.
- Sanctification, like justification, can be thought of as a promise, as something to be realized in the eschatological future.

But, now, what distinguishes sanctification? First, the term *sanctification* means to be "set apart," to be "made holy," and by implication, to be "consecrated" for special use or service. So the sanctification of a life can—unlike justification, which one might only say one has or does not have—refer to the continuing experience and the continuing reality of living as a Christian. We are justified because God has declared us just; and we can think of this in relation to the fully accomplished work of Jesus on our behalf (past), or in terms of its **eschatological** realization (future). In either case, the fact of justification should have a bearing on our experience, but I can hardly say, "I am experiencing the process of justification." Sanctification, however, might well refer to the ongoing experience of living as a Christian and growing in our love of God.

E. Y. Mullins made reference to both of these aspects of sanctification when he defined it as, (1) "the state of one who is set apart to the service of God, who belongs to God," and (2) "the inner transformation of one thus set apart, the actual realization of holy character."[2]

Sanctification includes the idea of growth or progress. That is the most distinctive feature within the concept of sanctification. Just as one cannot speak of justification as progressive, the other terms relating to salvation also do not carry the idea of a continually progressive experience. The idea of regeneration, for instance, is never understood in a progressive sense; after all, once you are born, there is no being more or less born. The same is true for reconciliation and redemption; these are absolute terms that do not allow for shadings or degrees of growth. But apparently the idea of salvation in the Christian experience does at least include a very important progressive element. A Christian grows, matures, and finds himself or herself moving from point to point in relationship to God and to other people. The idea of sanctification, however, is different in precisely this way: It is a term for salvation that includes implications of the others—the decisive "this" or "that," "yes" or "no" of God's action on our behalf—but it also implies and includes more. It includes the experience of growing, learning, changing, and personally coming to know the reality of salvation in the course of a human life.

The Two Sides of Sanctification

In the earlier chapter on the idea of justification, we noted the apostle Paul's two-sided expression for salvation: "Work out your own salvation with fear and trembling" (from this perspective it appears as if the human being is responsible for his or her salvation) "for it is God who worketh in you both to will and to do of his good pleasure" (Phil. 2:12–13, KJV; and from this point of view it is God whose work is really accomplished).

When we speak of salvation in terms of sanctification we are incorporating the two sides of salvation in one expression. Herman Bavinck, in *Our Reasonable Faith*, calls attention to this feature when he says that the reality of sanctification "places a heavy obligation upon believers."

---

2. E. Y. Mullins, *The Christian Religion in Its Doctrinal Expression* (Philadelphia: Roger Williams Press, 1917), 417.

He continues: "Sanctification is a work of God, but it is intended to be a work in which the believers themselves are also active in the power of God."[3] So whether one considers this idea from the point of view of God's work in us or from the perspective of our work in Christ, the experience that one refers to is the same. However much it is our work, it is no less God's work; and in that it is God's work, it calls forth obedience, discipline, effort, and sacrifice on our part. It is neither one nor the other alone; it is both. If it is only one or the other, then in reality it is neither.

Bavinck shows further how this two-sided expression of growing in holiness is thoroughly embedded in Old Testament as well as New Testament thinking: "In the Old Testament we read that the Lord Himself sanctified His people, and at another time that the people must sanctify themselves." In support of this he cites Exodus 31:13, "You shall keep my sabbaths . . . that you may know that I, the Lord, sanctify you." By way of support for the other side, he lists as an example Leviticus 11:44, "For I am the Lord your God; sanctify yourselves therefore, and be holy, for I am holy." Bavinck cites numerous examples of the Old Testament as *both* the work of God and the response of his obedient people (e.g., Lev. 20:8 and Lev. 20:7; Lev. 21:8 and Num. 11:18). He shows as well how this same style of thought, this dialectic of grace and response, of God's work and human obedience, is coming to light when it is said that, on the one hand, the Lord circumcises the heart (Deut. 30:6), but on the other hand we read that Israel must circumcise the foreskin of their hearts (Deut. 10:16; Jer. 4:4). The work of regeneration is said to be God's work (Jer. 31:18), and at other times we read Jeremiah saying, "Return, faithless Israel . . . acknowledge your guilt . . . I will take you, one from a city and two from a family, and I will bring you to Zion" (Jer. 3:12–14), making the rebirth of the nation appear to be their responsibility.

Bavinck carries this observation into the New Testament. He says that sanctification "is also presented as a gift of God in Christ and as a work of the Holy Spirit by which

---

3. Herman Bavinck, *Our Reasonable Faith*, trans. Henry Zylstra (Grand Rapids: Eerdmans, 1956), 478.

believers are sanctified." Then, in a revealing passage, he says,

> And yet these believers are repeatedly admonished to be perfect even as their Father in Heaven is perfect (Matt. 5:48), to do good works which glorify the Father who is in Heaven (Matt. 5:16; John 15:8), to yield their members as servants to righteousness unto holiness (Rom. 6:19), to be holy in all their walk and conduct (1 Pet. 1:15; 2 Pet. 3:11), to pursue sanctification and to fulfill it in the fear of God, and to do this because without holiness no man shall see the Lord (Heb. 12:14).

Even this *tour de force* by Bavinck can appear to some mere proof texting, and they might well call to mind that the apostle Paul (as the foremost example) can fairly be understood as holding a comprehensive theology of grace, a grace that prevails over the frailty, ineptitude, and misdirection of human works. While this understanding of Paul can be successfully defended, one must also explain why Paul, then, expended so much energy and so many words on instructing Christians in how they ought to live. The ethical exhortations of Paul are a major part of his letters, including chapters 12–15 in Romans, more than half of 1 and 2 Corinthians, and chapters 4–6 in Ephesians. In the letter most strongly addressed to the issue of relying on grace rather than works of the law, the Letter to the Galatians, Paul engages his readers in a long exhortation to be "guided by the Spirit," warning against envy and conceit, and reminding them to "bear one another's burdens" (Gal. 5:25–6:5). Then he puts the final touch on his letter about grace—over against the Judiazers with their imposing regulations—with the words: "Do not be deceived; God is not mocked, for you reap whatever you sow. . . if you sow to the Spirit, you will reap eternal life from the Spirit. *So let us not grow weary in doing what is right*, for we will reap at harvest time, if we do not give up" (6:7–9; emphasis mine). Evidently, Paul did not see these two sides of salvation as conflicting ideas, but spoke freely of both as the work of God. What man receives by grace is of God; but what man does in response to God is also by grace, and of God. Paul's argument, rather, is with those who see works as a *means* of grace rather than as participation in the grace of God.

It might be said that one receives the grace of God by faith. It can likewise be said that one participates in that divine grace by good works. These are two different things, but they are not two contrary things. In the final analysis, it must be insisted upon that they are two aspects of the same work of grace.

Living in Christ

There is no phrase that comes more frequently in the writings of Paul than the phrase, "in Christ." The Christian lives out of a new center of awareness. Before the person became united to Christ, the man or woman was centered in self. Now the new person has found an identity in Christ. In the opening lines of the Letter to the Ephesians, we find Paul writing of Christians being blessed "in Christ" (Eph. 1:3), chosen "in Christ" (v. 4), adopted "through Christ" (v. 5), bestowed with grace "in the Beloved" (v. 6), finding redemption "in him" (v. 7), obtaining an inheritance "in Christ" (v. 11); all this because "in him you . . . were marked with the seal of the promised Holy Spirit" (v. 13).

In Ephesians we have a compelling picture of what it means to live in Christ. Christ has led the way to God, and he did so by his own faithfulness to the image of God. First, as the Gospels (especially John) describe Jesus' life as one of living in imitation of God, now Paul describes the Christian life as one of coming to know Christ, not merely by an intellectual apprehension, but by the engagement of the whole life, following him in the way each believer is given to follow (4:7–12).

This way even Gentiles are taken up in the headship of Christ; so they are "no longer strangers and aliens, but you are citizens with the saints and also members of the household of God, built upon the foundation of the apostles and prophets, with Christ Jesus himself as the cornerstone" (2:19–20). For this way of Jesus Christ, the way of good works, is the way that "God prepared beforehand to be our way of life" (2:10).

This way comes to be known by the believer's being united with Christ, which means, from the external and temporal point of view at least, the imitation of Christ. When there is a solidarity of community imitation, following a pattern of behavior, speech, and affections that constitute, in the community and in individuals, a living out of the life of Christ, the quality that could be called living "in Christ" becomes apparent. Thus Gentiles are warned to "no longer live as the Gentiles live." Following that corrupt pattern of life, "They have lost all sensitivity and have abandoned themselves to licentiousness, greedy to practice every kind of impurity" (4:19). These patterns of life can readily be seen as wrong and destructive, because: "That is not the way you learned Christ!" (v. 20). By "learning Christ" was meant certainly more than intellectual learning *about* Christ, but the kind of learning that is implied in imitation and practice, engaging the whole range of human experience. It is following an example in work, thought, and love, ordering the whole of life by the discipline of following Christ. In the context of the church, it means following those exemplars, or following those strengths or virtues in others that conform to the life and mind of Christ.

Of course, the modern church furnishes many poor examples of Christian living; but so did the ancient church, and the real church (as opposed to an ideal one) at every juncture of history. But this does not deny the power and the importance of using the imitation of Christ, often mediated by fallible human beings, who nevertheless exhibit qualities of Christian life and Christian love that strengthen the church by the effect of example. Imitation is the only way the gospel has ever escaped the abstractions of doctrine and become a living reality among specific men and women.

In this way, new Christians are encouraged by the gospel itself, and its presentation of Christ, as well as by learning from the examples of Christians living around them (v. 21) to "put away your former way of life . . . corrupt and deluded by its lusts" (v. 22) and to "clothe yourselves with the new self, created according to the likeness of God in true righteousness and holiness" (v. 24). The practice of holiness in life cannot be said to result in a new person, as if that alone were the cause of a renewed life. But it can be said that God is capable of creating a new life; and that he does that by virtue of a *new way of life*, one that is learned of Christ, in Christ, and in the fellowship of believers.

■ ───────────────────────── ■

IMITATION OF CHRIST IN THE EARLY CHURCH
THE MARTYRDOM OF POLYCARP

"The Martyrdom of Polycarp" is an example of Christian writing about martyrdom outside of the New Testament. Polycarp was a second century bishop of Smyrna who was condemned to death for refusing to declare Caesar as Lord. Much beloved by the community, his death at 86 years of age came to be a source of inspiration and a pattern of imitation for the growing church. This writing is a good example of the church's attention to the need for exemplars and the power of imitation.

For nearly all the preceding events happened in order that the Lord might show us once again a martyrdom which is in accord with the gospel. For he waited to be betrayed, just as the Lord did, in order that we might be imitators of him, "not looking only to that which concerns ourselves, but also to that which concerns our neighbors." For it is the mark of true and steadfast love to desire not only that oneself be saved, but all the brothers as well.

He proved to be not only a distinguished teacher, but also an outstanding martyr, whose martyrdom all desire to imitate, since it was in accord with the pattern of the gospel of Christ.

Source: "The Martyrdom of Polycarp," in *The Apostolic Fathers*, trans. J. B. Lightfoot and J. R. Harmer, edited and revised by Michael W. Holmes (Grand Rapids: Baker, 1994),135–143.]

■ ───────────────────────── ■

All of the early church fathers knew the power of imitation. We find our values in society by unconsciously imitating the desires of others. It is not self-evident, for instance, that one style of automobile or clothing is to be preferred to others. Yet these desires spread through society like changes in the weather. They do so by the power of *memesis*, an imitation and unconscious adoption of the values of others. Culture, including language, depends upon this most powerful of social forces.

When we look at the life of Christ, we see one whose desire was to do the will of the Father, so that his life can be described as an imitation of the Father. He says, "The Son can do nothing on his own, but only what he sees the Father doing; for whatever the Father does, the Son does likewise" (John 5:19). The passion and intensity of his desire draws others. He invites his disciples, those who are called to an intimate learning relationship with him, to follow. The church thus becomes a fellowship knit together in its *imitatio christi,* and thus participates in the life and character of God.

What we know about the early church, and the church at many periods of spiritual vitality and growth, is that there was a heaven-sent contagion of desire for that which is good and that which is just. We are all, in a sense, naturally attracted to the qualities of what is truly good; yet we are like sick people who have to recover a healthy appetite. In the writings of Paul, and in works such as those of the apostolic fathers, we find that that appetite grows hardy most noticeably in the company of disciples who wish to taste of the kind of joy and passion that Christ himself exhibited.

A perusal of almost any letter in the New Testament will show the importance of this idea of imitation. In his Letter to the Thessalonians, Paul writes, "And you became imitators of us and of the Lord, for in spite of persecution you received the word with joy . . . so that you became an example to all the believers in Macedonia and in Achaia" (1 Thess. 1:6–7). The apostolic fathers carry forward this same theme, stressing the importance of exemplars among them and the faithful imitation of believers. Continually Ignatius is counseling believers to be "imitators of our Lord," [4] and

---

4. See, for instance, "The Letter of Ignatious, Bishop of Antioch, to the Ephesians," *The Apostolic Fathers*, 2nd. ed., trans. by Lightfoot and Harmer (Grand Rapids: Baker, 1994), 90.

he teaches them to find unity in their mutual participation in the manner of life that the Christian is to live.

The Pattern of the Christian Life

A great deal could be said about the manner of life that the Christian is called to live. We have already mentioned that the New Testament writers gave a major amount of attention to Christian conduct. From these writings we could find a number of matters that are emphasized strongly. For instance, we would find strong and continual encouragement in prayer, giving thanks, giving to the poor, caring for the widows and orphans—especially those in the church. It was frequently emphasized that a Christian ought to live peaceably and quietly, obeying the laws, honoring the civil authorities, avoiding gossip and useless controversies.

Some of the counsel given by New Testament writers was given in support of these basic commitments to lives of order, charity, and thanksgiving, but are couched within directions that applied to their culture more than our own. An example might be Paul's advice that women must pray with heads veiled: "Any man who prays or prophecies with something on his head disgraces his head, but any woman who prays or prophesies with her head unveiled disgraces her head—it is one and the same thing as having her head shaved" (1 Cor. 11:4–5).

It is well to remember that all traditions within any culture express a deeper conviction about life that might well be expressed in a variety of ways. When Paul commends a course of action that relates to his culture, but is almost without meaning in ours, it does not mean that we should ignore the more fundamental point such as, in this case, that Christians should live in harmony, showing respect and exercising humility. To follow the guidance of Scripture in these cases means not so much following the literal meaning, but, instead, following the more fundamental intent. The Word of God is timeless, yet it is necessarily addressed to cultural forces that change with time. The work of the interpreter is to be able to distinguish between what is the timeless Word, and what words are needed to address a particular culture. In that way, we are not misled by trying to imitate cultural ways that are now long out of use;

and, further, we are strengthened in our effort to interpret the revelation of God for our own times.

Therefore, when Paul, for instance, speaks of the need for salvation, the grace of God that transcends ethnic groups, the life of faith, and the supremacy of love, his words speak directly to our age as well as his. But when he speaks of the need for women to remain silent in the church, and not to wear their hair braided or to wear "gold, pearls, or expensive clothing" (1 Tim. 2:9–12), we must see through the cultural references to the deeper instruction concerning modesty, humility, and order. When Paul speaks of Philemon's rights with regard to his slave (Philem. 14), we remember that Paul's contemporaries took slavery for granted, but we also understand that the deeper instruction regarding how Philemon receives his runaway servant—"no longer as a slave but more than a slave, a beloved brother" (v. 16)— would ultimately be the kind of insight that brought slavery down, and undermined its legitimacy at least in the minds of Christians.

The Variety of Spiritual Gifts

Basic principles, therefore, supersede the various ways in which they are expressed. In the same way the gifts of the Spirit, which vary, are all linked to the underlying reality of the one Spirit of God.

This means, of course, that Christians will not all behave, or work, or worship in the same way. Nor will they manifest any one kind of personality, or interests, or tastes. The same Spirit working through all Christians will give rise to any number of ways, styles, kinds of work, and personal insights. "There are varieties of gifts," Paul writes to the Corinthians, "but the same Spirit; and there are varieties of services, but the same Lord; and there are varieties of activities, but it is the same God who activates all of them in everyone" (1 Cor. 12:4–6).

Paul lists spiritual gifts in this passage—wisdom, knowledge, faith, healing, miracles, prophecy, and so on—but this is intended to be an open list, not a closed one. It is not a categorization of all the spiritual gifts, but it illustrates the great variety of gifts and works that are liberated and that flourish where the Spirit of God is present in power, and where works of the flesh (i.e., self-centered works) are left behind. It is obvious that the varieties of gifts are distributed among believers, each exercising different gifts and manifesting the presence and power of the same Spirit of God in different ways.

When Paul speaks of the "fruit of the Spirit," however, in Galatians 5, he would have the readers understand these to belong in common to all believers in some degree. The intent of identifying these fruits of the Spirit is to draw the obvious contrast with the "works of the flesh," which include, "fornication, impurity, licentiousness, idolatry, sorcery, enmities, strife, jealousy, anger, quarrels, dissensions, factions, envy, drunkenness, carousing, and things like these" (Gal. 5:19–21a). Just as the works of the flesh Paul mentioned are not listed exhaustively (note: "things like these" in v. 21), the fruit of the Spirit is more a suggestive than an exhaustive list. Furthermore, it appears to many interpreters that the word "love" that comes at the head of the list is intended to comprehend or include all of the rest. So Paul is understood as saying simply, "The fruit of the Spirit is love," which manifests itself in "joy, peace, patience, kindness, generosity, faithfulness, gentleness, and self-control" (Gal. 5:22–23).

Love as the Ruling Virtue

Perhaps if, for a day or two, we could recall the early days of the church, we would find the most remarkable differences between early and contemporary Christianity would be the attitude toward the **virtues** of Christian living. A reading of the *Didache* or the *Shepherd of Hermas* should impress anyone with the fact that these earliest Christians were much more conscious of being involved in the development and refinement of virtue, of moral goodness. It was a matter to be cultivated, in private devotion, in the home, and within the church. It was the reason Paul called upon Christians to imitate good examples, and it was the reason for church discipline.

One was growing toward God, in imitation of God, along with other believers, whose practice of humility, prudence, and love grew up in the mutual strengthening fellowship of the church. We already know how Paul often sent words to the churches, as he did to the Colossians: "As God's chosen ones, holy and beloved, clothe yourselves with compassion, kindness, humility, meekness, and patience. Bear with one another. . . . Above all, clothe yourselves with love, which binds everything together in perfect harmony" (Col. 3:12–14).

The encouragement toward virtue and the perfecting of Christian practice is a frequent theme of early writers, such as Gregory of Nyssa (c. 335–c.395), who would write the following as a preface to his *The Life of Moses:*

> At the horse races spectators intent on victory shout to their favorites in the contest, even though the horses are eager to run. From the stands they participate in the race with their eyes, thinking to incite the charioteer to keener effort, at the same time urging the horses on while leaning forward and flailing the air with their outstretched hands instead of with a whip. . . . I seem to be doing the same thing myself, most valued friend and brother. While you are competing admirably in the divine race along the course of virtue, lightfootedly leaping and straining constantly for the prize of the heavenly calling, I exhort, urge and encourage you vigorously to increase your speed.[5]

The idea of virtue *(arete)* is naturally derived from the Old Testament's linking of the love of God to moral obedience. The church quickly found itself in partial agreement with the Greek philosophers, especially Plato and Aristotle, in their elaboration of the virtues. By the Middle Ages, there was broad agreement on the categories of classical and biblical lists of virtues. Seven virtues are typically named. Four are "natural"—that is, they arise from the natural capacities of people for good, although these virtues are compromised and misdirected by the fall. They are: wisdom (or prudence), justice, courage, and temperance. The other three are the theological virtues that are not natural to people, but gifts from God: faith, hope, and love.

It is good to keep in mind that the word *arete* could also be translated "excellence." It implied a certain strength or

5. Gregory of Nyssa, *The Life of Moses*, trans. Abraham J. Malherbe and Everett Ferguson (New York: Paulist Press, 1978), 29.

power to function appropriately, as a man, a woman, an athlete, a warrior. The English word *virtue* carries that same implication, with an even more direct sense of power or strength. The word is rooted in the same term that gives us *virile*. It implied competence in the sense of manliness, and was generalized to all areas of personality and character, calling for an excelling strength to perform.

The Reformers tended not to look favorably upon these lists of virtues, and regarded the biblical virtues of faith, hope, and love the only ones worth elaborating upon. Reacting strongly against the semi-Pelagianism of the Roman Catholic Church, with its emphasis upon merit, the Reformers of the **magisterial Reformation,** especially, were intent upon making a broader point, and in their minds, a more fundamental one. That is, sin and the grace needed to effect salvation had to do with a radical disorientation of human life, not with the refinement of natural qualities.

The idea of virtue, however, is rooted in its original meaning as a power or strength. So, the one who has virtue is one who has the strength to so live and act as a human being is intended. At the same time, this virtue is comprehended in the greatest of the theological virtues, love. Love is the keystone virtue, which gives the others content and makes them possible. To participate in the life of God is to take on the quality of love; it is to live out of the strength of his love.

It is in the context of spiritual gifts—the **pneumatikon,** or more generally, the "gifts," the **charisma**—that Paul speaks of the supremacy of love. He follows a very simple and direct line of reasoning:

1. The gifts are not for oneself but for others (1 Cor. 12:7).
2. The gifts are intended to build up the body of Christ, the church (vv. 12–26).
3. The various offices and gifts are distinct precisely for the sake of the whole body, which needs them all (vv. 27–30).
4. Therefore, the ruling concern of the gifts to the body of Christ is the binding together and mutual service of the members. In other words, the central purpose is love. The lesser gifts serve their purpose, which

comes to an end, but the purpose for which they are all given exceeds and supersedes them all: "Love never ends. But as for prophecies, they will come to an end. . . . For we know only in part, and we prophesy only in part; but when the complete comes, the partial will come to an end" (1 Cor. 13:8–10).

We have seen, going all the way back to the doctrine of the Trinity, that for Christians, the central reality is relationship. John was not simply engaging in a rhetorical flourish when he said, "God is love" (1 John 4:8). It is the nature of God, so supremely and so inseparably, that when we find ourselves participating in his life, we necessarily find ourselves loving others. John put it in a way that demonstrates how Christian practice and imitation run together with theology: "No one has ever seen God; if we love one another, God lives in us, and his love is perfected in us" (1 John 4:12).

Sanctification and Perfection

What is the goal of life in Christ? If it is love, it is more or less realized in human experience. Yet is there a fulfillment in the Christian life, a point of completion or arrival? Jesus told his disciples, "Be perfect, therefore, as your heavenly Father is perfect" (Matt. 5:48).

The question of whether, and in what sense, Christians are actually called to perfection or completion is an important one. It has been the source of controversy throughout the Christian era. It was especially so during the eighteenth century in Europe, England, and North America, where evangelical revivals had played an important part in the life and progress of the church. At the center of this controversy in those days was the Wesleyan movement in England, Wales, and North America.

Let's try to state briefly the terms of those arguments.

Those who argue for Christian perfection, as John Wesley did, fear that, without this sense of need to fulfill literally what Christ has called for, complacency and satisfaction with half-measures in Christian living and compromise with sin would be the sure result. When confronted with the argument that the Old Testament teaches that no one does *not* sin, John Wesley argued that, "Whatever was the case of those under the law, we may safely affirm, with St. John, that since the Gospel was given, 'he that is born of God sinneth not.'" Those arguing against perfectionism, however, say that the very expectation of "no sin" in the Christian life is likely to encourage self-righteousness, self-deception, and a host of sins that result from the unrealistic and unscriptural expectation that a Christian should have achieved sinlessness. Count Zinzendorf, whose **Moravian** theology influenced Wesley at one time, was appalled at Wesley's **perfectionism.**

"Why have you changed your religion?" he asked Wesley when they met in Gray's Inn Walks. Wesley denied that he had, and Zinzendorf launched into a stinging reproval of perfectionist teachings: "I acknowledge no inherent perfection in this life. This is the error of errors. I pursue it through the world with fire and sword. I trample upon it: I devote it to utter destruction. Whoever follows inherent perfection denies Christ."

When Wesley replied that he believed the Spirit of Christ "works this perfection in true Christians," Zinzendorf replied, "All our perfection is in Christ. . . . Our whole Christian perfection is imputed, not inherent. We are perfect in Christ: In ourselves we are never perfect."[6]

The danger, of course, for Zinzendorf's altogether imputed righteousness of the Christian, one that seems to leave aside any development in holiness, is that it threatens to break those bonds forged so strongly by the prophets between true religion and righteous living. Wesley's argument retains that obvious and strong connection, though it threatens to lose the Augustinian realism that admitted to the stubbornness of sin, a depth and strength of sin that roots itself in all human affairs.

The question that necessarily arises in dealing with Christian perfection is, "How do you take seriously God's call to righteousness, and yet not lose sight of the reality of sin?" Or, "How do you avoid cynicism and discouragement in the face of sin, yet not turn away from the goal of Chris-

---

6. Cited in Jürgen Moltmann, *The Spirit of Life* (Minneapolis: Fortress Press, 1992), 167–68.

tian living?" These are important questions, and they are important not simply for theological speculation, but for the practical life of Christians. The two sides of these questions frame the issues in every age, including our own.

Perhaps some of the earlier Christians, however, before the question of perfection had become too far polarized, were better at responding in a convincing and helpful way to this feeling of standing, theologically speaking, between "a rock and a hard place." Gregory of Nyssa wrote a *Life of Moses*, which is alternately titled, "Concerning Perfection in Virtue." I quoted a piece from the introduction of this work earlier, in which Gregory addresses his reader with his earnest desire to urge him on in righteous living. In the first part of this work, he endeavors to define the Christian idea of perfection.

He begins by conceiving of God as the One whose very nature is goodness, and thus as One who is the highest expression of all virtue. "Certainly whoever pursues true virtue participates in nothing other than God, because he is himself absolute virtue." Since God himself is infinite, and knows no limit, then virtue also knows no limit—it is one and the same as the nature of God: "The one limit of virtue is the absence of limit."

In this, he appears to be saying that the limitlessness of virtue makes perfection in virtue unattainable. In one sense he does say this, although he recalls (as Wesley does) the unequivocal command of Jesus to "Be perfect." He then counsels his reader in this matter by saying: "We should show great diligence not to fall away from the perfection which is attainable but to acquire as much as is possible: To that extent let us make progress within the realm of what we seek. For perfection of human nature consists perhaps in its very growth in goodness."[7]

It is interesting, in this regard, that the *New English Bible* translation of Matthew 5:48 (which the NRSV reads more literally, "Be perfect . . . as your heavenly Father is perfect") renders the passage, "There must be no limit to your goodness, as your heavenly Father's goodness knows no bounds." Such renderings shows evidence that the trans-

---

7. Gregory of Nyssa, *Life of Moses,* 31.

lators of the NEB had been reading their Gregory of Nyssa.
If we follow his insight into Christian perfection, we find a
means by which neither Augustinian realism about sin nor
motivation for ethical progress is sacrificed. Since the love
of God knows no end, the progress of love also is without
limit and without end. It is, rather, in loving and in continuing to grow in love that the command to be perfect is responded to faithfully. In this way, the doctrine of salvation
continues to lead Christians not to a false security of a non-
Christian and pre-prophetic pagan religion, divorced from
the pursuit of good works, but to a religion altogether dependent upon divine grace, one that grows in faith, and one
that issues in works of love. In this sense, we can understand the words of the apostle Paul, when he said: "Not that
I have already obtained this or have already reached the
goal; but I press on to make it my own, because Christ Jesus
has made me his own. . . .But this one thing I do: forgetting
what lies behind and straining forward to what lies ahead,
I press on toward the goal" (Phil. 3:12–14).

■ ─────────────────────────── ■

E. Y. MULLINS ON CHRISTIAN GROWTH

There is no reason to suppose that Christian growth
will ever cease. At the resurrection the body will be
perfectly sanctified, and the spirit at death freed from
sin. But as we are partakers of the divine nature, and
are to be conformed to the image of Christ, the eternal
son, we have an endless vista of growth opening before us. Christ is, as it were, a fleeing foal. We possess
him always, and yet there will always remain new
heights of attainment in him. He ever goes before us
to prepare a place for us.

[E. Y. Mullins, *The Christian Religion in Its Doctrinal Expression* (Philadelphia: Roger Williams Press,
1917), 422–423.]

■ ─────────────────────────── ■

Questions for Review and Reflection

1. How would you define the term "sanctification"?
2. What are the two sides of sanctification? How would you illustrate these two aspects or sides from the teachings of the apostle Paul?
3. How can you explain the relationship between works and grace?
4. What is the meaning of the term "virtue"?
5. What part does imitation play in the life of the church and the growth of the Christian?
6. What is "perfectionism"?
7. What arguments might be brought both in favor of and against Christian perfection?
8. What are the implications of Gregory of Nyssa's concept of perfection?
9. Comment on the similarity of E. Y. Mullins's insight on Christian growth (in the sidebar) and the teachings of Gregory of Nyssa on perfection.

■ ─────────────────────── ■

EXPECTING THE KINGDOM
ESCHATOLOGY

The Christian doctrine of the "last things," or **eschatology,** has much in common with the sentiment expressed by Shakespeare when he wrote: "There's a divinity that shapes our ends, Rough hew them how we will."

It has become almost customary among people writing about Christian eschatology to regret that this particular doctrine always seems to come at the end of any treatment of Christian beliefs. This habit, they say, tends to obscure the fact that eschatology is centrally important to Christianity and should not be simply left to a footnote or an appendix to Christian doctrine.

While the point is well taken, and causes us to remember that Christianity is supremely concerned with last things and is influenced throughout by its view of the coming Kingdom of God, the return of Christ, the final judgment, and the new creation, I can hardly imagine a more appropriate place to deal with it than at the end, or at least near the end. What is even more important than the placement of this doctrine is the idea represented in all of Christianity: namely, what determines everything is how things *end.* As

Shakespeare suggested, doubtless because he was thoroughly influenced by Christian thought, God determines the end, however we may be muddling through in the present. That idea of providence is not only the heart of eschatology, but also is very close to the heart of the Christian faith itself.

For that very reason, the doctrine of the last things has also been found at the center of controversy through much of history, and especially modern history. It is hardly possible to discuss what Christians believe about the **eschaton** without becoming acquainted with the many discussions and debates that have led theologians of the church to some rather distinct conclusions.

That is not to minimize that there are broad areas of agreement among almost all Christian traditions concerning the things most basic to a biblical eschatology. Toward the end of this chapter, I will highlight some features that we hold in common. These, however, will prove all the more meaningful once we survey the major issues that have occupied thoughtful believers from the time disciples heard the words, "This Jesus . . . will come in the same way as you saw him go" (Acts 1:11).

The Major Issues in Eschatology

The issues in eschatology are interrelated, making it especially difficult to separate them under distinct headings and speak of them as isolated matters. However, we can distinguish a number of typical questions that have been at the center of Christian thought about the completion of God's work of redemption. Without attempting to exhaust the possible questions, we can at least say that the following points arise frequently in any discussion of the last things:

1. Are we to understand the Kingdom of God, so central in the teachings of Jesus, as a future, concrete (even political) expectation; or is it a timeless, spiritual reality?

2. Was the Kingdom of God inaugurated with Jesus' first coming? Or will it only come into being with his second coming?

3. Did Jesus expect the Kingdom to break into his own time? Must we then include in our interpretation the possibility that Jesus' own expectations were of an imminent nature, but mistaken?
4. Are the "kingdom of God" and the "kingdom of Heaven" distinct ideas, or only distinct terms for the same reality?
5. Will Christ's return (technically called the **parousia**) establish the millennial reign of Christ?
6. Is the **millennium**—mentioned in Revelation 20—then, totally a future reality?
7. Will Christ return only *after* the gospel has effected changes in the world order, establishing what we now call the millennium?
8. On the other hand, is this millennium only a figurative reference to the present age—between the first and final coming of Christ?
9. Should Christians expect to endure the **tribulation** mentioned in Mark 13, Matthew 24, 2 Thessalonians, and the Revelation? Or will Christ's return to gather his saints preserve them from either part or all of the final days of tribulation?

All of these questions seem to circulate around two primary issues. First, what is the nature of the Kingdom of God? And, second, how is the parousia related to other expectations concerning the last things? Let's use these two clusters of issues as a way of sorting out the most pressing questions in Christian eschatology, as well as coming to an understanding of the most essential, underlying convictions in this area of theology.

The Kingdom of God

Biblical Sources of the Doctrine

There is no question that the term *basileia tou theou* (Kingdom of God) as it is used in the Gospels was derived largely from the political hopes and expectations of Israel. Yet even in eighth-century prophecies the idea of a reign of God meant much more than God's endorsement of a human political arrangement.

The account of Isaiah's call (Isa. 6:1–13) gives us an example of the idea of God's reign that is distinct from and transcends the political order. It was the year that King Uzziah died. This was a king who had been disqualified from office because he was stricken by leprosy. Leprosy was seen at that time, and in the Israelite community, as more than a physical misfortune; it was evidence of estrangement from God. Indeed we know that Uzziah was stricken with leprosy because of his presumption in performing what was only allowed to priests. The stricken leper in Israel was obliged to cover "his upper lip" whenever he went into public and cry, "Unclean, unclean" (Lev. 13:45).

Thus with this leper/king in the background, we can see that Isaiah's words denote more than simply a grand vision and a call to ministry. He realizes, because of the king's ailment, the guilt that really grips all of the people, "For I am a man of unclean lips, and I dwell in the midst of a people of unclean lips" (Isa. 6:5, RSV). Furthermore, this unfit king (Uzziah, the leper) is seen against the vision of one who actually rules and is holy. God is significantly called, in this passage, *ha-Melech*, the King.

From Isaiah onward the expectation of a king—a messiah, or anointed one—is always related to this theological conviction that it is a righteous God who truly rules, though he is not yet recognized by the nations. God destroys the army of Sennacherib, while Hezekiah, king of Judah, acknowledges that God is "enthroned above the cherubim" as true king of heaven and earth (Isa. 37:14–16).

The most prominent prophecies announcing God's disclosure of his kingship are found in Isaiah 24–27 and Isaiah 40–55. Other allusions to the coming kingdom are found in Obadiah 21; Micah 4:1ff; Zephaniah 3:15; and Zechariah 14:16–17.

The later the prophecy, generally, the more explicit are the announcements that God's kingship will come to pass. In Daniel, for instance, we find the remarkable vision of the "Son of Man." This figure approaches the Ancient of days, seated on his celestial throne. "To him was given dominion and glory and kingship, that all peoples, nations, and languages should serve him. His dominion is an everlasting dominion that shall not pass away, and his kingship is one that shall never be destroyed" (Dan. 7:14).

We also find these expectations of divine rule in the Psalms. These, perhaps more even than the prophecies, carry the sentiment of an impending kingship of God into the first century. We find these announcements of divine rule, for instance, in Psalms 47, 93, 96, 97, and 99. It is clear that, even though the express term "Kingdom of God" does not occur in the Old Testament (as it does prominently in the New Testament), the idea of God's rule and of a coming disclosure of that rule is a significant Old Testament idea.

In Jewish literature of the later intertestamental period, particularly in the apocryphal and pseudepigraphic writings, another term comes into common usage that also figures prominently in the New Testament. The expression *malkuth shamaim* (Kingdom of the heavens) reflects the growing Jewish reluctance to refer directly to God. Thus it is a circumlocution to suggest Kingdom of God, and comes over into the Gospel of Matthew as "Kingdom of heaven." This is almost certainly the term that Jesus himself actually used, but it is precisely parallel to the "Kingdom of God" and is used interchangeably in Matthew.[1]

This expression during this period is not nearly so prominent as in the Gospels, where it becomes the central message in Jesus' teachings. Yet it is already a term with broad application to Jewish expectations. It is, for instance, used when proselytes join themselves to the Jewish religion. The expression is that they have taken on the "yoke" of the *malkuth shamaim*. Again, foreign powers that act unjustly toward Israel were said to be attempting to throw off the yoke of the *malkuth shamaim*. Or, when Jews recited the Shema (Deut. 6:4–9), they were said to be taking on the yoke of the *malkuth shamaim*. So, in these senses, the *malkuth* refers to the general, spiritual, and timeless rule of God.[2]

---

1. Note, for instance, the parallel uses of "Kingdom of God" and "Kingdom of heaven" in Matthew 19:23–24.

2. See Herman Ridderbos, *The Coming of the Kingdom*, trans. H. de Jongste (Philadelphia: Presbyterian and Reformed Publishing Co., 1962), 8-9.

At the same time there is also an expectation of that which has not yet occurred. Often it is associated with the time of the messiah. Thus the *Kaddish* begins with the words: "Glorified and sanctified be his great name in the world he has created according to his own pleasure. May he establish his royal dominion and start his deliverance of his people, and may he bring his Messiah and redeem his people in the time of your life, and in your days, and in the time of the life of the whole House of Israel, with haste and in a short time; and thou shalt say Amen."[3]

In the New Testament, and especially in the synoptic Gospels, we will find a decided change in the tone and atmosphere of reference to the Kingdom of God (*Basileia tou Theou*) or Kingdom of heaven (*Basileia toun ouranoun*). In the first place, the very idea of the Kingdom takes on a prominence not seen elsewhere. But, more importantly, here we find an announcement of the *fulfillment* of the kingdom. In all three of the synoptic Gospels appear what might be called inauguration announcements concerning the kingdom that *was* expected and *is now* fulfilled.

> Now after John was arrested, Jesus came to Galilee, proclaiming the good news of God, and saying, "The time is fulfilled, and the kingdom of God has come near; repent and believe in the good news (Mark 1:14–15).

> From that time Jesus began to proclaim, "Repent, for the kingdom of heaven has come near" (Matt. 4:17).

> "The Spirit of the Lord is upon me, because he anointed me to bring good news to the poor. He has sent me to proclaim release to the captives and recovery of sight to the blind, to let the oppressed go free, to proclaim the year of the Lord's favor." And he rolled up the scroll, gave it back to the attendant, and sat down. The eyes of all in the synagogue were fixed on him. Then he began to say to them, "Today this scripture has been fulfilled in your hearing" (Luke 4:18–21).

These inauguration sayings are marked by a sense of historical urgency. Something entirely new has taken place or is about to take place. "The kingdom . . . is at hand." No one would miss the fact that these sayings speak not of timeless

---

3. Cf. Ridderbos, *The Coming of the Kingdom*, 10.

matters, but of something that has suddenly happened within time: "The time is fulfilled," "The acceptable year of the Lord." There is something here that has not always been present, and is just breaking in upon the historical experience of Galilean people: "*Today* this scripture has been fulfilled in your hearing" (italics added). All of these, as well as other similar passages, speak not of the timeless and eternal reality of God's kingdom, but of something concerning that kingdom that has to do with concrete, historical, and chronological experience.

From this tendency that we sense in the Gospels, a question arises. It is one that has come to be of major importance in understanding the nature and the theological significance of the Kingdom of God. That is, shall we understand the **kerygma,** or message of Jesus, his apostles, or of the earliest church, to reflect an imminent expectation of what would be realized in the course of time? If we do understand the gospel of the kingdom in this way, must we exclude the idea that it was also a timeless and spiritual reality? Or was there a sense in which what was outside of time (or at least not confined to time) now became "realized" in time? These questions, and similar ones, arise especially in modern theology where the influence of historical critical studies has played a major part.

We will return to these questions. But, first, let us look at the reasons the questions are not so clear-cut.

In addition to the evidence that Jesus and his early followers expected something, or were announcing something, of a temporal nature, we also can point to instances in which it seems that the Gospels retained the old idea of God's kingdom that is simply a manifestation of his lordship over creation. In this regard, we can recall especially Jesus' parable of the kingdom. Here the emphasis is most often on the hiddenness of the kingdom. In the parables of the "secretly growing seed" (Mark 4:26–29), of the "tares" (Matt. 13:24–30), of the "mustard seed" (Matt. 13:31–32; Mark 4:30–32; and Luke 13:18–19), and of the "leaven" (Matt. 13:33), the idea is one of a hidden kingdom, not visible to normal observation, that will only become visible at the end when "the harvest has come."

Jesus' contemporaries often tended to reduce the Kingdom of God to a historical, manifestly concrete, and even political idea. Perhaps the best indication that Jesus himself did not so reduce the kingdom is the consistency with which he led his hearers *away* from a purely temporal expectation. Allow me to briefly note instances when the transcendent and non-historical ideas of the kingdom prevail over an imminent and time-bound notion:

1. According to a passage that shows up in virtually identical form in all three synoptic Gospels, Jesus himself brought the controversy concerning the relationship of the messiah to David into the open for a final time. In Matthew 22:41–46 we read:

   > Now while the Pharisees were gathered together, Jesus asked them this question: "What do you think of the Messiah? Whose son is he?" They said to him, "The son of David." He said to them, "How is it then that David by the Spirit calls Him Lord, saying, 'The Lord said to my Lord, "Sit at my right hand, until I put your enemies under your feet"'? "If David thus calls him Lord, how can he be his son?" No one was able to give him an answer, nor from that day did anyone dare to ask him any more questions.

Some scholars will prefer to say that this passage comes from an early tradition that denies the Davidic claim to the messianic office. The arguments against this idea are quite involved, but I think also conclusive. We might simply consider the fact that all three synoptic writers included this passage even when it might prove inimical to an important thesis (particularly Matthew's claim for Jesus' messianic role in the old Hebraic sense of the legitimate heir of David's covenant). Apart from this unlikely idea that Jesus was simply dissociating himself from the Davidic legacy, we are left with an example of Jesus' consistent appeal to a higher and more transcendent understanding of the kingdom.[4]

---

4. See, for instance, the comment by Sherman E. Johnson, *The Interpreters Bible*, ed. George H. Buttrick (New York: Abingdon-Cokesbury, 1951) vol. 7, 526.

2. In another encounter with Pharisees on the nature of the kingdom, Jesus makes a similar point. Luke writes: "Once Jesus was asked by the Pharisees when the kingdom of God was coming, and he answered, 'The kingdom of God is not coming with things that can be observed; nor will they say, 'Look, here it is!' or 'There it is!' For in fact, the kingdom of God is among you" (Luke 17:20–21).

    Obviously there is more than one way this passage can be interpreted. This is largely because "is among you" or "is in the midst of you" *(entos humon estin)* can be translated "is within you." Some interpretations would be especially gratifying to nineteenth century liberals (as we will see later); or to Hindus, who take this passage as evidence of Jesus' pantheism. These psychological interpretations are generally rejected today in favor of one more consistent with the whole tenor of Jesus' proclamation: That the Kingdom of God is "right at hand," "within your grasp." It has to do with relationship, not private religious attainment.

    Nevertheless, whether this passage is translated "within you" or "among you," it yet serves us with another example of Jesus' resistance to the idea that the kingdom is merely an event within history—or even an apocalyptic event at the end of history. It is neither present nor future exclusively. It is both.

3. If the Kingdom of God meant to Jesus' contemporaries at least a quasi-political reality, we can see that Jesus consistently rejected that for want of a here-and-now (or even an imminent) reality. We find this rejection in the parable of the last judgment (Matt. 24:31–46), in Jesus' rejection of a political role at Caesarea-Philippi (Matt. 16:21–23; Mark 8:31–33), and in the temptation accounts (Matt. 4:8–10; Luke 4:5–8). In John we see this rejection of a political kingship in connection with the feeding of the multitude (John 6:15). There is, in short, no lack of evidence that the Kingdom of God did not, in the teachings of Jesus and Paul, come to be reduced to an immanent eschatological expectation.

This understanding will be quite important, as we will see, in discriminating among the various eschatologies that have come to light through history, and especially in modern times.

Kingdom of God in the Early Church

We have seen, in our survey of the biblical sources, that the Kingdom of God can easily be understood in two ways. One way tends toward an eschatological interpretation: It is something that belongs to the end of history, or beyond the end of history. The other way tends toward a non-eschatological interpretation: Though it may become manifest at the end of history, it is essentially a constant, timeless reality. In this latter case, the Kingdom of God is essentially not affected by events in history.

It can be safely assumed that the earliest church fathers were not burdened by this distinction. To the extent that they spoke of the kingdom, they tended to regard it as a future reality. George Ladd even says that during the first two centuries, "The kingdom of God in the Church Fathers was exclusively eschatological." Surely this is exaggerated in view of the many comments by the church fathers on Jesus' parables of the kingdom in Matthew and Luke that clearly interpret the kingdom as a present reality. Ladd is undoubtedly correct, however, in suggesting that, inasmuch as they distinguished the kingdom from the present church, they thought of this kingdom as a future, yet-to-come, eschatological reality.[5] We have good reason to believe that the dominating thought of writers such as Justin Martyr, Irenaeus, and Tertullian was futuristic, even though none (except perhaps Tertullian in his Montanist phase) would deny the significant presence of the kingdom.

It was not until Origen (about 185–254) and Augustine (354–430) that any significant theological issue was made of the eschatological or non-eschatological nature of the Kingdom of God. In those two instances, there was a clear effort to emphasize the *presence of the kingdom*. Origen rejected a literal future kingdom as anything that could be

---

5. George Eldon Ladd, *Crucial Questions About the Kingdom of God* (Grand Rapids: Eerdmans, 1952), 22–23.

discussed with confidence. Origen thought believers should concern themselves with moral and spiritual meaning of the kingdom.

Augustine, on the other hand, found it necessary to argue against theories that simply equated history with divine providence. The critics of Christianity maintained that the general decline of civilization (signaled especially by Alaric's sack of Rome) proved that the growth of Christianity and the neglect of the pagan gods were the causes of their misfortune, or, at the least, sufficient argument against the truth of Christianity. Augustine thus distinguished between the City of God and the fallen temporal order of the world. That city that God has prepared—the Kingdom of God—will not be disclosed until the end of history, though it is even now intermingled with the ambiguities of history.

The Augustinian argument prevailed. While it is often falsely claimed that Augustine equated the Kingdom of God with the Catholic Church, that turned out to be the way Augustinian thought was practically understood. Thus, through much of the Medieval period, the doctrine of the kingdom was applied almost directly to the church.

The Reformation brought no decisive change from the Augustinian position, or from the medieval Roman Catholic use of that position. The kingdom was still more or less identified with the church. Only the Reformers made a firmer distinction between the church as a visible institution and as an invisible communion of saints.

Kingdom of God in Modern Theology

Albrecht Ritschl (1822–1889) was responsible for bringing the idea of the Kingdom of God back to the center of theological discussion. For him, the kingdom was not an eschatological reality, nor was it the church as an ecclesiastical system. Rather, it was love organizing humanity in ethical action. The Kingdom of God is realized by human beings striving to attain that which is their highest calling; and that is determined by the religious "value-judgment" of love as the highest value:

> In Christianity, the religious motive of ethical action lies here, that the Kingdom of God, which it is our task to realize, represents also the highest good which God

destines for us. . . . For here there emerges the value-judgment that our blessedness consists in that elevation above the world in the Kingdom of God which accords with our true destiny.[6]

The eschatological aspect of the kingdom is replaced in Ritschl's thought by what might be described as its teleological character—that is, it is goal-oriented. Divine love is not simply a feeling of affection toward humanity, the object of love, but a Divine Will for the development of humanity in moral fellowship.[7] Thus, "love continually strives to develop and to appropriate the individual self-end of the other personality."[8]

Adolf Von Harnack was another great exponent of late-nineteenth-century liberal theology. While Harnack did not entirely reject the idea of the kingdom as something eschatological, he nonetheless emphasized—as if it were the greater part of that reality—that the kingdom is an interior, individual state in which one is connected with the power of God. By healing, and especially by forgiving sins, Jesus brings into being the Kingdom of God. "This is the first complete transition" from the idea of the kingdom as an outward thing experienced by the community in some historical sense, "to the conception of the kingdom of God as the power that works inwardly."[9]

According to Harnack, Christianity, thus conceived, "is superior to all antithesis and tension between this world and a world to come."[10] It is therefore decidedly non-eschatological in its highest and best expression, according to Harnack.

Of course, the problem here is that, by Harnack's interpretation, we are tempted to make the Kingdom of God a private affair. It is appropriated individually, experienced more on the private than the community level. It should, as

6. Albrecht Ritschl, *The Christian Doctrine of Justification and Reconciliation*, trans. by M. R. Macintosh and A. B. Macaulay (Edinburgh: T & T Clark, 1900), 205–206.

7. Ibid., 277–278.

8. Ibid., 278.

9. Adolf Harnack, *What is Christianity?* trans. Thomas Bailey Saunders (New York: Harper & Row, 1957), 60.

10. Ibid., 63.

Harnack describes it, have a good effect on the community, but the supreme arbiter of this judgment becomes the individual. This fact shows us one of the important elements of an *eschatological* hope. It gives expression to a destiny as a hope that belongs to people in community. In a sense it belongs to all of humankind. The loss of the eschatological reality of Christian hope is apt to be accompanied by the privatization of religion and the rise of a religion that no longer speaks strongly to humankind in community. That is what happened to the liberalism of this earlier generation.

Further, some scholars, as we see next, saw this interpretation as one that stood in conflict with the spirit of expectation so evident in the Gospels.

Consistent Eschatology. Before the end of the nineteenth century, certain students of the New Testament were calling attention to what should have been quite evident: Jesus, Paul, and the early church actually expected the end of the age. Whether that was to be soon or late or at an indeterminate time is not the point here; discussion over those points has continued for a long time. But clearly Jesus and his disciples were not talking about psychology; they were talking about cosmology. Something would happen to the world, not just to human consciousness.

This last point moved Johannes Weiss, and later Albert Schweitzer, to re-examine the eschatology of Jesus and the early church. Weiss and Schweitzer concluded that Jesus expected the apocalyptic arrival of the Kingdom of God in his own lifetime. This intense expectation colored all of his teachings and that animated Paul and the early church. Apart from this hope, one simply could not understand the New Testament.

Consistent eschatology, expanded and expressed by Schweitzer, includes four main features:

1. *Liberal critical theology mistakenly denied Jesus' attachment to Jewish apocalypticism.* Liberal critics reinterpreted the synoptics with the intent of expurgating the influence of Jewish apocalypticism, which they believed asserted itself in the early church after the death of Jesus but was not authentic to Jesus' teachings.

2. *This denial of apocalypticism also caused liberal critics to deny significant parts of the synoptics.* Schweitzer called attention to Wilhelm Weiffenbach's (b. 1842) denial of the apocalyptic in Jesus' sayings: "In the end Weiffenbach's critical principle proves to be merely a bludgeon with which he goes seal-hunting and clubs the defenseless synoptic sayings right and left. When his work is done you see before you a desert island strewn with quivering corpses."[11] This led to a clear insight, through various stages, by Weiss, that Jesus' teachings were *consistently* eschatological. Thus the "general conception of the Kingdom was first rightly grasped by Johannes Weiss . . . [and] we arrive at a Kingdom of God which is wholly future."[12] As a consequence, any true understanding of Jesus' life must acknowledge that Jesus did not establish the Kingdom of God; he only proclaimed it.

3. *The "liberal" Jesus was a world-affirming spirit that is now denied by the world-negating spirit of the true historical Jesus of apocalyptic Judaism.* Jesus' vision of an apocalyptic end of this world, and a dawning Kingdom of God, makes of this world a "lost region" soon to end in catastrophic judgment. In contrast, the liberals' Jesus appears domesticated, at home in the world of nineteenth-century optimism and progress. The two ideas of Jesus, Schweitzer said, could not be reconciled.

4. *Finally, however, the liberals ignored the evidence that the consistently eschatological outlook of Jesus became an embarrassment to the early church.* With the passing of time, the events of Jesus' life grew distant, with still no sign of the parousia. Therefore, the attempt to adjust to the conditions of ongoing history played a large part in shaping the character of Christianity. Nineteenth-century liberals had wanted to believe what was a later "adjustment" in the

---

11. Albert Schweitzer, *The Quest of the Historical Jesus* (New York: Macmillan, 1971), 232.
12. Ibid., 231.

teachings of Jesus instead of the (clearly more original) apocalypticism.

The principal objection to Schweitzer's line of thought has been predictable. Just as there is massive evidence in the synoptics that Jesus spoke the language and to an extent shared the vision of Jewish apocalypticism, there are likewise unavoidable indications that he reacted critically to that same apocalypticism. Also, it is difficult to get around the stream of teachings that affirm the presence of the kingdom as something to announce, not simply the future of the kingdom as an anticipation.

Reaction to Consistent Eschatology. It is apparent, of course, that if Jesus absolutely based his teachings upon an anticipation of the imminent and visible arrival of the kingdom, then they were based upon a mistaken calculation. Such a view would have some serious consequences in the interpretation of Scripture.

From the beginning, however, there were critical questions about this new interpretation that were not easily settled. Weiss, for instance, had launched into a reinterpretation of some of Jesus' teachings, especially those that stressed the presence of the kingdom. His reinterpretation appeared quite strained under close examination. Some critics, such as H. B. Sharman[13] and F. C. Grant,[14] came to conclusions quite opposite of those of Weiss and Schweitzer while seeing the same evidence. They concluded that it was the personal and present element of the kingdom that was essential to Jesus' teachings, while the apocalyptic emphasis was a later emphasis of the early, persecuted church.

In recent times Ben Witherington III has made a summary of the most telling arguments against the position of consistent eschatology. For instance, he points out that Schweitzer has attempted to reconstruct the whole of Jesus' attitude toward the end of the age on the basis of one verse, Matthew 10:23. "Largely on the basis of this text alone Schweitzer urged that Jesus expected the parousia of the

---

13. *The Teaching of Jesus About the Future* (Chicago: Univ. Press, 1909).
14. *The Gospel of the Kingdom* (New York: Macmillan, 1940).

Son of man . . . before his disciples had completed their preaching tour of Galilee."[15]

Another telling consideration is the prominence of Jesus' teachings that he did not know the day of the return of the Son of Man (Mark 13:32 and parallels). "Since it is not likely," Witherington said, "that the early church would invent a saying predicating Jesus' ignorance of such a vital matter, we must give this saying its full weight."[16]

Despite these objections, consistent eschatology (or "thoroughgoing eschatology") had important consequences for much of twentieth-century-theology biblical studies. Many commentaries and studies of the New Testament *kerygma* found a new point of departure in consistent eschatology.

Realized eschatology. The eschatology of C. H. Dodd put greater weight upon this obvious objection that Jesus' teachings are alive with the excitement that something is now present, and can be entered into: "The eschaton has moved from the future to the present, from the sphere of expectation into that of realized experience."[17] The teachings of Jesus were, according to this view, really non-eschatological. Jesus spoke of an unrealized transcendence now realized in him, his ministry, and his teaching. The apocalyptic element, so similar to Jewish first-century apocalypticism, was to be taken symbolically. In the course of time this rich symbolism of transcendent reality hardened into a literal interpretation. It became, as such, foreign to the spirit of Jesus' pressing people into a present realization of the kingdom.

Realized eschatology takes seriously the eschatological sayings of Jesus and the New Testament writers, yet it maintains that these sayings give way to a greater non-literal and non-eschatological reality. At the same time, we are bound to see that something of the eschatological tension and anticipation, evident in the New Testament itself, is lost through the reinterpretation of realized eschatology. The sense of expectation inevitably collapses into a sense of

---

15. Ben Witherington III, *Jesus, Paul and the End of the World* (Downers Grove: InterVarsity Press, 1992), 39.

16. Ibid., 36.

17. C. H. Dodd, *The Parables of the Kingdom* (London: Nisbet, 1935), 50.

indifference with regard to the future, and ultimately into hopelessness.

Dispensationalism. An interpretation of the kingdom doctrine, called **"dispensationalism,"** has found favor in only a few circles in higher education; yet it has been quite popular throughout the twentieth century. Stemming from a movement among British Plymouth Brethren that spread to the United States, it had been associated in Britain with J. N. Darby (1800–1882) and among American evangelicals with R. A. Torrey, C. I. Scofield, and H. A. Ironside. It was popularized broadly by the best-selling *Scofield Reference Bible 1909.* (Dale Moody, the Southern Baptist theologian, once joked that as a youth he thought even the notes of Scofield were inspired.)

Several notable evangelical institutions have also been influential proponents of dispensationalism. Foremost among them is Dallas Theological Seminary in Texas. The founding president, Lewis Sperry Chafer, wrote what has proven to be the most influential work of this movement. His multi-volume *Systematic Theology* is a sustained effort to reinterpret all the doctrines of orthodox Christianity in light of a dispensational eschatology.

In recent years, a number of able exponents of dispensationalism have seen their interpretation cut a wide swath in popular American theology. Among these are the scholar Charles Ryrie, whose *Ryrie Study Bible* and many books defending and defining dispensational thought have become standard texts for the dispensational ideas; and Hal Lindsay, the popularizer, whose *Late Great Planet Earth* has, at last count, exceeded five million in print.

The dispensational interpretation of the kingdom usually includes the following points:

1. The Kingdom of God is distinct from the Kingdom of heaven. The former is the reign of God over heaven and earth at all times. The latter is the manifestation of God's reign on earth.
2. The kingdom has manifested itself in various ways, or "dispensations," from the beginning of time. Each dispensation has met with rejection or failure on the part of sinful people, giving rise to a new dispensation.

3. The manifestations of the kingdom have included the following:

   (a) The theocracy of the judges, in which God ruled Israel directly through anointed figures.

   (b) God established the kingdom with the house of David in an irrevocable covenant (2 Sam. 7).

   (c) The kingdom announced by John the Baptist and Jesus constituted a literal and historical offer to Israel of an earthly kingdom. Israel's rejection of the King, however, *delayed,* but did not cancel, the offer of the kingdom.

   (d) The kingdom is thus postponed until the parousia.

   (e) The Kingdom of God, from the rejection of Israel's king to the establishment of a millennial kingdom, entered the realm of mystery, and remains hidden in the present age.

   (f) The secret rapture of all Christians will rescue them from the wrath of the Great Tribulation and will prepare the way for the establishment of the kingdom.

   (g) A Jewish remnant of 144,000 now recognizes the true kingship of Christ, and they announce the coming of the Davidic kingdom, or the Kingdom of heaven.

   (h) The ultimate manifestation of the kingdom will be inaugurated at Christ's glorious return and his reign over a millennium of peace and justice.

These are the main features of dispensationlism as they relate to the Kingdom of God. We will take note of other characteristics when we look at the issues related to the parousia.

The Eschatological Theologians. In the mid-1960s a number of theologians began to wrestle with the implications of eschatology as it had been approached in the twentieth century. Foremost among these were two German theologians, Jürgen Moltmann and Wolfhart Pannenberg.

Moltmann could agree with Karl Barth's early statement that "Christianity that is not absolutely and unreservedly eschatological, has absolutely nothing to do with Christ."[18]

To interpret the Bible in any consistent manner, one must give due weight to the eschatological orientation at its center.

Twentieth-century theology, however, had so far avoided the implications of eschatology. Karl Barth, for instance, had reinterpreted eschatology to mean that God's eternal transcendence is revealed in time. Nothing really changes for Barth, but what is forever true becomes manifest to us. This, claims Moltmann, is an evasion of the biblical eschatology that depicts God himself struggling in the present and passionately anticipating the future. The reality of God is revealed only in his eschatological future.

Similarly, with regard to another great mid-twentieth-century figure, Rudolf Bultmann, Moltmann is critical of any evasion of eschatology that reinterprets Christian hope as the eternity of the existential present. The "eternal now" of Bultmann, argued Moltmann, collapses the gospel into private experience. In *History and Eschatology*, for instance, Bultmann admonishes, "Man who complains: 'I cannot see meaning in history and therefore, my life, interwoven in history, is meaningless', is to be admonished: do not look around yourself into universal history, you must look into your own personal history. Always in your present lies the meaning in history and you cannot see it as a spectator, but only in your responsible decisions. In every moment slumbers the possibility of being the eschatological moment. You must awaken it."[19]

So, in Barth's approach Moltmann found, instead of the strong eschatological emphasis of the Bible, the revealing of cosmic *status quo*. In Bultmann, Moltman found a privatized revision of eschatology that made the history of the community meaningless. In opposition to both of these reinterpretations or evasions of biblical eschatology, Moltmann proposed a number of observations about the eschatological nature of biblical thought:

1. By virtue of its attachment to the idea of promise and fulfillment, the Hebrew prophetic movement

---

18. Karl Barth, *Romerbrief,* 2nd ed. (Munich, 1922) 298; ref. Romans 8:24.

19. Rudolf Bultmann, *History and Eschatology* (Edinburgh: University Edinburgh Press, 1957).

thought of God and the world historically. That is, reality is rooted in the future, ultimately in the eschatological future of the world.

2. Since God discloses himself in terms of *promise*, one has reason to see the transcendence of God, not in terms of an above and below (i.e., spatially), but in terms of the transcendent future (i.e., temporally).

3. The nature of God is ultimately disclosed in terms of the eschaton, the last things. Moltmann refers, for instance, to epiphany in Exodus 3, which can be translated "I will be, whom I will be."

4. The context of the promised future, however, is the present and its suffering and longing: its passion. Thus the resurrection, which points to the general resurrection of the dead in the future, is meaningful only because it is the resurrection of the crucified one. Thus, the promise is not an abstract wish, but relates to the concrete experience of the present and past.

5. Christianity is thus *messianic* in its orientation. It brings a vision of the future—a future of justice and peace—into the present with its injustice, alienation, and suffering. Its mission springs from holding this vision in the midst of this experience; it is a mission arising from the presence and power of the Holy Spirit.[20]

Pannenberg, also described as an eschatological theologian, nevertheless has an approach quite distinct from Moltmann. On the surface, one might say that Moltmann is more concerned with the problem of biblical interpretation, and Pannenberg more concerned with the philosophical problems that theology addresses.

Pannenberg's efforts are aimed against what he perceives as a widespread privatization of religion and of subjectivism in theology. Theology's reaction to the Enlightenment, with its scientific and historical doubts

---

20. These points summarize Moltmann's eschatology in *Theology of Hope*, trans. James W. Leitch (New York: Harper & Row, 1967); *The Crucified God,* trans. R. A. Wilson and John Bowden (London: SCM Press, 1974); and *The Church in the Power of the Spirit,* trans. Margaret Kohl (New York: Harper & Row, 1977). See also A. J. Conyers, *God, Hope and History* (Macon, Ga: Mercer Univ. Press, 1988).

about the Bible, was generally to retreat into the realm of private experience as a safe haven from the assaults on Christian foundations that were formerly thought to be rooted in factual history. Pannenberg sees this retreat to existential reinterpretation or to "conservative pietism" as throwing out the true intellectual resources of Christian faith. As one recent interpreter stated the matter, Pannenberg counsels instead, "an attempt to place Christian faith on firm intellectual footing once again, and thereby to provide an alternative to the subjectivist approach of much modern theology."[21]

This theology focuses on the Kingdom of God as the ultimate (and therefore eschatological) disclosure of truth. Very briefly stated, the features of Pannenberg's eschatological theology include the following:

1. All truth is provisional and partial until the fulfillment of truth in the eschaton. Therefore historical truth is not simply what happened in the past; but what happened can only be fully understood in terms of its future, and utlimately in terms of the coming Kingdom of God. In this way the future is "interwoven" with the presnt and past.[22]

2. The end of history impacts all that has happened before: it marks the fate or the goal of all things. Thus eschatological truth is the only universal truth.

3. The universal disclosure of the "deity of God" takes place first in the resurrection of Jesus. This is a proleptic revelation of the goal of history and is thus universal truth.[23]

4. The proper point of departure for understanding Christian virtue, Christian ethics, and providence is thus the universal proclamation of the Kingdom of God. The anticipation of the kingdom is inextricably tied to the love of God and neighbor, faith in God, and the hope that God's good will prevail.

---

21. Stanley J. Grenz and Roger E. Olson, *20th Century Theology* (Downers Grove: InterVarsity Press, 1992), 189.

22. Wolfhart Pannenberg, Theology and the Kingdom of God (Philadelphia: Westminster Press, 1977), 53–58.

23. *Revelation as History*, ed. Wolfhart Pannenberg (London: Macmillan, 1968), 139–45.

From the foregoing discussion we can see that, as we have approached the end of the second millennium, the eschatology of God's kingdom has come increasingly to the forefront of theological attention. While there are many points that distinguish "consistent eschatology" from "realized eschatology" and then again from the messianic eschatology of Moltmann or the revelatory eschatology of Pannenberg, there are a number of broad agreements that shine through this continued theological conversation.

First, the Kingdom of God and its expectation were central to the teaching and ministry of Jesus.

Second, the death and resurrection of Jesus—as these influenced the rise of Christianity—can only be properly understood against the background of eschatological expectations.

Third, whether Jesus, Paul, and others did or did not anticipate the imminent inbreaking of the eschaton, most recent interpreters conclude they were acutely aware of the dynamic impact of the future, and the end of all things, upon the present and past. So, the anticipation of God's Kingdom is in no sense an isolated future, but is intertwined with the truth of the world as we experience it.

Finally, the mission of the church and the vocation of each Christian can only be fully understood in light of God's purposes in universal history, and thus in light of eschatology.

Interpreting the *Parousia* and the Millennium

After the controversies and problems of interpretation surrounding the Kingdom of God, the area most problematic for Christians concerns the meaning of the *parousia* and the possibility of a future millennial reign of Christ. It is rather interesting—and perhaps significant—that these problems rise out of such thin exegetical and textual material. They concern whether Christ's return will occur (1) after a period (millennium) of Christ's spiritual reign in the world, (2) before a millennium of literal earthly reign, (3) after the present reign of Christ between his first and second coming, symbolized by the millennium, or (4) after a series of events that lead in quick succession to the literal reign of Christ for a thousand years.

Notice that all of these interpretations make some reference to the millennium, a thousand-year period of (symbolic/literal/spiritual) reign of Christ mentioned only once in all the New Testament (Rev. 20:1–15). It would almost seem that a disproportionate amount of attention is given to such narrow textual concerns. At the heart of the issue, however, is the very broad question of whether (1) there is something else to expect within history, (2) history will come to a sudden end, or (3) history is moving progressively toward that end. Let's look at each of the most common interpretations of the millennium and the *parousia.*

Premillennialism. The classical statement of the premillennial eschatology can be found among some of the earliest interpreters of the Christian hope: Papias, Justin Martyr, Irenaeus, and Tertullian.[24] Generally the proponents of this view hold that at his return (parousia) Christ will establish an earthly kingdom that will endure for a thousand years. This return of Christ is preceded by a period of intense struggle identified as the Great Tribulation. It is accompanied by the defeat of Satan, his binding so that he no longer deceives the nations, and the resurrection of the dead in Christ along with the gathering of all saints from the living and the dead (cf. Matt. 24; Mark 13; 1 Thess. 4, 2; Thess. 2; and Rev. 20).

The ensuing period of the millennium (not *always* taken as a literal thousand years by premillennialists) will take place as Christ reigns visibly on earth over a world of unprecedented peace and justice. At the end of this period, Satan is released from his bondage, allowing him to oppose Christ; he is defeated and cast into a lake of fire (Rev. 20). Then takes place the great judgment of the living and the dead, and Christ yields up the Kingdom to God the Father, and God becomes all and in all.

---

24. Papias' views are found in Irenaeus' *Adv. Haer., V,* 33); Justin Martyr in *Dial. LXXX*; Irenaeus in *Adv. Haer. V,* 33–35; and Tertullian in *De res. carn. XXV, Adv. Marcion, III,* 25.

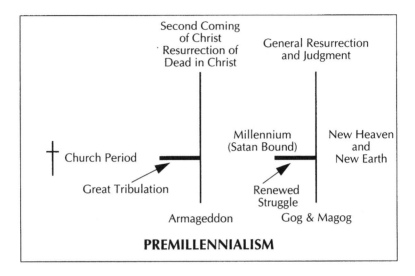

Foremost modern exemplars of this interpretation include Dale Moody and George Eldon Ladd.[25]

Postmillennialism. For postmillennialists, the thousand years of Revelation 20 refer to a future era that emerges out of the world-transforming influence of the gospel. Unlike the premillennialist view, the thousand-year reign of Christ is (1) invisible, but spiritual, and (2) not the result of a cataclysmic break in history, but the gradual, almost imperceptible changes in a society permeated by the gospel. It is called postmillennialism because the *parousia* occurs at the end of the millennium. The "great tribulation" of Matthew 24 and the "little season" of Revelation 20—both struggles with Satan—are one and the same (not separate struggles as in premillennialism). This struggle is to occur at the end of the millennial period, just before the *parousia.*

The *parousia* draws to an end both the millennial age and the history of this earth. With the *parousia* comes the resurrection of the dead, the judgment of the living and the dead, and the new heaven and new earth.

Major proponents of postmillennial eschatology include Charles Hodge and Loraine Boettner.

---

25. See Dale Moody, *The Hope of Glory* (Grand Rapids: Eerdmans, 1964); and George Eldon Ladd, *The Presense of the Future* (Grand Rapids: Eerdmans, 1974).

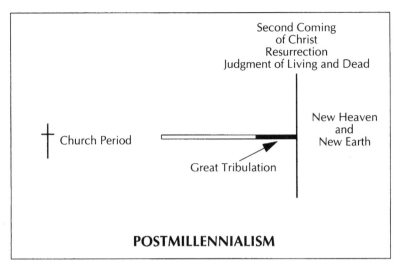

POSTMILLENNIALISM

Amillennialism. The eschatological position that has undoubtedly the broadest acceptance in the church is the amillennial view. In this view, the thousand years of Revelation 20 is to be taken figuratively, not literally. Furthermore, it represents not a future age (as in both premillennialism and postmillennialism), but the age in which we now live. The binding of Satan mentioned in Revelation 20:1–6 refers to the victory over Satan that took place with the first coming of Christ. It was the point at which Satan no longer could have his will with the "nations," so that they were no longer deceived, but were drawn to God through Christ.

As Anthony Hoekema pointed out, this defeat and casting out of Satan can be understood in the sense of John 12:31–32: "Now is the time for judgment on this world; now the prince of this world will be driven out. But I, when I am lifted up from the earth, will draw all men to myself " (NIV).[26]

The millennium, therefore, embraces the time from the first coming of Christ down to the *parousia.* This will bring to an end the last desperate attempt of Satan to resist God's kingdom (the tribulation of Matthew 24 and the little season of Revelation 20), and will bring in its train the resurrection of the dead, the judgment of the living and the dead, and the new creation.

26. See Hoekema's contribution to *The Meaning of the Millennium,* ed. Robert G. Clouse (Downers Grove: InterVarsity Press, 1977), 159–172.

Proponents of this interpretation include Augustine of Hippo, Thomas Aquinas, Martin Luther, John Calvin, Louis Berkhof, G. C. Berkouwer, Geerhardus Vos and many others.

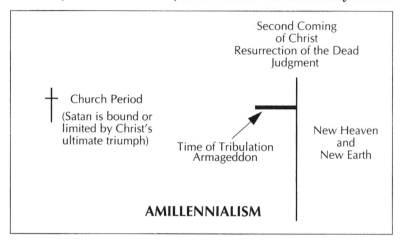

Dispensational Premillennialism. This interpretation shares the major features of classic or historic premillennialism with the following exception. It anticipates that the return of Christ and the resurrection of the dead take place in stages. First will be the secret, or hidden, rapture of the church from the world (1 Thess. 4) either before or during the time of Great Tribulation, followed by the inauguration of the millennial kingdom.

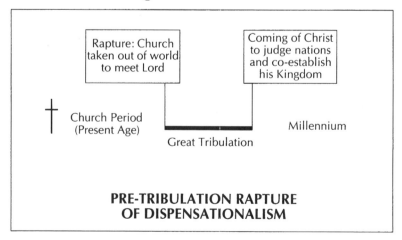

The great divide among all of these interpretations has to do with the expectation of a literal, future millennium. This expectation has long been known as *chiliasm,* from the Greek term for thousand. The chiliastic interpretations, historic premillennialism and dispensationalism, have been criticized for being too literalistic. The non-chiliastic systems, amillennialism and postmillennialism, have seemed unsatisfactory to some because of a tendency to affirm the *status quo* (since we are either in the millennium or moving inexorably toward that final state) and to expect nothing altogether new to occur in history.

Some students of the history of religious movements, such as Norman Cohn in his famous study on chiliastic movements, *The Pursuit of the Millennium,* have seen these expectations of a literal new age in history as profoundly disordering, giving rise to every variety of fanaticism—even turning into quite secular schemes of revolution, providing an excuse for violence, genocide, armed dictatorships, and discouraging the kind of civilizing thought that attempts to establish a basis for lasting social life.[27]

Others, such as Jürgen Moltmann, argue that Augustinian amillennialism takes the messianic hope out of the Christian message. Anticipating nothing new within history, it tacitly gives sanction to whatever authority exists. It is the triumph of a Constantinian Christianity that uses the Christian gospel as a theological affirmation of the political regime. Messianic hopes may be disordering, but that is because they are powerful and transforming. They are supposed to be.

It is not likely that theologians will come to an easy consensus on these issues before the eschaton itself. In the meantime, however, it is important to remember the features of Christian eschatology that are not generally at issue, and that unite any and all authentic Christian prospectives. These include the expectation that (1) God's work of redemption is not complete, but awaits a time of fulfillment; (2) that fulfillment will come as a result of God's grace, not human design; and (3) the influences of evil will come to an end, but the goodness of God, never.

---

27. See Norman Cohn, *The Pursuit of the Millennium* (New York: Oxford, 1970).

Questions for Review and Reflection

1. What are some of the Old Testament sources for the idea of the Kingdom of God?
2. What is the significance of the term "Kingdom of heaven"?
3. Compare and contrast consistent eschatology and realized eschatology.
4. Constrast the distinct eschatological expectations of premillennialism, postmillennialism, amillennialism, and dispensational premillennialism.
5. Summarize the arguments against chiliastic interpretations of eschatology.
6. Summarize the arguments against the non-chiliastic interpretations of Christian eschatology.
7. What part does the element of hope play in any interpretation of the Christian gospel?
8. In what way did the approach of eschatological theologians such as Jürgen Moltmann confront the problem of the privatization of religion? Why do you think Moltmann saw this privatization as a problem?

CHAPTER TWELVE

THEOLOGY, THE KINGDOM AND THE CHURCH

Dorothy Sayers once made the case for Christian theology, or "dogma," protesting the charge that matters like the Trinity and the Incarnation are irrelevant to the lives of rank and file church members. While defending the idea of dogma, she did not spare the clergy who, she rightly assumed, had been charged with the responsibility of passing on that doctrine of the church in some vital and understandable form. Instead, she found the ministry of the church in steady retreat in the face of the notion that doctrine is "irrelevant." "It is not true at all that dogma is 'hopelessly irrelevant' to the life and thought of the average man," she wrote. She then continued:

> What is true is that ministers of the Christian religion often assert that it is, present it for consideration as if it were, and, in fact, by their faulty exposition of it make it so. The central dogma of the Incarnation is that by which relevance stands or falls. If Christ was only man, then He is entirely irrelevant to any thought about God; if He is only God, then He is entirely irrelevant to any experience of human life. It is, in the strict-

231

est sense, *necessary* to the salvation of relevance that a
man should believe *rightly* the Incarnation of Our Lord
Jesus Christ. Unless he believes rightly, there is not
the faintest reason why he should believe at all. And in
that case, it is wholly irrelevant to chatter about
"Christian principles."[1]

The Value of Theology

Nevertheless, especially among people today who have a
practical cast of mind, we frequently hear the complaint of
having trouble seeing the connection between theologically
precise teaching and the struggles and aspirations of the
people who sit in church pews on Sunday morning, or who
are affected by the ministry of Christians. If this "ivory tower" approach to Christianity is a witness, some think, then
it is a highly esoteric form of Christian witness that reaches
only an intellectual elite.

This misconception of theology is perhaps widespread, especially in places like North America where the frontier
spirit often disparaged an overly learned "Eastern seaboard
and European" style that substituted intellectual refinement for authentic and "heart-felt" religion. The sense that
intellectualism can be a poor substitute for Christian reality, and that an overly developed estimate of one's intellectual competence can detract from the believer's full reliance
upon God, is a warning that we can at least say has some
merit. This broad indictment of anything that approaches
theology is false, however. I think we have had a glimpse, in
the chapters on the Trinity and the Person of Christ, how
even the most intellectually demanding of the topics and
questions in theology were born of a basic pastoral concern.

It is not that everyone in the church would deal with
these questions on the same level as that of a Gregory of
Nyssa or a Thomas Aquinas. But if the great theologians
can mark out the basic truth of revelation, using skillfully
the instrument of human reason, the result will be faithful
guidance in the life, work, worship, and prayer of Chris-

---

1. Dorothy Sayers, *Creed or Chaos* (New York: Harcourt Brace and
Company, 1949), 32.

tians. If those upon whom the great numbers of Christians rely to do this work fail in their efforts, (if they choose to emphasize the two natures of Christ, for instance, and fail to emphasize the unity of his person), then Christians at large are left with a concept of Christ that hardly relates to their own struggles as human beings. They fail to recognize the struggle that God himself underwent in order to be one with us. On the other hand, if theologians had not also fought the battle of the two natures (against Eutycheanism), they would have left Christians without the confidence that their salvation and hope is assured precisely because it is God who entered into the human condition.

Nevertheless, there remains this common prejudice that theology has no pastoral or practical relevance to the daily experience of Christians and others. This point of view doesn't surface in just one form; instead, it assails theology from several directions, questioning in each case the necessity of theology for the church. I would like to deal briefly, in this last chapter, with some of those objections to the real necessity of theology.

Objection # 1. Theology deals with such minute refinements in dogmatic language that it can hardly be understood, much less will it be of practical interest to most people.

If the story were better known, this objection might be followed with a historical allusion to the early Christian debate over whether the nature of the Son should be expressed as *homoousias* (of the same substance) with the Father, or *homoiousias* (of like substance). The debate involved two words whose only difference was an *iota*. This ancient theological debate comes down to us in the common saying, "It doesn't make an iota of difference."

No one can deny that a Christian who wants to say one person of the Trinity is of "like substance" with the other, and one who wants to say "same substance," may only be arguing over a theological split hair that apparently makes no real difference in how they pray, how they live, and how they witness. It seems that in every important way the two definitions are very close to one another. So why argue over such minuscule matters?

We are fortunate that many of the most influential early Christian thinkers, however, were very sensitive to these minutia. We might compare what they did to an ocean liner setting its course for a trans-Atlantic voyage. The navigator will be very particular that he is not even a tenth of a degree off-course. At first such fussiness over the precise course setting would make little difference; but half way through the voyage that tenth of a degree would make a difference of several hundred miles—the difference of ending up in Iceland instead of France!

B. B. Warfield once lamented the state of imprecision in modern theology and in the church as a whole. In calling to mind the original intention of the Christian thinkers who first formulated these doctrines, he recalled an extended comment made by a French theologian, Auguste Sabatier. Sabatier stated the case admirably:

> The promulgation of each dogma has been imposed on the Church by some practical necessity. It has always been to bring to an end some theological controversy which was in danger of provoking schism, to respond to attacks or accusations which it would have been dangerous to permit to acquire credit, that the Church has moved in a dogmatic way. . . . Nothing is more mistaken than to represent the Fathers of the Councils, or the members of the Synods as theoreticians, or even as professional theologians, brought together in conference by speculative zeal alone, in order to resolve metaphysical enigmas. They were men of action, not of speculation; courageous priests and pastors who understood their mission, like soldiers in open battle, and whose first care was to save their Church, its life, its unity, its honor—ready to die for it as one dies for his country.[2]

Objection # 2. God could not possibly be impressed with even the most skillful theology—so much lower is our intellect compared with his—so if God judges a Christian life on the basis of how precisely that life reflects the truth of theological dogma, then we are all bound for a derailment by virtue of the puniness and ineptness of any human effort.

---

2. Cited in B. B. Warfield, "The Idea of Systematic Theology" in *The Necessity of Systematic Theology,* ed. John Jefferson Davis (Grand Rapids: Baker Book House, 1978), 159.

It is undoubtedly true, as the best theologians have always admitted, that even our most heroic efforts and our most strenuous intellectual labors, fall miserably short of the goal when we set out to speak clearly and accurately concerning the things of God. Paul confessed that "now we see through a glass darkly." Mystical experience caused Thomas Aquinas to call a halt to his theological writings, saying, "All I have written seems to me like so much straw compared with what I have seen and with what has been revealed to me."[3] Indeed, the truest and best of theologians are humbled by the very experience of attempting to speak of God. Martin Luther wondered at the depth of the mysterious cross of Christ, saying that, "Since God is true and one, he is utterly incomprehensible and inaccessible to human reason."[4] Yet Luther wrote volumes and transformed Europe in an effort to speak a truth about God.

To engage in theology, however, is not to amuse ourselves with the idea that our thinking approaches that of God's. Instead, it is to recognize that God has taken into consideration our frailties. He has condescended to speak to us in ways we can understand: it is not pride or hubris, but humility, that should prompt us to think about God in any way we can, all the while realizing that our efforts must look altogether ridiculous in the councils of heaven. Nevertheless, our thoughts are lifted toward God in this craft of theology, and in this endeavor as well as any other we must make the effort (if not the result) worthy of the goal.

Objection # 3. Our response to God's revelation should be practical obedience, not empty speculation on the things of God.

It should not be surprising that some of the greatest Christian theologians have made this same objection. However, they would make a distinction between "empty speculation," that might include attempts to describe the physical properties of heaven or hell, or to answer the question, "What was God doing before he created heaven and earth?" To that latter question, both Augustine and Luther made

3. F. C. Copleston, *Aquinas* (London: Penguin Books, 1955), 10.
4. Roland Bainton, *Here I Stand: A Life of Martin Luther* (Nashville: Abingdon, 1950), 255.

half-serious allusions to the cynical answer that God was making a hell for people who asked foolish questions!

How do we distinguish between empty speculation and matters that are legitimate topics of Christian theology? The answer to that question includes, at a minimum, the recognition that *all* legitimate theological inquiry has a bearing upon human behavior. The connection might, at times, seem remote, as in the ancient attempts to precisely formulate a doctrine of the Trinity. But we will find consistently that the church's legitimate concern about heresy had to do with the pastoral problem of training Christians in living as Christians.

In the case of the Trinity, for instance, it makes an enormous difference eventually in our behavior and in our prayer life if we understand that reality itself, and the nature of God, are essentially relational. If we were to see God in a different way, and reject the idea of the Trinity for an idea of God as a great Monadic Power (a supernatural "Number One") whose every whim becomes a cosmic edict, and who resembles nothing so much as an Oriental despot, brushing aside the wishes of his subjects or granting them with the same degree of arbitrary and gratuitous "divine will;" then we have indeed found ourselves with a very different God. And such a realization might well call for correspondingly different behavior. It certainly is likely to influence the way I relate to my neighbor, who might as well expect my actions toward him to reflect no more of the give and take of personal interaction between two mutually sympathetic pilgrims than I imagine my God to show toward me. I become, in a sense, what I worship.

But, on the other hand, if I believe that God is somehow essentially relational, that relatedness is at the very center of his being, I might respond in a very different way. If I believe, as John said, that "God is love" (1 John 4:8), and if I believe on the basis of his essential relatedness and the inter-penetration of the Father, Son, and Holy Spirit, that this is the nature of God, then I might discover that there is every reason to treat my neighbor in a way that reflects that reality.

■ ──────────────────────── ■

THE PRAGMATICS OF THEOLOGY

"People outside of seminary raise issues that [scholars] Kant and Barth discussed, even if they do not recognize them as Kant's and Barth's issues."

"To say that [studying] theology is not practical is a contradiction. Any time you explain why a person should do something like 'love your neighbor' you make a theological statement."

[Seminarians Mark Lewis and Ben Gilder, quoted in a *Christianity Today* news article: October 24, 1994 (p. 76).]

I do not endeavor, O Lord, to penetrate thy sublimity, for in no wise do I compare my understanding with that; but I long to understand in some degree thy truth, which my heart believes and loves. For I do not seek to understand that I may believe, but I believe in order to understand. For this also I believe—that unless I believed, I should not understand.

[St. Anselm, *Proslogium,* trans. Sidney Norton Deane (New York: Open Court, 1903), 1–2.]

■ ──────────────────────── ■

Let's take another example from the realm of Christology. Many early Christians doubtless thought it quite harmless that some among them insisted that Jesus was not altogether human, and that these Christians refused to admit that Jesus had the same struggles with the flesh as any human being would. It was a fine point, they thought, and in either case Christians were saying that Jesus is the Son of God and that he was without sin. So why quibble over the precise degree of humanity in Christ, and why insist that he was just as bound to human flesh and human passions as the rest of us?

Well, those thinkers who could see further down the road of human behavior than most knew that such a discrete point of doctrine would make an enormous difference in the long run. If the flesh itself is the source of evil, then God has so constructed us that we could not help but sin and we could not be fully responsible in that case for our actions. If Christ is not subject to the same temptations of human existence as we are, then he could hardly serve as an example of human obedience. Nothing is left of hope, and nothing motivates us to follow Christ, if he is so constituted that he lives in a way we could not possibly emulate.

Theology that is truly a lasting legacy of the church has always contributed to the belief, worship, and obedience of Christians. It should always have a bearing on the Christian's wonder and love of God and love of neighbor. Theology should result in virtues that produce obedience to the demands of a holy and loving God. In short, it should have its effect on the way we live. Perhaps this will not happen directly, because not all Christians read theology, nor should we ever expect them to do so. But theology should, at the least, influence the way ministers are trained and the way the Word is preached from the pulpit. If thoughtful doctrine became the diet of every pastor, we should not have congregations fed on the watery pablum of modern notions from pop psychology, or the latest nostrums from the most current social movement.

That is not to say, however, that all theology is useful in the ordinary sense of the word. When Thomas Aquinas inquired as to whether Christian doctrine is "practical" or "speculative," he concluded that it is both; but it is to a higher degree speculative. This teaching of Aquinas corresponded to the teaching of Augustine, that there are those things that are for our use; and there are those things that are for our enjoyment; *and the highest and most valuable things are those that we enjoy*. Thus we can enjoy another human being, but it would be sin to attempt to use him. We are called to know God and to enjoy him forever, but to attempt to use God would be an impiety of the worst kind. So theology is practical in the sense that it allows us, and teaches us, to relate to all things in the right way. It teaches us to love our neighbor and to use our food to the glory of God. If we find ourselves using our neighbor, and loving (or enjoying) our food, then we can be sure that something in life is out of order. It is that proper order, of loving that which is highest to the highest degree, and receiving all things with thanksgiving, finding only the good that properly is given by these things, and not imagining in them the good that is ascribed only to God. It is this perspective that theology properly attempts to restore.

The Kingdom and the Word

Theology always has in view God's rule in the human heart, in individual behavior, and in the community of men, women, and children. It calls people to a new life, given by God, and a life that is reflected in a new way of living. Dietrich Bonhoeffer said that, in preaching and in interpreting the Scripture (and theology is an elaborate way of doing that very thing), God has "put his word in our mouth." Then he said, "He wants it to be spoken through us. If we hinder His Word, the blood of the sinning brother will be upon us. If we carry out His Word, God will save our brother through us."[5]

Theology stands as a practical link between two poles of reality. One is expressed as the "Word": It stands for the reality of God's communicating himself and his will to us. The Word calls for a response, but it does not enforce one. It implies God's dialogical relationship to his creation. He calls and waits. He speaks truth, and gives witness to truth; and as powerful as that Word is, it does not preclude the possibility that men and women of free will might turn their backs upon the truth.

The Kingdom of God represents a larger scope of reality and action. In a sense free creatures can respond as they will to God's Word, but they cannot alter the fact that God's Word is truth, and that the consequences of disobedience are to miss what is true, to deny what is real, and to therefore deny what is life itself. In this sense, God's Word becomes an appeal to recognize and receive what is true. Furthermore, it is an appeal to recognize and receive what is good. Ultimately, God's rule is both true and good—and it

---

5. Cited in Donald Bloesch, *Essentials of Evangelical Theology*, vol. 2 (San Francisco: Harper & Row, 1982), 71.

is also inevitable. I may choose to agree or not agree with the law of gravity; and I may resent it or deny it, but I cannot escape it. The kingdom is the reality of which God's Word speaks and into which it calls for us to enter.

Theology stands somewhere between these two. Theology is not the Word of God; it only attempts in many different ways to communicate that Word. It attempts to interpret the Word in such a way that Christians can respond to that Word with wisdom and loving obedience. Further, theology is not the Kingdom of God. Once a man or woman acts in obedience to God, that person no longer needs to explain to themself or others that obedience. The truth of a loving action speaks for itself. The reality of a genuine experience of God requires no apology, and it requires no doctrine to give it validity.

In the course of searching for true actions and real experience, Christians need signposts. When we arrive at our destination, after traveling to another city for vacation, we no longer look for pointers along the route. But we have not and will not arrive at our true destination in this life. Our need for signposts is quite evident. For that, the church has provided many witnesses—witnesses who sometimes are off the mark—but who also are indispensable unless we are content to wander in a signless wilderness, never learning from the careful thought and valuable experiences of others.

Questions for Review and Reflection

1. A very common question, asked by people with a variety of backgrounds, and often by those without a strong educational background, is a question of **theodicy:** "If a good God is also powerful, why does he not prevent pain, suffering, and evil?" This question, which occurs to so many, and is dealt with by academically gifted theologians and philosophers, arises often, and yet is difficult to answer. Does that mean, do you think, that the questions of theology are practical and common, even though the formal statement of theology often seems academic, difficult, highly refined, and not accessible to everyone?

2. Consider how theological principles carry over into practical concerns by completing the following:
   a) Since God is "three in one," the central reality of community implies, for human relationships. . . .
   b) Since God is incarnate, that is, "in the flesh," we must view one human flesh as . . . .
   c) If salvation is a gift, the relationships of Christians within the church should reflect . . . .
   d) If atonement is accomplished by God's humiliation on the cross, then the relationship of authority and discipleship in the church can be described as . . . .
3. What are some modern manifestations of:
   a) Gnosticism?
   b) Pelagianism?
   c) Arianism?
   d) Sabellianism?
4. Discuss the relationship of the idea of special revelation with the basic principles of modern natural sciences.

GLOSSARY

accident

In the philosophies of Aristotle and Aquinas, a term to denote a quality related to a thing, but with no independent existence. For instance, in the sentence, "Bill is tall, happy, and married," the qualifiers "tall, happy, and married" cannot be thought of as independent of the subject "Bill." Those qualifiers are accidents.

adoptionism

The doctrine holding that Christ, in that he was man, became the Son of God only by virtue of God's choosing him.

Apocalypse, apocalyptic

Literally an unveiling or revelation. Generally refers to futuristic disclosures of the end-time and to a variety of literature (of which the Revelation is the foremost example) that is highly symbolic, disclosing either a catastrophic future resulting in a new world, or the super-mundane experiences of the apocalyptic writer or central figure.

Apollinarianism

The christological view advocated by Apollinaris (310–390), in which Jesus is understood as possessed of the divine *Logos* instead of a human soul or mind.

243

Arianism

A heresy concerning the person of Christ formulated and argued by Arius (256–336), a presbyter of Alexandria. He held that Jesus Christ was not of the same substance as the Father and was a created being. For Arians, Christ was thought to be supreme among created beings, but not God.

Athanasian Creed

Also called the *Quicunque,* is especially important for its definitive expression of the orthodox Christian doctrine of the Trinity. The source is not known. It is not a creed in the ordinary sense of a document agreed upon in a church council. So, ironically, the two things one can say with certainty about the Athanasian Creed are that it is not by Athanasius and it is not a creed. Nevertheless, by the ninth century its formulation of doctrine was taken to be authoritative and an accurate expression of what all Christians believe.

atone, atonement

An English language theological construction meaning the act of making one, or of bringing into unity. It refers in Christian theology to the at-one-ment of God and his creation, especially regarding humanity.

canon

The canon of Scripture is the list of Old and New Testament writings. The word denotes a standard, a rule, or an authoritative measure. Scripture as canon is thus considered the rule and standard of faith and practice.

charisma, charismata

Gift, gifts of the Spirit, provided to the church for the sake of fulfilling its calling and ministering to one another.

chiliasm

From the Greek meaning "thousand," the chiliasts are generally those expecting or emphasizing the arrival of a thousand-year reign of Christ on earth, although there are more secular expressions of this expectation that are sometimes referred to using the same term. It is equivalent to the Latin-derived term "millennium," and is usually applied to those holding a premillennial theology.

cosmology

From *cosmos* (world) and *logos* (word or discourse), this term is defined as the discourse or doctrine of the world.

creatio continua

The doctrine or theological speculation regarding creation as a continual reality and not simply the act of God at the beginning.

creatio ex nihilo

Creation out of nothing; it is the orthodox Christian teaching regarding the absolute contingency of the world. In this doctrine is clearly presented the claim that all things owe their existence and essential nature to the purposes of God and have no nature that is truly independent of God.

cult

A system of religious worship, with emphasis upon the action and the order of events. A religion might be altogether defined by the practice of that religion, and not be given to a doctrinal expression. The Hebrew religion was at least partly distinguished from the religions of its neighbors by the tendency toward doctrinal expression and its criticism of its own cult.

Deism

A term first employed to describe the views of seventeenth-century rationalists who thought of God as the Creator, and yet denied his continued influence in creation. Thus, they did not believe, for instance, in miracles, providence, or revelation.

Deuteronomic theology

The theology reflected by the Book of Deuteronomy and the Deuteronomic or prophetic history in Joshua, Judges, 1 and 2 Samuel, and 1 and 2 Kings. A distinct feature of this theology is the emphasis upon Israel's choice between obedience and disobedience, and the consequences of blessing and cursing, life and death.

dispensationalism

A modern Protestant theology with British roots, emphasizing a view of history as divided into a number of divine "dispensations." In eschatology, dispensationalism insists upon a premillennial return of Christ and usually upon a pre-tribulational or mid-tribulational rapture of the church. That is, they believe the church will be taken out of the world during, if not before, the stressful times that precede the visible return of Christ.

docetism

Any Christian heresy that emphasizes the divinity of Christ by denying his full humanity. It literally means "seemism," and regards Jesus' humanity as the mere appearance of being human.

dualism

Any metaphysical or theological concept that views the world in terms of a strong opposition of good and evil. Gnosticism, for instance, involves a thoroughgoing metaphysical dualism, usually involving the identity of matter with evil and spirit with good.

dynamistic Monarchianism

A heresy maintaining the unchanging and undivided oneness of God, and considering Christ the Son of God by virtue of his attaining sonship and God's adoption of him as Son.

Ebionism

Derived from the Hebrew term for poor, Ebionism or Ebionites came to signify a movement out of Jewish Christianity that exalted the Law and considered Jesus Christ as fully human, but not divine. He was the human son of Joseph and Mary, but was elected Son of God at his baptism.

Ecclesiology

The doctrine of the church; a term derived from *ekklesia* (church) and *logos* (word or discourse).

economic Trinity

God is three persons in terms of his effect upon the world. The term stands in contrast with the idea of the immanent Trinity or ontologic Trinity.

enthusiasm

Any doctrine or practice emphasizing the experience of God as the determination of valid religious truth.

eschaton, eschatology

The last things, the doctrine of the last things. These terms refer to the end of history, embracing the Christian expectation of the return of Christ, the resurrection of the dead, the judgment of the living and the dead, and the new heaven and new earth.

Eutychianism

Also called Monophysitism (meaning "only nature"), Eutychianism tried to protect the doctrine of the "one person" of Christ by denying his dual nature, human and divine. The doctrine of Eutychianism tended to relegate the humanity of Jesus to a level of no real importance and to emphasize his divinity.

filioque

A Latin term, meaning "and the Son," appended to the Nicene Creed by Western (West European) churches in the early eleventh century to clarify the idea that the Holy Spirit is sent by the Father "and the Son." The Eastern Church resisted this addition, and the resulting controversy is seen as a central factor in the dividing of the Eastern and Western churches in 1054.

fundamentalism

Historically this term refers to the early twentieth century movement in American Protestantism seeking to recover and strengthen the churches' adherence to certain fundamentals of the Christian faith. Conceptually, it can also refer to any religious movement seeking to correct or combat modernity by strict emphasis upon foundational beliefs.

general revelation

A term referring to any disclosure of God that does not rely upon the unrepeatable events of history. The disclosure of God in creation or in common human experience can be referred to as "general revelation." The term is used in contrast to "special revelation."

glossalalia

The practice of "speaking in tongues" heretofore unknown or practiced by the speaker, referred to in Acts and by the apostle Paul.

gnostic

An early movement, or class of movements, within Christianity that was thoroughly dualistic, denied the full humanity of Jesus, and was condemned as heretical by the church fathers. The designation comes from the Greek word *gnosis* (knowledge), referring to their claim for a special, esoteric knowledge leading to salvation.

hierarchy

"Sacred rule," referring to ranks or orders within creation or in society that are ordained by God or the divine powers.

incarnation

In-flesh-ment. This term refers to God's becoming human in Christ.

Islam

The religion founded by Muhammed (c. 570–632), and referred to by this Arabic term meaning submission or obedience. The adherent of the religion is called Muslim.

justification

The act of making just or right. To be justified is to stand in a right relationship to God and to satisfy his requirement of righteousness. If one is declared righteous in Christ, one is thereby justified.

kerygma

The central or essential message of the gospel of Jesus Christ. The term was especially used by Rudolf Bultmann and his followers of the mid-twentieth century.

liberalism

In Protestant theology the term for any movement emphasizing the openness of religion to popular culture and which seeks to redefine the basis of Christianity in terms of contemporary philosophy or values. Historically it was a nineteenth-century movement centered in German Protestant circles.

libertinism

A philosophy or religious construction that rejects the restrictions of law or custom in favor of autonomous freedom.

materialism

Any system of thought that sees all reality residing in matter and its complex interaction. Thus materialism rejects any idea of the spirit or of a trans-material reality.

Millennium

The thousand-year reign of Christ mentioned in Revelation 20.

monism

A metaphysical view based upon the assumption of the essential oneness (unity) of all things.

monotheism

The doctrine of one God, who is personal and transcends the world. Of the great world religions, Christianity, Islam, and Judaism are monotheistic.

Moravian

Church of the United Brethren (*Unitas Fratrum*) that arose from the refugees fleeing Moravia after the Thirty Years War. It was a missionary movement, with a pietist theology, that influenced much of eighteenth-century religious life, including the Wesleyan revival in Britain and Methodism in North America. An early leader was Count von Zinzendorf.

naturalism

Any system of thought that excludes what is beyond nature from its explanation of things.

Nestorianism

An early heresy taught originally by a pupil of Theodore of Mopsuestia named Nestorius. He taught that the two natures of the person of Christ must be thoroughly distinguished, giving the impression that the Son of God was related to the Father only in view of his moral obedience and their mutual sympathy.

nihilism

A metaphysics rejecting the meaning and purpose of anything; all philosophical and religious questions are answered by the ultimate "nothingness" (*nihil*) of existence.

nominalism

A medieval philosophical position that rejected realism and the existence of universals as having prior or independent existence from the "things" that are examples of the universal category. These universals, instead, are the "names" of things; thus: nominalism.

ontologic Trinity

The idea that the Trinity of God is grounded in his being, and is not merely his manifestation in the world. In orthodox Christianity, the economic Trinity is grounded in the ontologic or immanent Trinity.

ontological argument

An argument for the existence of God put forward especially by Anselm of Canterbury in his *Proslogian* (1079).

ontology

A doctrine of "being."

original sin

The doctrine that humanity has inherited the bondage of sin from the father and mother of the human race, Adam and Eve. Thus, human beings share a collective guilt and a collective liability for the sins of the human race, and sin cannot simply be considered as the province of individuals.

Panentheism

The concept of God that states that all is identical yet does not comprehend all of God. Process theology is an example of a Panentheistic system.

Pantheism

The universe is identical with God. God is all, and all is God. God is not in any sense distinguished from the world.

parousia

The Greek word literally means "coming" or "arrival," and refers to the second coming of Christ.

Pelagianism

An idea of salvation based upon the merit of righteousness. This doctrine was promoted by Pelagius and was opposed primarily by Augustine of Hippo (354–430).

Perfectionism

The proposition that Christian sanctity requires, or tends toward, a state of perfection. This matter was debated with the rise of Wesleyan movements of the eighteenth and nineteenth centuries and continues in varying forms in the twentieth century.

perichoretic Trinity

A doctrine of the Trinity articulated by John of Damascus (675–749) in which the Trinity is viewed as mutually subsisting Persons; the Father, Son, and Holy Spirit are always understood in terms of their relationship to one another.

person

In trinitarian doctrine a reference to the Father, Son, or Holy Spirit as distinguishable, yet one. The classic definition (Boethius) is that of an individual substance of rational nature.

preservation

The doctrine that understands God to be maintaining his creation by active and attentive participation in it.

prevenient grace

The (generally Reformed) doctrine that God's grace extends to preparing the individual for a conscious turning to him.

privatio bonum

This usually refers to an Augustinian teaching that evil is not, in itself, something that exists, but is only the privation of good.

process theology

Christian theology that takes process philosophy as its organizing principle. God has not fully come into being, but is coming into being, comprehending himself in his future.

providence

The term designating divine purpose and intention within, and through, the events of history, in creation and nature, and in personal experience.

realism

In medieval philosophy the view that universals are real and they exist before things, *ante res*. The view stands in contrast to nominalism.

redemption

In the Bible it is the idea that God pays the price to restore human beings to fellowship with him. It includes the restoration of God's relationship to the individual, the corporate body of the church, the nation, and creation.

Reformed

A theological tradition that is historically drawn from the writings of John Calvin (1510-1564). It is also frequently referred to as "Calvinist."

romanticism

In philosophy, literature, and the arts, an attitude that expresses itself in a confidence in the self-expression of nature, humanity, and history. It generally sees reason as inadequate to comprehend the richness of the romantic unfolding of the dynamic processes latent in humanity, nature, and history.

Sabellianism

A kind of Monarchianism in trinitarian doctrine, a heresy that saw the three persons of the Trinity as distinct, temporal manifestations of God.

sacrament, sacramental

A rite or service of the church understood as instituted by Jesus Christ. Roman Catholic theology names seven sacraments (baptism, confirmation, eucharist, marriage, ordination, penance, and unction), and most Protestant theologians would name two (baptism and the Lord's Supper). Baptists in North America generally refer to these two as ordinances.

salvific

Having to do with salvation.

sanctification

A doctrine of salvation expressing and emphasizing the aspect of growth and change in the Christian experience of God.

soteriology

The doctrine of salvation.

sovereignty

Regards the absolute authority of God in governing the world.

special revelation

In contrast to general revelation, it is the kind of divine self-disclosure taking place in unique and unrepeatable events. Special revelation is available to all men and women only in terms of tradition.

synoptic Gospels

The first three Gospels, those of Matthew, Mark, and Luke.

teleological

Having to do with the "end" or "goal." The term derives from the Greek *telos* meaning "end."

testimonium

The inward witness of the Holy Spirit, confirming and illuminating the witness of Scripture.

theism

An alternate term for monotheism.

theocentric

That which centers in God.

theodicy

The issue of justifying God in view of the existence of evil. It deals with the question of why, if God is both good and powerful, evil exists. The term is constructed of two Greek words: *theos* (God) and *dike* (justice).

Tribulation

In eschatology, the period of suffering that precedes the end of history, or (in premillennial theology) before the millennial reign of Christ.

Trinity, trinitarian

Refers to the doctrine that God is three persons—Father, Son, and Holy Spirit—and yet one God.

virgin birth

The doctrine, based upon Matthew and Luke, in their accounts of the birth of Jesus, that he was born of the virgin Mary.

NAMES INDEX

SUBJECT INDEX

SCRIPTURE INDEX